"*in interview with Christopher Higgs April 2, 2013"

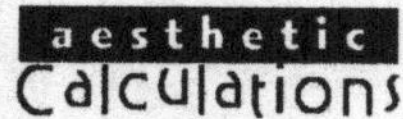

Published in Australia by Aesthetic Calculations 2022

Aesthetic Calculations
The Nicholas Building
4th Floor, 37 Swanston Street, Melbourne
Victoria, 3000
Australia

aestheticcalculations.com

ISBN 978-0-646-86425-9

To Winfried

preface

I want to start with the opening line of One Hundred Years of Solitude where we see a well-known example of the process I want to describe for you, which is the process that is the present concern of this novel: 'Many years later, as he faced the firing squad, Colonel Aureliano Buendía was to remember that distant afternoon when his father took him to discover ice.' Also, from Juan Rulfo's 1955 novel Pedro Paramo, a favorite of Marquez, the sentence: 'Years later Father Renteria would remember the night his hard bed had kept him awake, and driven him outside,' a few words changed here and there; a few added, a few taken away. 'Influence? The distinction is not as clear-cut as the words suggest.'

The work of others has always been a part of what we've done here. To say there aren't many writers who have not used the work of others is to reify a very interesting approach to the anxiety of influence. All words are from elsewhere we could say, but there are certain passages that achieve that moment in which the subjectivity of the author is conveyed inimitably, and we could say then that these are those author's words. If one wants to, one can find all sorts of examples; Pierre Menard, a character in Borges' Don Quixote trilogy, aspires to rewrite the original novel, word for word, three hundred years later. Jean Rhys is planning a retelling of Jane Eyre for her next project. Peter Carey aspires to breathe fresh vitality into Dickens' work. JM Coetzee and Daniel Defoe are two of my favorite authors. It's all a matter of perspective.

As TS Eliot wrote in The Sacred Wood, 'Immature poets imitate; mature poets steal; bad poets deface what they take, and good poets make it into something better, or at least something different.' The Waste Land, a modernist masterpiece, is an anthology of brilliant lines from other writers. That is, you take something and turn it into something new; you personalize it.

This is a novel of allusions, much like the work of writer, John Hughes, who in the preface to his second book, Someone Else (the title itself gives the game away), writes that:

"As a young man, I saw myself in all that I read. It was as if I had created a novel in my head, the characters would not be still, they rose up from the pages of their different books and argued and fought and merged and grew inside me, but with an autonomy that made them as real to me as you are, sitting here now. I was not alone in this ... everyone I knew at the time seemed to be acting out some kind of fantasy, but in the intensity of my imaginative identification, an intensity fueled by the almost febrile world of the works themselves, and the way in which I viewed myself and the world around me almost entirely through these works, I was, perhaps, a little more extreme, a little more possessed. I wanted to be haunted. In my imagination I was a character that Beckett or Chekhov had created, I lived in their works as their characters lived in me ..."

When it comes to literature, writers have always talked via other people's voices. Whether we like it or not, we spend a lot of time immersed in fictional worlds. Over the writings (and cultures and histories) of others, I've always held that we can only write about these fictive locales (a kind of literaro-geographical palimpsest). As John Hughes says in No One:

"Australia is a strange place. It exists only in its imagining of other places. This is not just because of recent migration; it's been happening since the colony's inception. We're born here and imagine being there, in Asia or in Europe, reading their histories and their literature. Over the years I've come to think that Australia exists in this absence, defined, not like other countries, by how its inhabitants think about it, but by how it thinks about other places – not in our imagining of it, but in our imagining from it, our imagining here of somewhere else. The whole notion of an Australian literature could be distilled to the image of a painter who exhibits enormous canvases – on the French heroic scale; think Gericault's Raft of the Medusa – but who only paints in one small corner the most detailed scene, like a perfect miniature."

The present novel can be thought of as inhabiting that small painting.

All music, in the words of legendary singer-songwriter Bob Dylan, may be described as folk music. Take classical music as an example. Its history is littered with examples of folk forms and melodies being incorporated into the compositions. We could go on and on with the names of great composers like Beethoven, Brahms, Liszt, and Bartok. Even in the 21st century, contemporary musical sampling is only the newest incarnation of a centuries-old tradition. Each and every one of us is an artist since we all take. What more can we do except rehash the same old tales? For as long as people have been recycling Homer's for Dionysian festivals, whether it was the ancient Greek tragedians, Shakespeare, or novelists, it has always been a part of the process. A person's actions are more important than his or her possessions.

For most of its life, Clear-cut as the words was called 'Tardiness' because I wanted to write a novel that took such sloth as its theme and whose protagonist feels forever late to the party, discovering that even his own life was someone else's. The original idea for the protagonist was that he would gradually begin to discover that even his life was not his own because it too, had already been written (that unlike Borges' Pierre Menard, re-creation for him was unavoidable!). This is why it had to be so literary. Pastiche of the great nineteenth century novels was the dominant mode, but coming into the twentieth century too, because Russian I wanted the protagonist to discover that not only his past, but his future preceded him too (that he was late even to his own life!). He was to be a historical composite. It isn't plagiarism, because obviously if I had thought it was plagiarism I would have concealed it (no reasonable thief wants to be caught!), but I am no thief. Like TS Eliot, I want the appropriated passages to be seen and recognized as in a collage.

Clear-cut as the words is, in one way, a story about second-hand stories. History comes to us as memories – fragmented, contradictory, incomplete – and we have to make sense of it in self-conscious and allusive stories. We all suffer the anxiety of influence, but as my analyst always tells me, the liar's error is that he thinks he knows the truth.

All of our memories of the past are based on someone else's story; 'This is what occurred,' claim eyewitnesses to the events in question, 'Is there anything more I can do?' 'How can we be sure?' Consciously and unconsciously influenced behavior. To be creative, we rely

on influences like memory and the unconscious, even on the creator, though the process may stay mysterious (just as memories can and must be lost from time to time). From time to time, memories thankfully can be lost; lost to time or sometimes lost to burglary.

I've been known to say two things...

A life that can be described is a life that does not exist. There's a danger of falling back into a life we didn't want to lead, and dying there, without *ever* waking up from the dream we've been living.

To tell a person's narrative is to tell their own tale.

Sam Lieblich
1st November 2022

As a writer, you cannot write about the living and not think of them as already dead.

The only photo my mother gave me after my divorce was of her as a child. An easy-to-follow tutorial. In the print's upper-right corner, you can see her. Her right arm is tucked behind her mother's back on a high stool to the left of her. Behind them, only the heavy folds of a curtain can be seen. My mother is between the ages of 7 and 8 when she was a youngster in 1923 or 1924. When I first saw her, she was dressed in what seemed to be the national attire of the country she was visiting: a white cotton tunic with tiered sleeves, as well as a floral belt around her waist, and a flower garland tied to her hair. She may be decked up for a party, but her outlook on life is anything but festive. She can't fake a grin as well as her mother does when it comes to shooting photographs. Her mother, a famous opera singer, never wore a national costume. As a result, she is dressed in a fashionable clothing and a smart hat. When the photo is taken, it seems to be a time capsule that simultaneously captures and unleashes the past and future.

Another picture was given to me by my mum. In it, a huge mob of people is rushing along a road that glows as black as snakeskin. As though the road is slowly devouring them and regurgitating the indigestible portions, there are old shoes and ragged garments scattered over it. Over the years, I've spent many hours looking for my mother in this picture. What other explanation could there be for her gifting it to me? But every time I think I've found her; she disappears like night in lamplight. As a hermit crab whose shell isn't its own, she's crept inside this picture.

Even if his parents had him late in life, a lone kid learns a lot. As a child, I believe my mother wanted me to be older. I felt as though she was always looking at me from the side rather than directly at me. Throughout my youth, I had no idea who my grandmother was. My mother was a lady always fighting against the tides of fate (a childhood she could not bear to recall; a war that took her whole before dumping her; a husband she didn't expect to love but then lost; a kid she didn't want). She was displaced, remote, and closed. Beyond that, I'd hardly given her a second thought.

As a result, we grew up and went our own ways. She became old and alone, as she had been for all the time that I had known her. After I moved out of the house, of course, I hoped well for her, but I wanted her to see me. I was the only child of a widowed mother and though I adored her, I always knew that she would never have a happy life again once I left; both her actions and personality were a factor. It doesn't mean she was constantly depressed or that she was unhappy with her lot in life, she was, in fact (weeding her flowerbeds, raking leaves), it was never sufficient. There were times when she seemed to be on the verge of losing her cool and becoming a fish out of water because she was so irritated, acerbic, and frank. Despite the almost 50 years she would spend without my father, her life never seemed to be truly lived. She was apprehensive and defensive, yet every time I left her, she cried because I accounted for the majority of her resources. Yet, in the end, it wasn't enough. This lack of resources underpinned all we attempted.

In the lengthy pauses that followed most of our meals together, mother would tell me she was thinking about the time before I was born. I didn't press the issue since I knew I wouldn't get a more detailed response. Only a week before she died, in the nursing home where I had buried her against her will because I lacked the will to do anything otherwise, would I get the answer more than 50 years later.

During my mother's pregnancy, she developed cataracts in both eyes and lost her vision for two months. Doctors couldn't explain why her sight returned or why it had been lost since she was forty-four years old during her pregnancy (as I already mentioned was a late one); an emotional response to an unexpected pregnancy was considered to be the cause of the woman's symptoms.

When I lived with her in our modest Rose Bay home for 18 years, and subsequently when I visited her in her fisherman's cottage in the lizard place after she had moved out of Sydney, not a single loving gesture was exchanged between us: no touching, no hug, not even a passing kiss. Instead, we went about our business as usual, reciting our catechism or retreating to our rooms until the time came for us to dine together at the little kitchen table, as was the habit.

Although, she leant her forehead against mine and caressed my hand for a brief moment after we finished eating one evening, it would be the last time I saw her at her house. I didn't know at the time, but it was her last meal with me at home. My attention was drawn away from the rest of her face when I saw that she had her eyes closed. It was only when she opened her eyes that I noticed them in all their glory, their light blue irises flecked with green.

'Do you see them?' she whispered in my ear as she lifted her hand and pointed above my head. Nothing could be heard from the garden, which faded into dusk via the window and was entirely quiet. 'There,' she muttered, looking at me with increasing astonishment. 'Aren't they obvious?' At this point, her hands were at her breasts, as if she were nursing something in there. 'The four-legged companion animals, they're coming closer,' she murmured as she sat back in her chair and looked away from me.

Her candor was exceptional that morning; how else could I have known her mind was already at odds with itself? She told me that she had fantasized about what it would be like to love a kid before she became pregnant. She said that if she hadn't gone through the process of giving birth, she would have believed what she thought to be real. However, when she held her kid for the first time, she realized that this must be the case with everything we picture.

How could I not have been inspired by such words? I don't know. My understanding is that imagination can never teach itself its limitations; it is like a kid in this, since it does not know them. Only the body understands what is going on within. That's why it's so difficult for us to understand what should be obvious: what's important and what's real, because how else would I have known that the baby she was referring to wasn't me?

I was waiting outside a room at a nursing facility in the lizard place in the early winter of 2015 for a nurse to complete her work with my mum, I hadn't seen her in two years for circumstances that aren't in my favor, and still her face looked like she'd aged twenty years. It's hard to comprehend the extent of the damage. However, I did not approach her immediately, instead, I waited for the right moment when she glanced my way and showed me any signs of repulsion – or better yet, dissimulation. You might argue that I'm trying to take advantage of the situation, but given our previous history, I was desperate for any and all advantages I could get.

The chamber resembled a cave; the window was completely covered by a thick black curtain. A halo of light appeared around its perimeter, but it went no farther. Mother and the nurse were having a conversation. Her words appeared to be perfumed with the scent of tomb flowers as she spoke with a little accent. She talked with her chin in her hands and a forward bend in her torso. Although there was just darkness, it reminded me of a sunflower.

The nurse switched on the bedside light as if she'd read my mind, casting her shadow on the wall in the shape of a monster I recognized yet had never seen before. My mother didn't feel the need to step in during this moment of silence and because her gaze was a bit unnerving to me and I was shy, I was unable to leave the doorway. If the nurse hadn't detected my presence, I would have turned and snuck out the door. Since my mother had been hospitalized, I had not returned to the hospital.

As she welcomed me and invited me inside, her voice was filled with astonishment. 'It's your son, Mrs. Thomson,' she remarked to my mother, pointing to the doorway as she spoke. 'John. His visit is to see you,' she says.

'Who?' My mother gazed at me as if she were peering into a wide abyss where she could take nothing in. Even though I'd refused to see her for almost a year, hearing that one word was the worst thing that could have happened to me. The way she looked was eerily similar to staring into a tomb. I smiled at the nurse as my skin became numb. It was still possible to flee (I hadn't even entered the room by this time).

It was clear that the nurse was going to have to abandon her patient. 'You have a lot to catch up on,' I told her.

When I first saw her wheeling my mother away two years ago, I thought she must be Greek because of her accent, or Lebanese - the Levantine. In addition to a skin tone that reminded me of varnished wood, the fin-like nose, and a pair of eyes as black as oysters, I was struck by the whole appearance; in addition to the fact that she was as skinny as a grasshopper, she had a lengthy birthmark that went down her left cheek which she seemed to be covering by letting her hair fall on one side of her face.

As I followed her down the hallway, I asked her 'How is she?'

The wide window that looked out into the vast sky let in plenty of natural light. I was able to see the tops of the trees from my vantage point. To me, as a youngster, the leaves were so far above me that they seemed to be struck by sunlight from underneath, turning them green, crimson, and yellow. It was as if I was attempting to

10

touch the stars at night or anything else that was out of my grasp, so I would lift my hand and see them between my fingers.

'She believes you're dead,' she says. Sorry for the inconvenience. As far as I know, she didn't believe me.' The nurse said, though she didn't mention whether she thought I was bad. She spoke with the same brevity as she moved; without any shadows, this is how it appears.

'In the event of an emergency,' she continued, 'It may happen very quickly.'

'Will she be able to tell the difference between us?' I asked again.

'She can now converse fluently in Italian, English, and what sounds like Russian while she's sleeping, all as if they were all one language. As soon as I arrive, she informs me, she speaks to a cat that hides in the wardrobe since animals are not permitted. The sprinkler in the ceiling is making her believe that someone is attempting to poison her. She observed a guy hanging from a curtain rail with a noose the day before and asked "Would you mind if I lowered him and buried him?"'

I repeatedly said 'I'm sorry' to the nurse as she narrated these to me.

'However, she tends to sit in her chair with her eyes closed most of the time which is not at all uncommon.' The nurse concluded.

She grasped my hand when I put it out as that was all I could muster as an answer. I wished she could feel the strain on my heart.

I believe she smiled at that point. The gap between us grew gradually, like the warmth she'd left in my palm as she walked away from me. Then she walked to the end of the hallway and was out of sight.

I was devastated when I learned that I would have to place my mother in a care facility. The base hospital in Nelson Bay called to check on me. From Sydney, I took a direct route north. There, I was welcomed by her doctor, a tall guy with long, curly hair in black suit who talked with a huskiness that made it difficult to understand him. He warned me that things wouldn't work out. My mother had been worse than I realized and had spent days in her room alone (the nurse had of course, not informed me about this). He had a soft spot in his heart for my mother; everybody appeared to be doing that.

We went to the room where she was being kept, her eyes were shut, despite the fact that he spoke about her (I mean, he talked to us as a group). Using the clipboard at the foot of the bed, he informed us of the dreadful news that we were about to receive. He had done tests and scans on her brain and the outcome was not favorable; her mind was deteriorating and recuperation was not an option. He felt bad saying it. What I said to him is a blur in my mind. Most likely, I was rather verbose in my enquiry. I'm not sure I ever shed a tear.

'What are your plans for the day?' I muttered. When the doctor walked out of the room her eyes opened at that. I took it for granted that she'd heard what I'd said before I even asked.

She turned away from the window and gazed down the hill at the sparse trees and she responded, 'I know what I don't want to do.' My heart sank when I realized that I would be entering a house like that.

'Maybe you'll feel better soon,' I added.

She did not respond to that. Instead, talking as though to no one but herself, she said, 'I want to die. I don't want to be preserved.' Though I resisted, I could see a glimmer of recognition or acceptance in her eyes at that point. 'I can't believe it, John. My mind has deceived me.'

I answered, as if I hadn't heard her, 'It doesn't have to be a home. You're welcome to join me.'

I'm not sure what possessed me to say that. We were both aware of the hollowness of the words. The last time she visited me in Sydney was when I was married to Anne, and she had a grandchild. Then, there were all the years after my divorce when she hadn't been back. Those words should not have come out of my mouth. I could have just said, 'Whatever you desire,' and that would have sufficed, but I didn't say that. I felt remorse for what I had said, but rather than take it back, I put my plans for the future on hold instead.

Since it was all too easy to believe what she said when she cursed me and said she didn't want to see me again, I left her to die in a nursing facility in the lizard place alone; a lengthy, drawn-out death, because it was all too easy to take her at her word. Everything we could have done to help each other had vanished in that split second.

The fact that someone was in the room took her a few seconds to come to grips with. I was as soundless as a cat because the carpet was so thick. Her eye doctor had told her two years before that having the cataracts removed was pointless since her eyesight had degraded so much. She lifted her head, smelt the air, and glared at me as if I were just another apparition. To be gazed at in this manner was weird, yet it wasn't as horrible as I expected. The look on her face reminded me of a horse's desire for its rider: not the equine longing per se, but rather, the lugubriousness in her gaze. I'd seen it in her mother's photos as well, even when she was at her peak of success. My family's journey through flesh and blood.

'It's me,' I said. 'John.'

'Do you have any food for lunch?'

Her voice caught my attention for some reason. As if I hadn't realized she could talk. I pondered what a ghost may bring in terms of cuisine.

'Do you want to eat?' I asked.

'No.' she said, then continued, 'My name is "Mum."'

'I know,' he said.

'How did you know that?'

'We have a new family member. My wife and I are parents to a boy. He's working abroad. In the meanwhile, he is now back. It was a mistake for him to go.'

She burst into tears. When I saw her there, propped up on the huge cushion she'd filled with duck feathers when she was a youngster and carried about for all those years as a nomad in Europe, it wounded my chest. She told me once that it was big enough to be my bed. My first idea was that it would be large enough to be her bed once again, given how much smaller she had shrunk to be. She seemed to be weak and transparent. In my imagination, the white sheet was visible through her neck. Leaving her in such a state makes me feel guilty.

I confessed to her that I'd been looking at some photos.

I want to hug her, but she's resting in such a position that I can only brush her shoulder. I'm curious what she sees when she looks at me. Even under the light of a lamp, the room seems dimmer than usual. Shame, on the other hand, is difficult to hide. I can only detect bone under the fabric of her nightgown. When she switches position on the bed, she exudes the vase water scent of long-dead flowers. Her face was like a flower with petals crushed into the papery skin.

12

As I reach inside my jacket pocket, I pull out two photos and hand them to her. She can't see them, and even if she does, she has no idea what to say. I carefully wriggle her right arm out from under the blankets so she can make a fist around mine. It has a powdery texture similar to that of a bare shelf. The sobs died down. With the sheet's edge, I dab at her tears. I can't see what she sees as she kisses the images near enough to kiss her face.

'Dad.' I said. 'Your husband.'

'What happened to him?' She asked.

'Dead.' I reply.

She shook her head and flipped the picture over to the other side.

'Your mother,' I remarked with a proud tone. She's wearing a silk robe in crimson. Outside the frame, cherry blossoms are falling like snow.

'Dead?' She asked in a monotone.

'Yes.'

She asks, as if it was a secret, 'Why didn't anybody tell me?' Is it possible for you to ignore such little matters?

It's as if she's finally discovered a method to transcend mortal blindness and see beyond the grave, the souls of the dead by placing the images on her lap and running her fingers over them like a form of braille.

A dreadful notion, but I wonder whether she sees me the same way I do.

She suddenly exclaims, in a voice I recognize, 'You know, I never met my father.' I'm not sure who she was addressing. I'd pushed her to the brink of annoyance for years, but she'd never once mentioned him. Many things were known about her mother, but nothing was known about her father. Maybe she's just telling me now because she thought I was someone else all this time. It seemed as if I were in a cage and she stared at me as if I were a different species. It was a strange experience, but I like the sense of anonymity; It was a welcome respite. In her eyes, I was nothing more than a ghost of what she was seeing; I wasn't going to let her down. What evidence did I have to the contrary? We have a place to call home. My mother was not an exception to this rule. She may not recognize her kid, but at least, he will now know the truth.

After that, I started regurgitating (there is no other term to describe it) the jumbled pieces of a tale that I would never be able to put together, but which would consume my thoughts for the next two years. We may only ever remember the past as a bitter aftertaste, a poison that lingers long after the rest of our memories have been excreted. My mother, on the other hand, was no exception to this rule.

However, I had no idea what was going on at the time. I felt like I was in a trance. The lampshade's watery glow is a result of its fine ribs. As it drifted over the walls, it caught shadows in its folds. When you think about it, is it not supernatural how the past returns, or how much of our lives are spent living in the shadows?

To retrace all the paths my mother took that afternoon, with its stuttering pauses, incoherent rants, and fevered, anxious monologue would be tedious because it occupied me for the next two years and marked the end of a long recovery from what I only later came to realize was a disease that, like any other, I had caught long before. In me, something that had been dormant for so long sprang to life with the reckless abandon of a predator. During those two years of stillness, I believed I had put my mother's spirit to rest, thinking that by forcing her to live here against her choice, I had destroyed what little good we had left between us. But nothing is ever really done. She talked as though she were strolling on a weed-slick rock shelf, like a ship in a wave. When she spoke, I was taken by surprise by her style of speaking more than what she said, and I couldn't help but be taken aback by what she had to say and how she spoke.

It was only after the war had finished and she was reunited with her mother for a short while that she learned anything about her father. The plot, at least in terms of its skeleton, was straightforward: Before the Russian Revolution, a Russian guy falls in love with an Italian opera diva - her mother! My mother was conceived, but the love was not allowed to mature.

A tale so unbelievable it could have been plucked straight from an opera, but despite my best efforts to dismiss it as a figment of my imagination (reminding myself that reality is often stranger than anything we can imagine), I accepted the story with the same gullibility with which I had accepted my home world's speeding through space, however ethereal.

There was something about the entire situation that made it seem like a storybook, and I couldn't describe it. I was moved by the simple mystery of this faraway guy she had never met, not by the fact that my mother had been born fatherless (I had been without a father for much of my childhood, too), but by the fact that I was the descendant of some forgotten Russian aristocracy.

That afternoon, I must be cautious not to let this subsequent understanding influence my memory of it. Our memories aren't actually of the past at all; it's as if the future is clinging on to the past like a spool. The future is always a part of our memories, even if we don't realize it. We know how much time has passed between the moment we're attempting to relive and the current moment we're finishing from. This means that the future is always known in the past not as something yet to occur, but as something that has already occurred.

That winter day two years ago, my mother seemed to be mining in reverse, digging up out of the depths and disclosing what she could see to me on the other side of the hole she had dug for herself in the dark. The plot revolved on the gaping fissure in the ground. It had to have been terrible, yet all she could see in her eyes was exhaustion, as if she had travelled a long distance just to be there. There was a brief glimpse when it seemed she saw me, but I don't believe it was really me she saw. She lingered. How long had the moth been hitting the lampshade with its wings? Preparations for supper were going on outside the door. Strokes of lightning in the hallway; soft, yet insistent tones. I waited patiently for the aroma. Do they really expect me to provide for her nutritional needs?

'Mum, it's time to eat,' I said.'

However, she'd fallen asleep by this point. At least, her eyes were shut. It was a relief, even though for a brief moment, I considered kissing her, disturbing her reverie, and digging into my pocket for two obols (it was definitely the place for such money) in order to send her back to the medium she had previously inhabited so strongly and in which I now stood alone. What more can I say if that's a paradox? Everything we experience is jumbled up with its polar opposite. Actually, I had no intention of welcoming her back. Seeing her eat was too much for me to bear; 'Not like this.' As a child, I'd never had to deal with a situation like this. Just being that close to her was a memory I couldn't recall in a long time. Her face was like a worn-out pair of shoes.

As I pulled back the curtain, I took a glance outside at the silver mist that had settled on the ground. As we sat in the dark, I looked out the window and saw our reflections one on top of the other, in the silver light. Nothing could have been done to avert the inevitable (I don't understand how there could have been), so, I knelt down and began to pack my tiny bag. There was still a long way to go.

The theatre has never been a favorite pastime of mine. I sat in the dim light of a packed theatre, witnessing men and women their own age pretend to be others their own age. I like puppets instead; there's no faking it with puppets. Puppets hold my attention for long periods of time. I'm still undecided about my feelings regarding TV.

The Greeks were on the mark. They didn't try to conceal it from the audience. There was no need for disguises, since they just said the words. What an accomplishment! The Greeks are one of my favorite ethnic groups (I'm referring to their ancestors). Thank you for all your help. An American studio contacted me a year or two before I placed my mother in the home to adapt Euripides' Medea for the big screen, which was a great opportunity and my first performance outside of Australia. Their phrase for it was 'zeitgeist,' and they felt I might help bring it out of the play. If my agent had told them anything about me, it would have been that 'he could speak wheat out of his ear and weave a silk purse from a sow's crotch before breakfast if there was money in it,' but I'd only ever written for television, so it can't have been the whole story.

In any event, I've never been a team player in my whole life. The thought of someone peering over my shoulder drives me crazy. It is much worse if they had their mouths wide open. Even if I don't really care what happens to the screenplay after I complete writing, the truth is that I like to work alone while writing a script. That is the attitude I've had for more than 30 years of writing, and nothing has altered my mind about it. For all my writing experience, nothing I've done in the last three decades has brought in close to the amount I've made now and no one could ever say that I lacked moral principles in any of my dealings. For the love of God, I'm a TV drama writer! I'd even write a play if I were offered the amount of money we're discussing by a Bezos here. I wouldn't have to sit through it if the contract was explicit.

Of course, the only thing that came out of it was the money. As soon as I put pen to paper, Medea vanished from the cultural consciousness. I enjoyed the experience, and now that I had the cash, I decided to devote some of my spare time to writing my own work instead of just watching TV.

Writing screenplays of trailers for films that didn't exist and then developing adverts for things that didn't exist, gained me a modest reputation in the advertising circles when I returned to Sydney from Cambridge in the 1980s. It's safe to say I was a self-promoter back then, as you may have guessed. There was something about it, regardless of whether I was just showing off. Creating a need for something that does not exist and making us want what we already have is the goal of all excellent advertising, right? I know I didn't develop the wheel, but it gave me a little of prominence and allowed me to go into the television business.

Seeing that made my mother scream in horror, to say the least; 'Not a job for a son of immigrants. It's amazing to me how much you haven't matured,' she added.

Probably because she felt I did it out of spite, complete pig-headedness, and too much Teflon in my metaphysics.

Having my mum perform a scarification ritual on me was an honor. Being the subject of a Picasso two-nosed picture or a Bacon eviscerated four-legged companion animal was a strange and disconcerting experience. To live up to her expectations, you'd have to be some kind of superman posited or perhaps longed for, by a 19th century German Philosopher who wished he was a composer. In passing this judgement on her, I don't intend to be cruel. She was correct up to a degree, as was her wont, but she was also inaccurate in jurisdictions she was unaware of because every individual, like the human animal, is more than the sum of its cells, even if he is full of flaws. When it comes down to it, self-love is a precondition for loving others, and my mother could not bring herself to do that.

It wasn't only for the sake of making up with the lizard place that I'd gone back to the town, but also so I could put her home on the market. There was no Rockefeller in me; I had just purchased a little time with the writing. The nursing home wanted its pound of flesh, and I had no clue how long she was going to survive. An indestructible rock like hers could be relied upon to stand up to any challenge. What on earth had happened to her? I'll be honest, I didn't have the notion to sell the home until after two years of self-imposed exile. It still didn't seem right after seeing her like that. My fears resurfaced, and I couldn't sleep for hours. The philosopher Heraclitus once said that 'you should never tread twice in the same river', but I don't believe he was thinking about memories when he made that statement because you may retrace your steps in the same river over and over again in your mind. The only difference is that you don't get wet in your memories.

Her new home was located in the lizard place, from which I left for Cambridge the next year. Only the weatherboard home on the cul-de-sac that was not part of the construction boom was notable about the house itself. After rain, its corrugated iron hair looked particularly good with its eyes and mouth positioned in an anthropomorphic manner on each side of the entrance. A place for bathing and excreting; a place for cooking and eating; a space for sleeping and procreation; and a hole under the floor for nightmares are just some of the biological functions that make up its interior. Shades of dark and ornate are all that can be seen. Because I had never lived in the area and had only been on a few occasions, it brought up few memories. I began planning my exit as soon as I stepped foot in the door.

I woke up about 4 a.m. since there was no use pretending that I could sleep any longer, went into the kitchen, make myself a cup of tea and turned on the light. If what happened in the past still haunts and corrodes us, is it truly a shock? It's like worms living in the flesh of the deceased, isn't it? My father was always around me, even though he didn't reside here. To make a long story short, he walked all the way from Rose Bay to the Gap before jumping. While retrieving him from the rocks below, the cops decided to leave them on the cliff's edge. My mum likened it to two birds. Seven-year-old me can still recite them. I couldn't figure out to whom she was reaching out for support at the time. There was a moment when she extended her hand to me as if she had already arrived in a new universe.

The tea has cooled in the cup, and the bag has turned into a bloated corpse. Standing up, I make my way to the verandah. The weather is pleasant. At a distance, the sky appears clear save for a thin layer of fog and an oceanic band. I don't know whether it's the fog or the darkness, but I have vivid memories of my father taking me eel fishing, I don't think I was older than five at the time. I saw the animals he was looking for in the flash of the torchlight, frozen in the light, with their blank eyes full of everything that they couldn't see.

My cup of coffee sits in a pool of light on the kitchen table as I peer in through the open door. Close your eyes and I'll be able to see her as well. On how many such mornings had I sat across from her, waiting for the sunrise? I used to believe she slept only when she had to. This arrangement will always trump everything she says in my mind. Like the light from a constellation, the conversation is its afterglow.

With her ash-grey hair pulled back and styled with hairspray, she had a look that alternated between sorrow and exhaustion most of the time. Even in the garden, she wore cotton pants and jackets she made herself. It seemed like she never got sick, never even had a little cold. Despite the fact that she was adored by everyone in the neighborhood, she had no friends and didn't even attempt to create any; my mother was certain that she had nothing to say about herself. Of course, her actions said volumes, as did her refusal to be sidetracked from any duty, whether it is dusting the flowers with her white-gloved hands or sorting the laundry into little heaps. However, when it came to her life before meeting me, she was mute. There was a certain inaccessibility to her silence, which made her seem like someone who understood something about life that she would not reveal. It seemed to her that all words were an overabundance. She appeared to be saying that 'if you're going to talk, you better speak better than the quiet!'

Her life was sketched out for me once, but she left the notebook practically empty. She barely wrote down a handful of words, mostly placenames, that she hoped might hold the answer. 'Haven't I told you enough already?' she remarked when I begged her to tell me more about the events. 'You're the author,' I said. Though she had deceived herself in a manner she would rather die than allow it to be present in her life again, the few things that she did tell me were so enticing to me that today they appear to me to take their meaning from another world about which I know nothing; smokescreens. She once told me, 'Childhood is a difficult period.' Everything in this world appears to exist so it may keep on supplying you with new things, until you realize that the majority of those new things are holes. Although, I know now that she was talking about more than just growing up in the interwar period, that realization must have been devastating. It was as if she was saying that life is nothing more than a scab covering a wound, like the feelings of dread you get when swimming in deep water and not being able to see the bottom.

My occasional trips to her in this kitchen, particularly towards the end, the discourse was of a different kind. As soon as she sat down, she'd tell me, 'John, you're not ageing gracefully. It wasn't always like this for you. You have changed your hair, right?' Eventually, she'd have had enough and withdraw to her room to sleep (or whatever was going on behind her closed eyelids) and I'd have to face the glaring day and drive back to Sydney.

However, I had no intention of leaving the city that morning. At first glance, I assumed it would just take me a month or so to clear out the home and get it ready for sale, I had no idea I'd be stuck there for the next two years, like Sisyphus, with no closer to the conclusion than when he arrived.

Before seeing my mum, I drove to Shoal Bay because I was restless and unable to confront what I had come here to accomplish. There were just a few riders to be seen on the route, all of whom were stranded on the climb out of Dutchman's Bay. As I drove by, their taillights pulsed like tinsel in the dim pre-dawn light.

After the divorce, I began swimming in Nielsen Park on a regular basis. On the weekends, I was able to see my son, James. On Saturday mornings, I would drive over Bondi to fetch him up. Whenever I learned that my ex, Anne and her new 'partner' were going on a weekend trip to the seaside, I would not show up. I know it's trivial, but it still made me laugh. The phone was ringing nonstop. Hearing it resound was a pleasant experience. I had a feeling this swim was going to be a blast. No, I didn't think of him.

The clouds loom over the highway as if they were extensions of the hotels that line it. In between the unending concrete blocks, there are glimpses of fishing boats on the tiny road that leads to the bay. As it approaches, the jetty - a fishing trawler with two small funnels -makes no noise at all in the calm sea.

My favorite time of day to go swimming in Sydney is on rainy mornings because I'm usually the only one and can park right next to the beach. To this day, after what feels like an eternity (hundreds of years), I still get goosebumps when I visit Nielsen Park, with its little netted cage scarring the bigger harbor and reflecting rainfall into chandeliers of light as they bounce off the surface. I get out of the vehicle, lock the doors, and get my towel and umbrella from the trunk.

The Moreton Bay figs' bearded ancient shapes define a path to the changing pavilion, where parrots flit about like windblown leaves. My eyes refuse to concentrate as the trees emerge from their ghostly negatives and I can't escape the feeling of staring at a tapestry, the warp and weft of positive and negative space, but never quite resolving which one is which. The water flows through the leaves in an unending variety of blues and greys. As though I'm standing in front of the final landscape painted with the type of beauty that only dying love can provide; a fleeting, tragic, fragile love on the other side of sadness.

Quickly taking off my shoes and clothes on the concrete stairs, I plunge into the water and immediately begin to swim. I use a combination of breaststroke, backstroke, a turn at the net, freestyle, and a type of frog kick on my back to navigate the pool. The rain falls on my cheeks, and the sky's jagged backbone pierces my ears with thunderous cracks. The harbor's neck, the CBD's staved fangs. As I swim in the ocean, I encounter everything from churning jellyfish to gobbets that kiss my arms. It's a fantastic feeling to be completely alone. When it rains, the water takes on a silky sheen.

It's not Nielsen Park, but Shoal Bay is a beautiful place in its own right! As the headland snouts into the ocean, it looks like an enormous lizard. The sand is fine and golden, there are no other people around, and the water is refreshingly cool. A fossilized seahorse has washed up on the shore. The restroom facility where I shower and change is covered with a lattice of huge figs, and the water from the shower is colder than the sea. Back at the vehicle, I'm greeted with an acrid sting on the ball of my foot; I've perforated the skin of a seed pod by standing on it. Between my toes, there are lace trails of blood. To wipe it, I stoop down and reach for my towel, but then I reconsider; It will eventually dry out but I'm hobbling because of the sharpness of the pain.

A biker loses control of his bike on the slippery road and slips in front of the vehicle as I drive back to Soldier's Point, where I've been told you can have a wonderful breakfast. I swerve just in time to avoid colliding with the rider, who lands on his back against the little island of safety in the center of the road - It's a stunning location. The bay and the surrounding vegetation seem as quiet as a black-and-white image as the road bends to the right. For a split second, I'm torn about whether or not to aid the guy. The thing is, I've already moved on from that particular setting.

In the rear of the café, at a modest table, I read my book, ordered scrambled eggs with grilled tomato, bacon, and a long black I like savoring my cup of joe for as long as possible. I'm not a regular reader of the news, so, I sit back and enjoy the unfolding of the day: In the midst of the commotion, two elderly men are playing chess on an outside table as schoolgirls in sports uniforms offer their moms, coffee. The cyclist's astonished expression resurfaces in my mind, and I can't help but smile. I didn't see any accusation in his eyes since we were both thinking only on where we were going; what lay at the foot of the hill.

What a fragile foundation expectations have when faced with the realities of life. Everything happens so fast that you find yourself on the wrong side of a wall you weren't aware of and unable to turn around.

I go from the parking lot to the elderly home's door on a morning brilliant with sunlight, as if it were the day after a holiday when the fun is ended. I arrive at the nursing home to clear skies.

My mother is being fed in her bed by a Levantine nurse whose name escapes me. Neither is aware of my presence, so I silently observe them from the hallway. Though I can't put my finger on it, I'm disturbed by how the nurse walked away from me yesterday. In some ways, it reminded me like watching the end credits roll on a movie. It's strange that I have no recollection of her name, considering that she was the only person with whom I interacted throughout my mother's hospitalization. It, too, has vanished from view. The natural opening up that occurs after familiarity in others is a shrinking of immediacy that seems like a growth (a concealed expansion) – like the root life of a growing tree, even in this short period of time (it was only afterwards that I learnt of the tragedy that befell her).

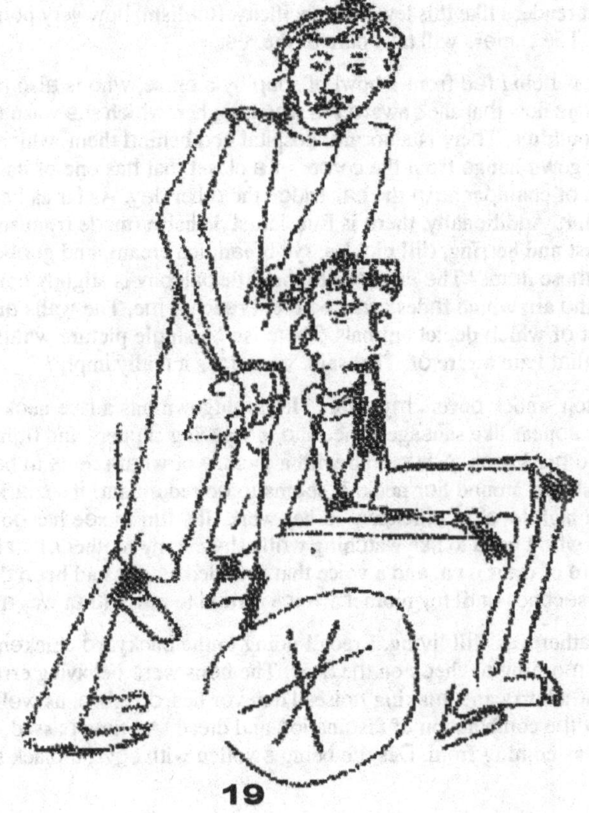

It's hard to tell if guilt is good or negative. It seems to have a powerful magnetic field. Seeing how well-cared-for my mother is, makes me think in this manner, maybe because of the jealousy it evokes in me. Whatever the situation may be, my mother is being fed by a nurse whose name escapes me, and she is conversing freely with her in a way that I could never imagine. The American wheelchair I purchased for her before she was in it is sitting there. In the event that she has to go to battle, it's engineered to withstand the rigors of combat and comfortable enough for her to spend lengthy periods of time at her leisure. As a result of her poor sight, she's no longer able to read or watch television. God knows what she does all day sitting there with her eyes shut (while I was busy grinding away at my axes for two years)! When she was able to see, she never looked at any of my work, but I don't hold that against her at all; I'm unable to view it as well. There are few people who can sit for hours looking at their bread and butter without tiring of the task. I entered the company knowing what I was getting myself into, and so far it has treated me nicely. I have nothing further to add.

Despite the fact that the air conditioning vents are rattling like snakes in the background, my mother is animatedly waving her hands as if she were attempting to clear the way for someone else. How many times have I listened to her rattling on a tune that had a deep groove? I don't know how many times. Quite a few things may bring up memories.

To be honest, I've been losing my creativity for a while now, and that's not good for business. I'm no longer interested in eliciting or explaining emotions or feelings. It's as if I'm already bored with it before I even begin. All of this information is unnecessary, and what's the point? Take this space. I'm taking a look at it at the moment. It's there in front of me. It shows up in front of me. What's the big deal if you can't say it? In any writing program, the instructor will tell you that readers like this level of specificity. Realism, how very pointless it is! It annoys me to the core. The camera will take care of the rest.

My mother is being fed from a bowl of soup by a nurse, who is also taking care of her. She's self-conscious now that she's aware I'm watching her, which she wasn't before. They converse between mouthfuls. There is a normal hospital bed behind them, which is a mattress on a cart. A dressing gown hangs from the corner of a closet that has one of its doors half open. I saw half-bottles of champagne in the bar fridge the other day. As far as I can tell, my mother still enjoys a drink. Additionally, there is Russian-style halva (made from sunflower seeds), as well as liverwurst and herring, dill pickles, rye bread, ice cream, and gubbets of blueberries. Who buys all of these items? The entrance to the little balcony is slightly open, allowing the curtain to sway in the air, which fades away before it reaches me. The walls are covered with generic prints, most of which depict animals. There isn't a single picture whatsoever, not even on the nightstand that I am aware of. That said, what does it really imply?

A grey cotton smock covers my mum. Her nightgown has a lace neckline, which I can make out. Calves appear like sausages since she is wearing slippers and tight circulation socks that go almost to her knees. A huge bib with a picture of what seems to be Winnie-the-Pooh and Piglet is fastened around her neck. It seems to be redundant; It's sparkling and spotless. The nurse has a high level of efficiency in her work. It's fun to see her go about. That Rose Bay hairdresser who I used to like watching while she cut my mother's hair had hands that seemed to have a life of their own, and a voice that sounded as if it had been there for all time. It was a matter of seconds until my mother's voice turned to mush (that was a poor choice of words).

When my father was still living, I recall going to the backyard chicken coop he'd constructed early in the morning to check on the hens. The hens were behaving erratically, as if they were in the eye of a hurricane, making noises I'd never heard before, as well! I was both awed and horrified by the combination of fascination and dread. As time passed, it became clear where the crazy was coming from. Despite being swollen with eggs, a black snake that had crawled through the chicken wire was still attempting to push itself out the same manner. Suddenly my mother was there, this abrupt presence, shoving me away without saying anything, she fought the snake silently with a shovel, repeatedly slamming it down on its black back and head until it was shattered in half. In the early hours of the next morning, I saw my father demolish the chicken coop and break the necks of the chickens one by one.

As my mother chatted happily with the nurse, it seemed as if they had known each other for years and she was a young woman again, so caught up and interwoven with the thread of her words that she might never return – that somewhere beyond my grasp, things were trying to move into place, but as in a dream, where there is confusion and certainty at once, and no way of untangling one from the other.

'John is here,' the nurse says, her voice raised so I can hear, yet she continues with her work. My skin tingles when she gently dabs at the corners of my mother's lips after lifting the bib.

My mother goes into a complete frenzy, her hands folding over her lap like a sophisticated lock.

Now I can almost taste the soup. Cabbage, onion, and maybe chicken fat don't sound bad, do they?

As I write this, the nurse is cleaning my mother's face with a moist flannel besides the soup tray and adds, 'She's been awake since four.' She hasn't turned to look at me yet. 'You said you'd be here at six, and she told me that.' She accused me in the same cool tone that appeared to be her natural pitch, and she did so without irritability. She wouldn't admit it if I'd been a bother to her this morning because of my tardiness.

'I told her nothing of the like,' I responded, my voice rising with defensiveness. There must be a better

way to put it. 'She doesn't even know the time anymore,' a friend said.

It wasn't until the end of the conversation that I realized I'd been talking about my mother as if she weren't present. She froze like a lizard on the verge of a train track when she saw me. Was she even aware of my existence? I hadn't yet entered the room to its full extent.

'You may be interested to know that she's been patiently waiting for you.'

Why, what do you ask? I'd been relieved of the anxiety I'd had about how she'd react to me after two years — she had no idea who I was. It was so delightfully unexpected that my joy was clouded by the significance of its meaning. Inside the nonexistence of my mother's blind look, it felt surprisingly quiet. Only this nurse, whom I'd only just met, was able to make me feel the remorse I should have. When I attempted to explain myself to her, every word I came up with simply served to bury me deeper.

'I'm so sorry.' Finally, I replied, 'It's not your fault.'

However, another music was in the works in her head. When she said it, it was if she knew what I was thinking. 'Don't be alarmed. In my own country, guys speak about honor even if they don't know what it is. They're actually referring to 'self-esteem.'

If they were supposed to reassure me, they were strange words. She shifted her attention away from my mother in order to focus on the words she had to say and ultimately turned her attention to me. Her gaze was not one of accusation. There was a time when I thought the words had originated from somewhere else. Since I was a child, I've been obsessed with the idea of being a better person, and you'd think by now I'd have realized that you can't just wiggle your nose and become the person you want or think you could be.

In a mocking grin, I added, 'I feel like I've disrupted something,' and left the room. What I didn't know was what impression she'd developed of me while we were talking. There was more of her in the room than there was space for. It seemed as though she couldn't believe I was there, much as James did when he was a baby. Doesn't every kid have some kind of distrust towards their parents? And it's a surprise we don't kill them all considering what they know about us.

'No,' she responded, 'we've been talking about Italy before the war. In addition, there's Lebanon. Her interest hasn't waned.'

She turned her head to look at me as if she had finally realized I wasn't the only one here for a brief minute. When she sat down, her hands were free. Her wedding band was twisted in her hand. I was aware of it, but my attention was drawn to the nurse. Something sweet and kind about her gaze suggested that she had just asked me a question, and that the only thing that mattered was how I responded. Her thick lashes, which made her hazel eyes seem darker than they really were, frisked me amiably and without any resistance. I was able to detect the subtle motion playing across her face throughout the quick examination, and I immediately understood why my mother was drawn to her. The light of her eyes and the grin on her face seemed to come from some unseen source, as if she couldn't control it.

I focused on my mother, who had her eyes wide open, as if she were sensing something. I had no clue what she was seeing. Even though I was standing right next to the bed, near enough to touch her, she still hadn't recognized my presence. I couldn't get the feeling

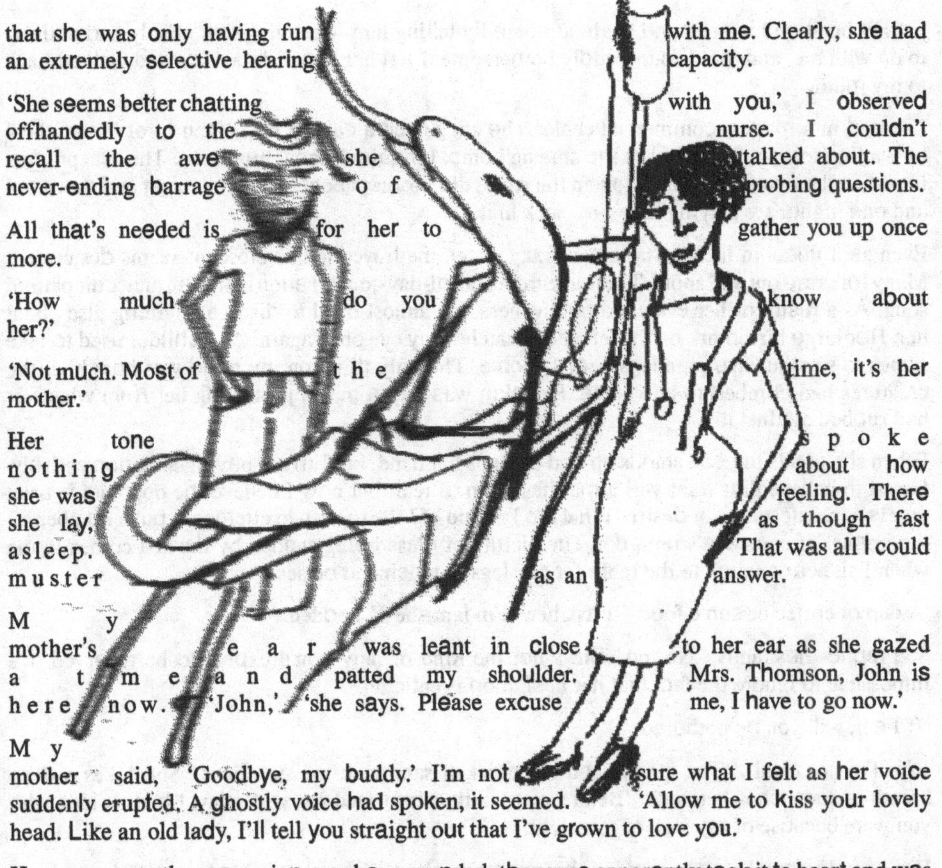

that she was only having fun with me. Clearly, she had an extremely selective hearing capacity.

'She seems better chatting with you,' I observed offhandedly to the nurse. I couldn't recall the awe she talked about. The never-ending barrage of probing questions.

All that's needed is for her to gather you up once more.

'How much do you know about her?'

'Not much. Most of the time, it's her mother.'

Her tone spoke nothing about how she was feeling. There she lay, as though fast asleep. That was all I could muster as an answer.

My mother's ear was leant in close to her ear as she gazed at me and patted my shoulder. Mrs. Thomson, John is here now. 'John,' 'she says. Please excuse me, I have to go now.'

My mother said, 'Goodbye, my buddy.' I'm not sure what I felt as her voice suddenly erupted. A ghostly voice had spoken, it seemed. 'Allow me to kiss your lovely head. Like an old lady, I'll tell you straight out that I've grown to love you.'

However corny the expression may have sounded, the nurse apparently took it to heart and was delighted. When my mother's lips kissed her cheek, she blushed, straightened up, and gave me her hand with a smile that appeared to shift between her mouth and eyes. I was happy to press it, as if it represented something special. She walked slowly towards the door.

'So sweet,' my mother said, before closing her eyes once more.

I responded, 'Wait,' and followed the nurse out into the hallway, my mind boggled by my mother's metamorphosis. I felt compelled to whisper even though no one else was around. 'I have something to say to you,' I said.

She patiently awaited my response.

'Would you want a cup of coffee?'

'In Nelson Bay,' she replied, as if she had anticipated the enquiry. 'If you like, I could meet you there at 4:30 p.m.'

There was nothing in her demeanor to suggest that she found my proposition out of the ordinary. It's possible that demands like these were prevalent.

She gave me the details and then walked down the hallway to the kitchen, where she sat down at a table. My smile stayed on my face as I kept an eye on her. I saw her approach a cleaner, put her hand on his arm, and begin animatedly telling him something that plainly had nothing to do with me, and that I found oddly bothersome. I left her to her discussion and walked back to my mum.

Located in a modest commercial center, she suggested a café to try. When I get there, she'll be waiting for me. Before I left the nursing home, I inquired about her name. The receptionist introduced me to Cassandra. How in the world did I forget about that? Arab night and thousand and one nights are playing hide-and-seek in it.

Even as it floats in the crystal-clear, fizzy water, the frayed lemon crescent seems desiccated. Many folks are out and about. The murmur of end-of-day conversation is like an unaccompanied song. As a result of her evident attractiveness, it's almost hard to discern anything else about her. Her large birthmark on the left cheek catches my eye once again. As a child, I used to take James to see the cave paintings near Broome. The only thing on my mind was how high the creatures had climbed to be visible. Her skin was like a mask, protecting her from whatever had rubbed against it.

When she greets me, she stands up and extends her hand, but I'm not paying attention entirely. I used to believe that want was a manifestation of fear, but now I believe the opposite is true: fear is a manifestation of desire. What am I afraid of? It's foolish to attempt to put a number on the impact of someone's remarks. The picture of glass being sanded by the sea comes to me when I sit near enough to the table for our legs to touch and be seen.

'A cup of coffee or some food?' I ask her. 'I'm famished,' I added.

She replies hesitantly, 'No, no.' She's not the kind of lady you'd expect to be reserved. It's impossible to ignore the fact that her hesitation is enticing.

'If I eat, will you be bothered?'

'No, I'm not at all. 'The quiche and the chicken sandwich are excellent.' She takes a deep breath and stretches her neck. 'Before your mother informed me yesterday, I had no idea who you were because of my lack of foresight.'

However, I remembered her saying that my mother had said nothing about me (and I wondered again at the game my mother might be playing), so I let it go. I ordered the chicken sandwich and a cup of coffee when the waitress arrived. Cassandra didn't say anything as she nodded her head.

When I asked, 'What did she say?' Afterwards, I inquired about it.

' I've heard you write for TV. I checked out your profile. I've seen pretty about all of them.'

'And what do you think?'

'Affirmative.' In her gaze, she locks on to mine. It's disconcerting how quickly the air of mystery gives way to openness. 'They're not the same. Nothing about the characters changes, they're only made more genuine via revelation. Even after spending a lifetime together, you barely scratch the surface of what each person has to offer the other. My favorite part of your tales is when you tell the truth, people do not change.'

It was the longest I'd ever listened to her talk, and I'd never feel the same way again, despite all that happened thereafter. There was nothing better than a good cup of coffee to accompany a great chicken sandwich. For all I knew, she may have spoken about my scripts for hours and hours and hours.

'I'm grateful,' I said. The truth is that I haven't written anything worthwhile in a long time.

How haughtily I went fishing. The woman, on the other hand, refused to be lured in by the bait. For that, she gained favor with me. She seems to have a natural aversion to dishonesty. Despite the fact that I had only just met her, she seemed to be quite alone.

She asks, 'What were you hoping to get out of this?'

Two young women are unloading a car's hatch with portable hangers and bags of clothing as seen from the window of a nearby café. A temporary retail establishment set up on the sidewalk. You can't help but appreciate their will to succeed. They seem to be just a few years old.

I admit that it isn't simple. When he was fourteen, an American writer whom I much like once said, 'I felt my father knew nothing,' His father had learnt a lot in seven years, he claimed, by the time he was twenty-one. That's OK with me, however my thoughts on the matter vary. In a way, it's like being eighteen, when I believed I had it all figured out. In my mid-fifties, I'm shocked by the amount of information I've forgotten.

Almost laughing, she flashes a grin. 'When I was in elementary school, a Vietnamese friend of mine informed our instructor that time flies quickly. She'd only been in Australia for a short time, but she was already enjoying learning new terms in the language, but she was mistaken. Time isn't a hook; rather, it's a sneak, like in the game 'What's the Time, Mr. Wolf?' that we used to play. Years have sped by without notice, leaving you aged and wondering where your life has gone.'

She stated that with no remorse at all. In my wildest dreams, I can't comprehend how she was able to maintain such a level of calm. Even more so, given where and with whom she worked.

'You were raised in Sydney?' (That's what I told you).

'Yes, but before we came here, we spent two years in Major metropolitan area in South-Eastern England.'

'Ah.'

'What?'

Despite her puzzlement, she didn't seem annoyed by my incoherence; rather, she seemed to have become used to it. There is always a silver lining in every situation.

'I like your accent.'

'Oooh, that. It's completely unrelated to Major metropolitan area in South-Eastern England. For a long time, I called Parramatta home. You may call it a stew if my accent is anything.'

I joined her in her laughter when she eventually did. It was a pleasant get-together. Even her uniform's grey skirt and blouse seemed to be of high quality and elegance.

'Would you want to have it back?'

'No.'

She was as direct as ever. In her chair, she seemed to be moving away from me. A reduction of the charge between our legs that didn't quite meet may have been the cause, even if it wasn't physical.

When asked about her accent, she answered amiably, 'You didn't bring me here to speak about my accent,' as if that had made up for her being so direct. Before raising her glass, she stroked my hand. I thought she had stung me. The moment I took a bite of my sandwich, I couldn't stop myself from scanning the surface for a sign of damage.

'No.'

Now it's my time to be sarcastic. I was at a loss as to how or even whether I wanted to tell her what I wanted to say. As a son who hadn't seen his mother in two years and hadn't made a single phone call, she must have developed an opinion of me.

As she put it, 'the ones who want to do good are usually the ones with the guilty conscience. Whoever is actually to blame doesn't give a damn.'

Wasn't this clear to begin with?

'You'veforgotten where I work.' A grin brightened her face. If you conceal it, the more others will notice, it's like trying to remove a stain with a rag.'

Nonetheless, I wanted to make it clear that guilt isn't the sole factor here. I wanted to explain and defend myself, but I also wanted to hear her speak. It wasn't simply her voice that got me, although it sufficed. My mother had been sleeping peacefully that morning, and so I remained silent about what I'd been thinking. That debt (what I owed) was more than just a financial duty. After two years of ignoring my mother's presence, how could I be here now, with no explanation other than this silent summons that sounded like an ember beneath the ashes of an extinguished fire, and I would keep returning even though she had no idea who I was and might sleep (or pretend to sleep) for as long as I was there? How could I explain this? Because this commitment, this duty, was also a gift in some sense, because without it, everything else in my life seemed drab and dreary. Some people know this instantly; for me it took two years.

'I'm reading,' she responded when she realized I was ignoring her, despite the fact that my gaze had not shifted from hers. 'It's as though we're breathing in the same air as our ancestors. Aren't you in awe of it? To say this is a novel about dying is an understatement. When you hear your mother's voice, you hear an echo of other voices that have been silenced for generations, according to the writer. It's like a secret pact between us and them that we'll remember, pay homage, make restitution, and maybe even put to rest.... No matter how hard you try not to be struck by how incomplete everything seems, working in a profession like hers will always leave you feeling that way.

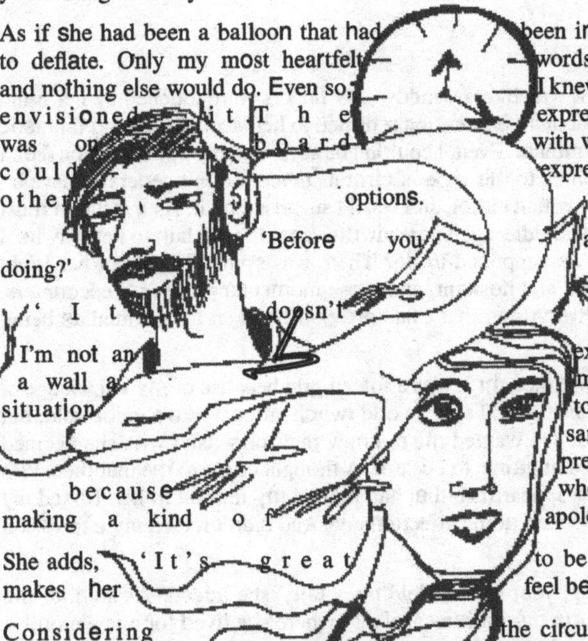

As if she had been a balloon that had been inflated by the words, she seemed to deflate. Only my most heartfelt words would suffice as an exchange, and nothing else would do. Even so, I knew it wouldn't turn out the way I had envisioned it The expression on her face indicated that I was on board with what she was saying. If only a grin could express such sentiments. There are no other options.

'Before you arrived here, what were you doing?'

'It doesn't matter,' she said.

I'm not an expert on anything, but I can see a wall a mile away. I take advantage of the situation to eat another mouthful of my sandwich. She must have felt her previous remarks were too harsh, because when she speaks again, it's as if she's making a kind of apology.

She adds, 'It's great to be sitting here with you,' as if that makes her feel better.

Considering the circumstances, it's not surprising that I had forgotten we were in a café until she said those words. We were the only ones there.

I say, 'It's a little unexpected.'

'When I awoke this morning, it wasn't what I had in mind.'

'What were you thinking about?'

'I suppose it would be a typical day.'

Inquiringly, I said, 'You're bored?'

'Not at all. I really like what I'm doing. If anything, if I ever imagined of anything, it was that I would be doing precisely that.'

That has to be difficult.

'No. They're just like little kids,' he says.

As the saying goes, 'it's going to cost something.'

For some reason, I couldn't let this go. Her response this time was a simple grin, which appeared to me at the moment to be filled with some kind of promise at that modest café by the sea. A strange feeling came over me: I thought I'd seen her grin before.

'Have you ever lived outside of Sydney?' I inquired.

'Later.'

'Where's Granville.'

It all made sense now.

'Are you here with your family?'
'No.'

I felt the wall again, but this time it was like a window. My fingers were touched by her hand as she went for her drink, and the demure expression returned to her face. Something fantastic seemed to be about to happen for a minute. Even, I couldn't be sure, and my apprehension didn't go away anytime soon. When it comes to this type of circumstance, I don't generally have an issue. However, I wasn't unfamiliar with it either, so I wasn't surprised by it. As a result, it must have something to do with her. If a middle-aged screenwriter couldn't explain to her why he'd brought her here, what else was she supposed to do? There was something about her look, the way she alternated between bold and hesitant, and those momentary physical encounters. There was something about her. Everything that I had previously taken for granted as being unaffected suddenly felt tainted.

When she smiled back at me again, I thought it was a forced grin because of my knowledge of being shut off. When I looked into her eyes, I saw an odd twitch, almost like a quick cold, but it was more like an acting exercise. She wanted me to know that she wasn't who she seemed to be. Why, then? It was an odd kind of game, to be sure. A thought came to me that there was something more intangible than her appearance that had piqued my interest in her. I fixed my gaze on her smoky irises. But she looked at me affectionately and didn't return my expression of challenge.

'As we waited for you this morning, your mother told me a tale,' she added. 'As a child, she said she spent time with her mother in the Italian canal city where she lived for a few months. In the midst of the Carnival season, this incident occurred. In the morning, they got up early and headed off. She described how chilly it was and how she felt like she was breathing in a mist. She believed the breath had made the mist thick. The way she speaks is beautiful, but you already know that.'

She stopped, but I didn't want to interrupt her since I wanted to hear the rest of the tale. Her knowledge of my mother's background was becoming more apparent to me—certainly more of the truth. It was as though a stranger had taken what was mine.

'The mist dissipated as they approached the Grand Canal, and a small number of guys, costumed as Turks, were seen strolling on the river. Once again, she exhaled, and the fog began to gather in around her as she remarked it was just a short walk. However, her mother was deep in contemplation and said nothing to her as she turned to face her. I didn't push her any more since interruptions typically disrupt people's flow of thinking. However, I had the impression that she was attempting to communicate with me in some way... There are instances when individuals start something that doesn't end because they want it to.'

Despite the fact that I couldn't be sure whether it was her or my mother's notion, it was a wonderful thing to say. However, its significance only dawned on me in retrospect. Resentment lingered over the fact that my mother talked to her caregiver in a manner she hadn't spoken to me in years - and probably ever.

Despite being brand new, the nursing home where my mother was confined had rapidly begun to resemble the old-style nursing facilities that it had replaced. It had been constructed to meet newer standards and with the greatest of intentions, with an eye towards cleanliness, comfort, and even elegance. All of this new modern airport lounge preoccupation, from the botox-faced receptionist smoking outside the entrance to the stale tea and cold scones waiting for fuck knows who's rescue outside the common room, made me feel ill.

I smelled the toilet before I saw my mother's corpse wrapped in a blanket. A little, fork-like hand connected to the short arm-bone, slender and straight from wrist to elbow, rested on top of the blanket. The head rested on the pillow in an odd position. She had sparse hair on her temples and a tight forehead that seemed almost translucent. Her face looked like a corpse since she hadn't been bathed or made up, and her artificial teeth were missing. I thought that couldn't possibly be my mother's horrible body. But when I got closer, there was no room for doubt. It didn't take long for the horrible reality to sink in: this dead corpse was my live mother. That's when I felt what I should have felt upon my return three days earlier but didn't: sympathy and terror at the prospect of her imminent death.

With one accusatory stare, the maniacs' eyes seemed to recognize me for the first time, and that gaze immediately formed a live connection between us. I was resentful of my good fortune in the face of such adversity. I couldn't shake the image of yesterday afternoon in the café. My mother gave me a warm grin as I clasped her hand. Even though it was barely discernible, the severe look in her eyes did not budge, and yet there was still a grin there.

She struggled to say, 'You didn't expect to find me this way.'

'No,' I responded, tripping over my words. 'Yes,' I answered. As if they had not told me sooner.

It was simple to fabricate the facts. When she didn't react, I had no idea what more to say, particularly since she didn't look away from me. She suddenly awoke and started to speak. She was full of accusations against her doctor. She sobbed and begged me to take her home right away, lamenting the fact that she should never have been brought here. She didn't give up!

'This place is filthy,' she replied.

I shook my head and stated 'I'd go locate a nurse', so I could get some relief from the agony, but as soon as I entered the hallway, I paused. After all, she was the one who stated she'd look for a nurse for me. The next time I visited, I sat down next to her bed and, after making sure she wouldn't have to turn her head to look at me, I started talking to her by lifting and pressing on her skeletal hand. My Dictaphone was still in my jacket pocket, so I pulled it out, switched it on, and set it down on the bedside table with my free hand. She didn't mention it if she had seen it. In the end, I didn't care what she said, since I didn't want anything to go to waste.

Maybe it was cruel of her, but I was her son, and here she was, helpless in her bed, the drawbridge finally thrown open, like she had never been before. As a result, I subjected her to a barrage of questions. She took advantage of her predicament to get what she deserved. At the same time that I saw the absurdity: that I was eliciting memories just as her memory was crumbling, with dozens of queries, to be precise. What's so great about Australia? How?

Amongst whom? What brought her and my father together? Her mother's fate is unknown. When was the first time she heard about her father's story? How? I'm curious how she felt, and so on. Since she no longer held the perspicacity of headspace she once did, she replied; garbled, incoherent, fragmented, mad, but not with any hesitation and without the use of deception, she was maskless. It seemed like way before Cassandra came, she had been talking in this manner for an hour. My Dictaphone was returned to my pocket as well. Then, as suddenly as it had arrived, her liveliness had gone. It was as if she felt what was happening between her nurse and her son and detested it. Her face set again in the reproachful look that was now its default; I'm a hundred years old, yet I'm still struggling for life!

How long has it been? Everything in her head had been smashed to pieces by a flood, like one of those Picasso paintings in which nothing seems to fit with anything else, but somehow it all makes sense at the end. It wasn't that she had a stable condition of memory, but rather a continual rushing out of amnesia. Words scabbed over by her insanity seem to be scabs on the wound. I could still see, as I had as a child, the vestiges of a narrative she wasn't telling - its suppression must have been geological – there in her eyes, hands, and voice, a corporeal memory no less coded but for which I had yet to find the key. For some reason, I felt like I was witnessing someone who had lost their memory transform into flesh. There were so many possibilities, but one memory was flickering in the back of her eyes but there was no line or hook for it to latch on to; it was like watching a person who had lost their memory transform into flesh. I have no idea why that made such an impact on me, not just at the time, but even when I went back and transcribed and edited it all. I'm not really clear who she was speaking to at this point.

Hanging by the feet of two guys. So, mama said: 'I know where their heads are.' They weren't going to be here tomorrow, either.

'It was known as hand palace prior to Neolatry's reign. Mama informed me that it belonged to him. I was told... what was that?

'A slew of letters from Johnno.

'It was a night shift. Were you the one? He'd had a leg amputated. Remove your blouse's buttons so that I can view your breasts, please. I went for a jog and returned with a hasty retreat; he had expired.'

She was contemplating something out the window. She scanned the skies for what seemed like an eternity.

She had a rigid way of doing things. She never gave me a pat on the back. However, this time she grabbed my head and kissed me... kissed me! 'You looked into my eyes... I continued waving, waving, waving at nothing...

'He picks up his spectacles that had fallen off. There has been a lot of rain recently. They arrange us in a queue. Everywhere you look, there are puddles. The soldier's pleading is audible to us. He bursts into tears. Shoot him in the forehead as he's on his knees. With a gun in hand.

'We went exploring in the woods. Refused to leave anything out. According to a rumor, since the youngster is already half-dead, he will succumb to his injuries. You seem to get my point of view... We camped in ditches and beneath bushes. There were People from the European country that was unified in the 19th century and was famously geopolitically aggressive in the 20th century wherever we looked. There was no other option, according to the guys, except to battle our way out. We were doomed to perish regardless of what happened. At night, they came to us. Not enough ladies

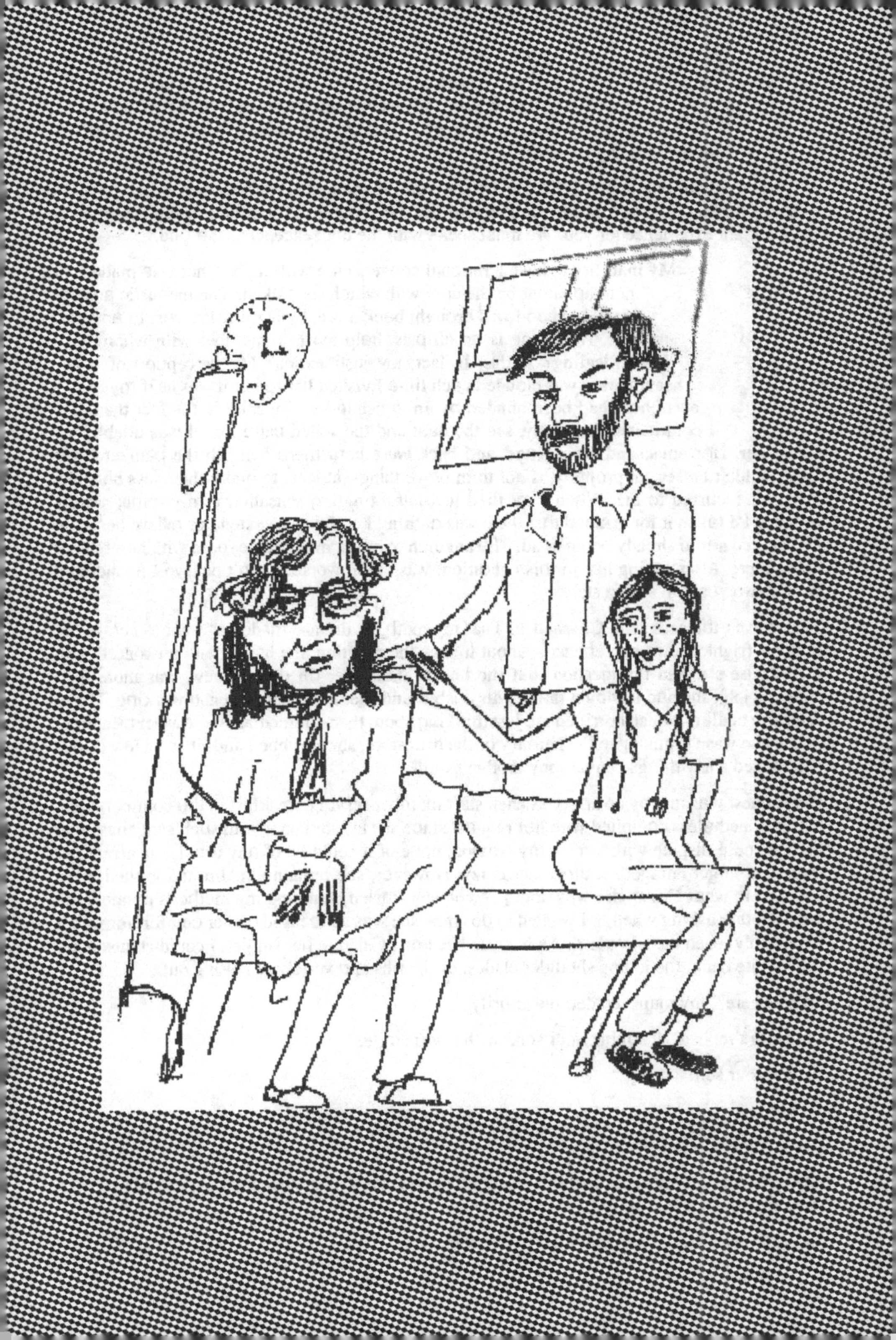

showed up.

There were so many males, yet only three of us were there. You're on board, right? At one point, it seemed as though we were going to perish...'

Rather than look at me as Cassandra entered the room, she immediately began speaking to my mother. As she looked around the room, she told me, 'I'm afraid this isn't going to be a pleasant experience for you. We must speak with the housekeepers,' she said.

My inability to have a rational conversation with my mother was made all the more apparent by the ease with which she talked. The monastic austerity of my boyhood was brought back to life by her disclosures. In a world where everything is an ellipsis, help me to remember with whom I was dealing? Is this, in fact, my justification? My perception of her situation was clouded each time I visited her room; it was as if my awareness had been blinded by an invisible veil. In spite of the fact that I could smell her body, see the dust and the soiled bathroom, I was unable to aid her. Her emaciated shins, legs, and back were bent there beneath the blanket, as if they couldn't be set out properly, if not to improve things, at least to make them less horrible. It hadn't occurred to me. When I recalled it, I felt a tingling sensation in my spine; simply because I'd taken it for granted that there was nothing I could do to extend or relieve her pain, I'd equated her to already being dead. The anguish of being in the same room with her, but not being there, after seeing her in this condition, was much worse. I can't believe I abandoned her for two years in such a state.

That wasn't the case with Cassandra. That my mother's disease made her want to act, rather than be frightened or apprehensive about it, was the reaction she had when confronted with it. Because she had no question that she had to assist her (in this, I knew, was more than simply a job), she had no doubt that it was doable, and she immediately began working. Those same particulars, which horrified me just thinking about them, immediately drew her attention. When she wasn't running to the laundry or the drugstore, she scrubbed and rinsed a few things and tucked a few things beneath my mother's quilt.

Her request was met by an angry kitchen staff member serving breakfast in the common area, but he nonetheless complied with her request since she insisted on it with such gentleness that no one could dispute with her. In my opinion, none of it could be of any use. I was afraid my mum would get enraged. It drove her crazy. However, she remained calm and looked to be engaged in what Cassandra was doing. When she started changing my mother's panties, she didn't bother asking whether I wanted to go since she was so focused on her comfort (or was it to possibly teach me a lesson?). As her arm became twisted in her singlet, I couldn't unsee her little white back, the jutting shoulder blades, or the ribs and vertebrae poking out.

'Who's here?' my mum scolded me angrily.

Cassandra replied, 'It's John, your son,' with a soft smile.

'Is this your son?'

'Yes.'

'Do not come to this place, please.'

As Cassandra adjusted her arm and snuggled her back into bed, I murmured, 'I'm not looking,' more forcefully than I meant.

'Go grab me a cup of tea, I'm thirsty,' she said.

Even though every syllable was delivered with a ferocity that made my pulse pound, I was enthralled. Surely, she had finally figured out who I was. As soon as I returned with the tea, I saw a completely different person, as well as a completely different environment. Disinfectant and musk took the place of the thick enuretic odor, and there was no dust to be seen everywhere. When I woke up, my mother was dressed in a new nightgown, her lace collar wrapped around her slender neck as she slept on clean sheets, supported up by high pillows. New hope filled my heart as I watched the scene unfold.

In a profoundly unnerving look, my mother told Cassandra, 'I am already better,' and smiled. 'If only you could assist my kid,' I begged. She grabbed Cassandra's hand and started to kiss it, but she quickly changed her mind, as if she was afraid it might be uncomfortable for her. Cassandra grasped both of my mother's hands in hers and pushed them together, as though her thoughts were continuously focused on what my mother needed. My mother told me to 'flip me on my side and leave,' and I obeyed.

Cassandra gave me a look I'd never seen before and beckoned for me to take her seat next to the bed, which I gladly did. She said, 'I believe it's best if you do it.'

Even though it was terrifying for me to wrap my arms around that dreadful body, to hold those parts beneath the blanket that I did not want to know about, I succumbed to her command, placed my arms under the blanket, and grabbed hold of my mother. Cassandra swiftly moved the pillow over, plumped it, and fixed my mother's thin hair, which had once again adhered to her temples as I rolled her over, feeling a chilly arm wrap around my neck.

When I was a child, my mother held my hand in hers. That's what I thought she was doing, but I didn't know where she was sketching it at the time. With a heavy heart, I bowed my head in submission. She kissed it as she pulled it to her lips. I trembled with weeping and walked out of the room without looking back, unable to utter a single word.

Even if it's unfathomable to contemplate death, I can't help but be fascinated by its incessant ingenuity. It's hard to imagine anybody except a genius coming up with dementia. Despite all my pondering, I still have no idea what I'm talking about. I still don't know how to talk to this dying individual. In a state of uncertainty, I have no notion what to say or how to appear. Unrelated topics are offensive, yet being quiet is difficult. Whether I look at her or not, she'll assume I'm interested in her. If I walk on eggshells, she could bite off my head. I don't think Cassandra cares at all about it, and she seems to know just what to do. She tells tales, she asks questions, she smiles, and she touches her, she speaks as if there is a future where everything works out. My mum is overjoyed. My mother's physical health has nothing to do with what she's being asked to do. It's there, and it doesn't do anything. It's only a matter of time before Cassandra enters the room again, and I'll gaze at her with the same terror as I did this morning when I saw her.

It's possible that if I weren't her son, she might treat me differently. Because she, too, is familiar with death — in the same way that a wife is. However, she let me into her world with a sigh of relief. It's as though every phrase is accompanied with a goodbye glance, nearly from the other side. Now, as she recalls, she is older than she was back then. She would have recounted one narrative in Europe, but now, after seventy years, she fills in the blanks with her whole life's worth of experiences. And then there's the looming specter of death. It's as though nothing in a human being makes sense until one considers death.

When I first played the recording, she immediately replied, 'I can't... I'd rather forget than think about it. I made it out of the conflict unscathed. Quiet! Keep it a secret if you don't want to be exposed. I was there, and I can tell you that... because of your age...' (Me? Was she speaking to me, or was she just joking? Her son, who is fifty-five years old?) 'My whole life has been shattered. For a period of two years, I didn't consider myself a woman at all; I was completely devoid of blood. My body had stopped breathing... While in Naples, Italy, my future husband proposed to me while he was in the camp and said, "The war's done. Despite all the bad news, we're still here. Let's tie the knot." I was on the verge of tears. I wanted to smack him about the face. "How do you know that I'm married?? Now? After all this - are you going to get married now? What do you think?" First and foremost, I need to transform myself back into a lady. "Yes, I'll marry you," I say to him as tears stream down his cheek. His face was scorched purple, and I could see he knew everything.

I sat at the dining table at her home that night, unsure of what to do after I had left her sleeping in her bed. Instead, I should have prepared a meal, settled down for the night, and contemplated my future plans for both the home and for her. In her agony and agonizing sorrow, it occurred to me that Cassandra may be doing all of these things in her own kitchen with the same directness of action and speed of judgement that men are fabled to display before a war. But all I could do was listen to the voice that arose from the Dictaphone, which I had only now realized was in my pocket.

I returned to my mum after a three-day journey. Twelve missed calls from my son were found after I finished transcribing all she had said on the recording the next morning.

In James's eyes, the more ambitious the plan, the better. In a fit of irrationality, I agreed to spend a few days with him in the place where people like to surf or grow old in Queensland later in the year. Nonetheless, I entirely forgot about it in the midst of everything going on around me. The flight was scheduled to take off in the afternoon. He had a deal going on, and he felt I may be able to assist him out with it. 'Business relationships' and the development he was engaged in with indigenous landowners. I explained to him what occurs when you construct a home on sand. However, he said, "as you know, Dad, up here it's just sand."

Sand and swamp, he had it right. The Russians were also present in the swamps. Not the teddy bears of Stalinist diaspora, all sons of exile, but the type that don't need to loan money to expect their return; they take it as their due because their due is to take until they're taken by some predator even larger or more unhinged than they are - loan sharks whose only capital is their teeth, and who'd heard of James Thomson and his supposedly political connections and who wanted to take advantage of them. Who is to blame then? He had become a millionaire as a result of it. In fact, he'd have me think, he made squillions of dollars from nothing more than the mere purchase and sale of that marsh and sand! From across the world, you could detect the scent of chum. I was surprised, though, by what my son expected me to undertake in his bizarre plan to put the original owners of the property against the Russians. I had no idea what to do. Rows and rows of white teeth were all I could see from this vantage point. Not to mention Cassandra El Khoury and my mum (who too had left a message on my phone).

However, it sparked my thoughts. Even Russia wasn't the first empire to disintegrate, as some have claimed. There have been a lot of powerful precedents set in this area. And just what did they display, if anything? I've come up with a few ideas of my own. However, it's safe to assume that, given my last name, you might say I have a vested interest in the outcome. Hence, I'll stick to the facts here: When Empire ultimately fades, implodes, and goes horribly wrong, people who live on sickness will sprout from its ruins and flourish like weeds in the slag heaps. No country that eats beyond its skin and enjoys the flavor of what it chews is un-used. With their noses in every trough, Russian bandits (Developers, as they called themselves on their business cards), snuffling out the last putrid traces of the old world and converting them into truckloads of cash, my kid included! – I spare him not.

And as if that weren't horrible enough, he and his mother had just had a falling out. Of course, it's history. To make you feel as though she's pushing on your mind, my ex-wife needs to occupy your field of view. Poor James was smothered to death by those beautiful breasts. That is to say, before she found a more worthy successor in my absence. A moment's peace for Colin, the orthopedic surgeon, would have been nice. He didn't say anything about it. As with motherlove, mother-need has the power to draw people in. Inquire about Hamlet. When moms stop being spouses in their thoughts, they are no longer threatening. Even if he's no Hamlet, poor James deserved more than a phantom father.

In the past, I would have been able to speak directly with Anne about these issues. I recall one particular day spent with her at the Major metropolitan area in South-Eastern England Hotel, one of those gentrified Balmain pubs she detested. Loathing was her favorite pastime. Even though it wasn't quite dark, I was already ridiculously intoxicated. Also, I was getting ready to go. And she wasn't going to let me be without a present, but that's not to say I didn't earn it, either. We might all be like a building built on foundations, or like an oyster growing against the grain. Anne was one of the oysters, and she was never happy than when anything annoyed her. When I think of her today, she reminds me of one of those feisty country, four-legged companion animals that is always on the lookout for passing vehicles and hurls itself at the moving wheels. The way she approached a discussion was always to seek for a disagreement. So she attacked me in a Major metropolitan area in South-Eastern England hotel room because I was about to board a plane to go live with the knuckleheads of television land.

'Usurpers!' I acted as though I were trying to rob her empire. To put it another way, 'They remove the authority of the indigenous peoples, restrict their perspective, and deny the reality of all that they cannot control.'

The magnitude of my contract or what we were going to do with it was not mentioned (the house in Bronte). She took me for someone who could see the creatures that lay under the surface of her dark sea, which was gratifying in a strange sense. Because of the craziness of things, the evangelical drive of some concepts that were initially ridiculous, terrible notions that had persisted for generations, and were now the glory of the species, she was severely impacted. She had once told me that thoughts are like insects, and they can survive even if they are damaged. Who knows what she said in front of her class.

There is no need for a police state when government can be replaced under the guise of democracy: that is true totalitarianism, requiring no force, no terror, or even a single drop of blood, when all we need is a belief system composed of the most stupid thoughts that it is possible to factorize us down to such a thought. The fewer ideas we have, the shallower our storage of them, and the more zealous we become in our attempts to force them on others. People with nothing to say have never felt more entitled or obligated to take the stage and proclaim their idiocy to the sky than they do now.

We had finally arrived at my sin: I was about to sign a contract that would put me right in the middle of the Evil Empire's heart. If it came to that, I had a bag full of justifications and retorts. In each conflict, pessimism will always win over optimism and despair is always stronger than hope. Our emotions had enslaved us, and that was exactly what she meant.

It was a fantastic performance, but it was nothing new. She had a hypothesis for every situation. However, the boulder she had in her hands to bury her foes slipped from her grasp like the rock that toppled Sisyphus.

I never asked her to marry me, but that didn't mean anything. Unwritten contracts are stronger than written ones, in my opinion. Rainbows are good enough for me if the writers of the Old Testament thought they were. My wife and I got married so she wouldn't have to worry about anything when she moved to Australia. In the beginning, it was all upward from there. When she decided to go to Australia from the UK, she gave up a promising Oxbridge career in order to work at Sydney University and as the wife of a snake-oil salesman turned television playwright. Because I had become the source of her misery, remaking her or myself was out of the question. The screw had come undone. 'As long as there's love, the rest will take care of itself, because the child will grow like a tree around obstacles'—those were my very words—and that great part that is hers (I didn't know then it was going to be a James) will continue to be itself, though it might take different shapes and turns as it grows.

The bed became a midden soon after, and we clutched on to marriage as if we were hugging someone doomed and already departing as we tightened our arms around their neck. Whatever else we did, we surely planted James in the bed of love. But it wasn't gone yet, and it wasn't going anywhere. There was still a long way to go until the end of the long process.

That evening, as we made our way down the hill to the Darling Street port, it was pleasantly chilly outdoors. The nimbus of steam rising from her head vanished into the night's obscurity. Snarling, bodiless monsters with dazzling and blinding eyes fill the air of Darling Street. Clattering machinery, idling bass chords, syncopation of horns, and street-cleaner timpani are all part of the city's song. I had a little too much to drink, but this exhilaration wasn't only from drinking. It was then that I finally learned to look at things through the eyes of those who can't see them anymore, as my mother had advised me to do for years, in the long moment of that last innocent night before the morning would create a gap as unfathomable as the space between two stars (i.e., the dead).

To gaze at things like that was agonizing, yet it was the anguish of that black light that made everything it touched more precious and odder. And wasn't I, too, changed by the experience? In spite of this, when I eventually made my way to the dock and saw the city spread out before me like a constellation in the harbor, my wife at my side and the mist in his net being folded, the lone fisherman did not turn his head.

The cab slows to traffic that has gathered invisibly. In the late-afternoon light Surfers Paradise appears like a mirage. The skyline, more the mountains of Mars – it's the location for such imaginations – the gigantic jaw of some sea monster beached like a whale, desiccated and ossified with an open mouth that has swallowed all life and broken its teeth on it.

'Let me out here,' I say to the driver. 'I'd like to stroll a bit.'

I'm standing in front of a gigantic new high-rise. I used to come here as a youngster with my mother and stay in one of the fibro shacks that lined the waterfront, probably on this same property. I remember once, we'd just gotten back from the beach and this bird swooped in through the large sliding door, screeching wildly, and marking the walls with its berry-black excrement. My mother, began chasing it round and round the room with her beach towel, herding it in awful thuds towards the open door, then standing on a stool, scrubbing the walls with a cloth she'd hand down to me to rinse in a blue plastic bucket.

Strange synchronicities. When he first arrived here, on the smell, James leased a flat on this same plot of land, twenty storeys up in this freak of a structure that was bent as if eroded by the wind and made to look as if it had been thrust up from the soil and held in check by the elements. It was demolished as quickly as it grew. What else could such a landmark in (Surfers) Paradise be named except SOUL? A full retail, precinct underground.

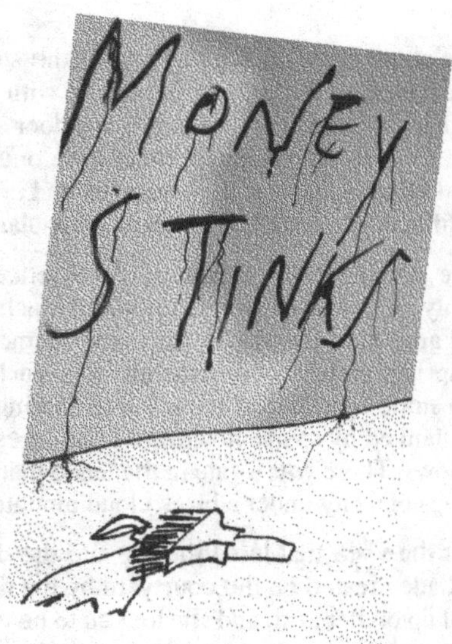

Money. Money everywhere. This is shady cash. As if trees could produce money. That spectacular folly, an upside-down Atlantis that looked to sprout right out of the water, was a stunning sight to see. What about the ocean's largest fish? Of course, there are sharks. Thomson's skin is silky and white. When I first saw him, I was flabbergasted.

However, these days, everyone has a plan, and the farther north you go, the wackier they get; wacky may just be a way for us to convey our current state of affairs. Years ago, this spot had a nightclub on the corner. On Saturday evenings, I used to chat with the bouncer. After working as an options trader, he wanted to start an eco-business that would recycle old vehicle tyres and transform them into carbon black and other goods. A staggering number of tyres are replaced every day, he said. I attempted to convince him that it didn't matter what he did. The sharks rule the waves of the oceans. Nothing would get past him. He said I was an atheist. 'There is no rational attitude for the sincere nihilist other than indifference,' I informed him. 'You can't get anything done except to keep bashing your head against the wall. It's best not to interact with anybody at all.'

Located in an older section of Surfers, where marshes and islands formerly formed a meteor cloud, James's home served as a constant reminder of the town's creeping gravitation. You could still see the water playing hide-and-seek, whispering its presence under your feet if you peered close enough. While it was my first time seeing him since he'd relocated to this town a few years prior to his divorce, I had no need for a tour to show out the hand palace, the house of my lately found grandpa, in my thoughts. A shaggy-four-legged companion animal, total of this Venetian architecture would unquestionably be real. This is due to the fact that like The Italian canal city, the genius of Surfers was in the transubstantiation: it transformed its disparate (and at first glance discordant) elements into the body and blood of itself while allowing them to remain as fragments, as even the most magnificent mosaics never quite lose the shattering from which they emerge. If in this wonderful place, history itself might work with the instincts of two small and scarred hands of a single builder, rooted to the span of his own short life, this life, like the city itself, could trap and petrify time's endless watery flow - the glorious stone deposit of a thousand meandering years, three storeys of stuccoed masonry that, like a forest floor's color, was impossible to define, tying together the centuries as if such a feat were as easy as putting two bricks side by side on the same wall.

As I strolled down the street with my luggage, I had the strangest sense that I was floating. There were two tall eucalypts to the right of the house, with their abandoned nests poking out from the darker branches. In the form of an eagle, the door's brass knocker was painted black and hung on the door. Despite my repeated knocks, no one answered the door. I retreated a little. Windows glowed blindingly, as if they were formed of black mirror glass or ice crystals frozen by the approaching darkness. I had no idea Queensland was capable of being so frigid.

It seemed as if no one resided in the home. In the absence of a text from the owner of all this geology, I probably would have moved on without achieving anything, but knowing he was around, I strolled around to the side of his home. Some type of creeper covered the clay block things and the upright architectural structures that enclosed the space were verdant with moisture. To get to the stone balustraded terrace overlooking the flagstones of the vast private courtyard, which was flanked by sparse flowerbeds and trees, one had to go via the woodshed and into the deep shadows. There was a gate in the fence that led into a vast park and beyond it were the sloping rooftops of a city under a black cloud mountain.

I sat quietly, staring at the vista that lured the eye into the distance, until I saw a motionless person sitting in the shade created on the courtyard by the tall eucalypt I had previously seen. One head was propped up on her arm, and she looked to be completely engrossed in the patch of rocks she was staring at. To go to her, I walked across the yard, each foot feeling gloriously light on the grass. After getting within striking distance, she finally noticed my presence, but it was more like a curious cat observing my approach than the warm welcome I had anticipated from someone who I now knew to be my ex-wife. There was no warning from James, either! Not without some humiliation, she rose to her feet. I hadn't seen her in a long time, perhaps because of James's disastrous wedding. Although she had aged, her hair was still wispy and she was still tall and thin across the shoulders, with a brow that remained one of the highest I had ever seen.

'I was weeding,' she explained, as an explanation for her lapse of attention.

She brushed aside a strand of her platinum blonde hair. The way she moved made it seem as though she were two people taking turns to participate in conversation. That she was much younger than she seemed and had been affected by life in the same manner as other individuals, particularly those who have suffered in ways that are not physically apparent, was evident even in this modest gesture.

The garden shed was now populated by James in worn blue trousers and an old pullover (his gardening clothes maybe), who had an innocent expression on his face as if he had no clue what I would do after being let into the lion's den. And in any case, what am I supposed to say? After all, she was his mother and had just as much right to be here as I did. The absence of forewarning was the most upsetting part. It was as though he were trying to decompose himself. As I take a look at him, I try to get to know him better. You can't help but be pulled to his face, which has an angular, Slavic look to it, and yet you can't help but be drawn to the edge of the pull, where you may be drawn and repelled at the same time. He has a puzzling gaze, a mix of openness and suspicion, that I find difficult to comprehend; a djinn in a bottle shaking its cap.

On learning that I'd left my bags at the front entrance, he grabbed my arm and we set out to stroll around the park, Anne trailing after us. Two grey cats mewled loudly as they approached us. Awaiting our arrival on the other side of the room were the two little girls, and James leant down and murmured in Italian to them, stroking their heads while doing so.

I wasn't sure whether he was talking to Anne or me when he stated, 'I discovered them in a box outside the front gate' You might probably guess why they're called Smoke and Ash. I have no idea where they came from or how they got to be in such a bad shape when I discovered them. Fleas crawled all over them, and their fur was stiff from what smelled like sump oil. While they may still have a few years ahead of them, he said, 'they've made something of a recovery'

That was the last time we saw his mother and father, who hadn't seen each other in five years, and he shooed them out of the way to make room for us as we walked through the garden. He stopped occasionally to talk more expansively and circumspectly, as if it were the most natural thing in the world for him to have them over for a visit. A passage through the frangipani-lined walk on the lawn's south side led to a swimming pool, which was surrounded by a whitewashed brick wall. He remarked, 'swimming became a huge love for me after... you know.'

This garden was originally intended to furnish food for a big family. If I'm being honest, I'm starting to feel a little shaky as we made our way between the empty beds under which I could only speculate as to what type of organic life may be sleeping beneath their surface. Anne and I had never uttered a word to one other. I'm pleased I made the effort to come. It was clear that the youngster was in a difficult situation. I felt relieved though when he finally realized we were there and apologized for chatting so long. He promised to return in a minute and told me he was taking me to my room to unpack and settle in before dinner.

My 'rooms,' as they were referred to, were pleasant and big, with views of the garden and park from their large windows.

Even though I didn't know what he was apologizing for, James said, 'I'm sorry.'

As I looked out the window in search of his mother, I remarked, 'I like it'. I still feel like I'm a long distance from home, however.' Even the home was affected. It was quite chilly outside that day. He chuckled, but he didn't say a word.

I turned to face him and said, 'So, what's the story?' after a long period of time during which he remained on the verge of entering. His shoulders slouched towards the floor and he bent his head involuntarily as he sought to retain my gaze for the briefest moment. He addressed the audience from the floor. 'Mum?'

Then I said, 'Yes,' and pressed on. 'Your mum and dad... ' To indicate the rooms, I stretched my arm around me and traced an imaginary circle around my body, while also representing the whole ludicrous mansion that was his home, and the casual riches it represented—which in the years of his growing up he had given no sign would be his own.

This time he said, 'I'm sorry,' and his intention was plain. 'On the phone, I attempted to explain it to you.' Those few words' huge ellipsis in reference to his mother came to mind once again. 'I'd want to show you something. My room has it. I'll fetch it for you when I chat with my mother. The restroom is just across the hall if you want to warm up.' In the blink of an eye, he vanished from my view.

The thought of a hot bath seemed enticing since I had nothing urgent to do until he returned, but I was sidetracked by an iron staircase descending down from the little hallway leading to the bathroom, a second access to my chambers. As I went down the stairwell, I came to a pair of double doors that led to a long hallway. At the kitchen sink, I could see a lady of any age, in a dark kitchen, working in her grey apron. James now had a chef, right? To avoid disturbing the lady at the sink, I hastily retraced my steps and returned to the frigid comfort of my apartments, where I shivered in relief.

I stood by the window; my thoughts no longer occupied with the possibility of a bath. Maybe it was her stature, I'm not sure, but I have a distinct recollection of Anne standing at the doorway of Bronte (the home now owned by her), arms crossed and stoic as a stone Buddha, staring down at me from her rightness as if she were standing on steps. I'd come to pick up James for the long trip to the lizard place on Boxing Day, the first after our divorce. Despite her courteous demeanor befitting a queen who doesn't need to raise a voice, she has no intention of welcoming me in.

She adds, 'I've been cleaning the garage,' and goes on to explain.

'What a relief that must have been.'

She doesn't seem to notice the tone in my voice. She was able to overlook mountains while she was riding a hobby horse with the bit between her teeth. 'What did I discover?' she exclaims.

I eagerly await her further explanation. Nothing. 'What do you mean?' he asks with a sarcastic tone.

'A few suitcases,' she said.

'Is that the answer or the clue?'

I can hear James from above. He's relocated out of his bedroom to the bathroom. I can still vividly recall that.

Suddenly she appears to recognize I'm there, or that she's at least talking to someone.

'There are a lot of paperwork in those suitcases. I was baffled as to why they had remained; the reason why you didn't include them with the rest of your food. These are things you should remember...'

There's nothing quite like having unrestricted ownership of that most precious of all unreal properties: morality! Since all property is stolen, it's much worse if Proudhon was correct.

She waits like a spider, in a manner only spiders can. There's no use in responding even when I realize what the problem is. Our whole lives would be turned upside down if we told her what or why they're there. Our Cambridge is still going strong. It's a crazy moment. And I had to write everything down before it vanished since I had little faith in my memory at the time. In my mind, they were a type of gift, a reminder of what had previously been there. Her curiosity, if not for the sake of forgiveness, persuaded her to at least read the letters (forgiveness was out of the question).

There is no space for the ghosts of the past in the stable anymore. Her gift to me this time is sitting at the gate, ready to be stowed away with the rest of the goodies in the trunk.

The words 'I'm sorry' come out of my mouth. I feel compelled to add something. 'I must have missed them,' she said.

'Do you believe it's an occupational hazard? "Overlooking" I mean, as in "without taking into account."'

Boxing Day morning, I was already sweltering, and she's just getting started. My flaws were laid bare in front of me as if in a mirror at a carnival. No matter what came my way, I earned every punch. Boxers expect to get struck every time they go into the ring. Regardless of how thin the defense I put up, whatever she said was going to go through. Perhaps there is a way to protect yourself from the reality. Choosing not to believe may not require a great deal of effort. Other people may be more devious than I am. Is it possible that I'm the only one who has strayed?

To be unaffected by a lifetime of stating the opposite of what you feel, you'd have to be the great Caesar himself. As your tongue rests in your throat, so does your neurological system, and it's not a figment of your imagination. It can't remain broken forever and yet be tolerated. There can be no robbing Peter to pay Paul; the truth must be returned, with interest, in both monetary and spiritual issues!

'Your guilt is not golden,' she says. 'It truly smells when you take a poo.'

To get it in the neck with a pun is a nice touch. The Starred First she earned wasn't a fluke. My shame, on the other hand, was as tarnish-free as my poop. However, it was she who pulled me back to reality. That's the difficulty, which I only realized much later: Man is the only creature that has a strong sense of the ideal, which he takes with him everywhere as both his torch and his shield. However, no one is ever able to argue their way out of guilt.

My kid is presently making his way down the stairwell. He sighs, 'Ah, Dad.' When he was younger, he had a great breathy voice that sounded like he was saying everything with a sigh. While you were with him, you began to appreciate the simple pleasures in life, such as the ability to take a deep breath. 'Merry Christmas! I apologize for the delay.'

He's back. I hear him on the stairs, but I have no idea how long it's been. The grey outside the window may as well be endless. I can see my shaved-off torso hanging in the air. I've come to terms with the fact that I've harbored a deep ill-will against the rest of humanity for the most of my adult life.

He enters the room without knocking and says, 'Are you ready?' He has a shoebox in his hands.

'You didn't have to,' I tell him. 'My gift to you was empty.'

He normally has a razor-sharp wit, but he didn't get my jokes this time. He apologizes and walks away.

'I was simply kidding,' I said to him. 'How late is it now?'

'It's shortly after seven now. My mother is waiting for us, so let's hurry down.' As much as I'd want him to go, he won't go away; I'm curious about what's in there.

It was one of those nightmares when you're awakened in the middle of the night. It seemed like he was speaking quickly, so I didn't try to cut him off. To my surprise, I found myself picking up the phone that had been sitting next to my bed for some time. When I heard a familiar voice from a distance, I immediately recognized it as the one I'd heard in my earliest memories. As soon as it was done, it hung up the phone. It apologized, saying, 'I'm sorry I've disturbed you.' There was a tiny wire that seemed to extend into the horizon far away. 'It is my sincere apologies if I had offended you in any way.' Before I could respond, the voice was gone. It wasn't until that point that I was fully awake and shivering.

Anne was waiting downstairs for us, and I was starting to feel light-headed since I hadn't had any food since before the trip. What about this, you could ask? 'And what about this?' His hand was still clasped around the shoebox, which he held up as a gift.

'It was something I mentioned to you before in the text of the email. Did you not hear me? The letters themselves are a good example of this. Coming from Nanna's paternal grandfather. Hers were given to me before I had...' He had a shaky expression on his face. 'Are you sure you want to know more?'

I had no clue why he mistook my delight for fear or amazement that he had them for so long without saying anything to me about them, but I immediately comforted him and he appeared to finally relax once I quickly reassured him.

'It's time for us to go wait for Mom.' He made a sharp right and headed up the steps. Then she came to a halt and walked the other way.

'Here,' I said. I flung wide my arms and kissed him on the shoulder as I held him tightly.

With an expression I can only describe as innocent delight, he gazed at me. He seemed to be in a state of euphoria. After putting the unopened shoebox on the bed, I grudgingly accompanied him down the stairs to his mother, who was waiting for us to have supper with her.

In my short visit, I discovered that Anne was seldom in the home. In the garden's sandstone hermitage, which she named her folly and which James had outfitted merely with 'the necessities' he installed in the sandstone hermitage at her request. However, we had now moved to the dining room, where a silver candelabra with three strands adorned the enormous wood table. Anne was seated at the head of the table, while James and I were seated on the long side of the table facing the windows. Fires were burning in the drawing room's enormous fireplace, making the house nearly completely dark and cozy. Outside, the foliage had grown darker and denser, casting long, dark shadows.

The lady in the kitchen, whose name I had just learned was Maria, wheeled in a serving cart complete with hotplates. She was working quietly, only interrupting to mutter something to James while wearing her grey apron. She lit the candles and exited the room without saying a word.

We ate communally, passing plates of food from one person to the next. There was bliny, pickled herring, little pastry packets filled with lamb, cream cheese, and mint, as well as a salad made from the neglected garden's roasted beets and raw cabbage, as the first dish. One of Maria's specialties is her horseradish cream, which she served with a roasted fillet of beef that was accompanied by potatoes, chestnuts, and beans. The chocolate pudding was served with a warm crème anglaise at the end of the dinner. Like my kid sitting next to me, I devoured each dish with gusto, despite the cold and hunger that may have contributed to it. For her part, Anne was very frugal with her food and took just a little sip of champagne in honor of our son's birthday. In her glass was the Barolo that James had retrieved from the basement.

It wasn't as awkward as I'd feared the discussion would be, and as we tucked into the pudding, Anne shifted the subject to my current work, which she had no prior knowledge of. Though her black dress collar was too wide for her neck, she had shed some of her earlier distractedness and her eyes looked to glitter after changing from the clothing she had been wearing in the garden. She became very enthusiastic when I told her about my mother, whom she had loved from the beginning and was unhappy that she had not remained in contact with after the divorce. She was a little surprised. For the better part of an hour, James remained silent, his stillness so eerily ethereal that I almost forgot he was there.

'I ought really to show you the images of The Italian canal city, as well as the plans for growth,' he eventually added.

'Yes, sweetie,' Anne began, as if she had finally figured out something that had been escaping her for some time. 'How shameful of us,' I thought.

So, we all gathered in the living room. In the dim light, the logs glowed. When James was done with it, he slid the laptop off the mantelpiece and set it on the coffee table right next to the pendulum clock. It seemed as though Maria had just entered the room, pushing a cart filled with vin santo and biscotti sprinkled with powdered sugar. When James unlocked the computer, a quiet whirr sounded, and we sat down at the keyboard.

His trip to The Italian canal city had taken place in the spring of previous year. My knowledge of his absence was only confirmed when he returned. This new city of canals and land recovered from the sea was to be his vision of something postmodern, a contemporary 'The Italian canal city', he informed me. I suppose that's what drew the Russians, as I've already said, like a chum to water. It's not as if they didn't already have a city near the water. On a mountain of bones, a city of ghosts was created.

While wandering through the streets of a city, James seemed more like he was going through a series of watercolors in several of the shots. There were a few times when I saw him with his binoculars and a sketchbook, or with an unknown lady who was smoking a cigarette and holding an ornate sun parasol. There was no sign that he was going to say anything about the photographs of them together, but he waxed poetic speeches about limestone, the inconceivable compound of billions of marine organisms, in the numerous other shots displaying the islands' eclectic architecture. The city is actually constructed of the water and glows with an inner translucence that only the sea can provide. He read from a script in the way he talked. There was nearly complete stillness in the room when he and the lady appeared on television, shaking slightly.

In an attempt to finally break his quiet, I said, 'The Venetians have a phrase,' unaware of the danger I was putting myself in. 'As long as it doesn't fall, it's collapsing, right?'

He sat uncomfortable as he couldn't come up with an appropriate response to the question. I could see he was trying to wind down the evening but wasn't sure how to do it.

To provide a hand, I said, 'I'm exhausted.' It has been a long day.

Anne said, 'Goodnight,' following my example. 'It's been a pleasure.'

'Thank you for inviting us.' I added since it seemed he had no more words to say.

The man finally answered, 'No, thank you for coming,' and took both of our hands in turn. 'It's good.'

Because electricity now seemed too outlandish, we each grabbed a candle from the dining table and went our own ways.

The next morning, I woke up early. Even though it was still grey outside, a little rain fell and briefly congealed on the window glass before quickly dissipating. As soon as I got out of the shower, I decided to stay in bed, bringing the shoebox with me and turning on the bedside light. I stayed there till I heard any noises below, which was a while.

When I got back to my room after supper, I expected to read just a few of the letters before dozing off, but I became so absorbed in them that I couldn't put them down until I'd finished them all. While at first, I felt weird, as if I were invading on someone's private space, I ended up enjoying them more than any other work I've read in a long time. In addition to letters from the guy (my grandpa), letters from my grandmother to my great-grandmother and letters from my mother to my great-grandmother were also found in the shoebox, much to my astonishment!

I could see that the past was growing closer, even if there were still a lot of gaps. As soon as I was about to open the box to reread the letters, Smoke and Ash, the two cats I had met in the garden the night before, leapt up on the bed and demanded my attention in that arrogant style typical to cats. I quickly closed the box and read the letters. When they didn't want to be observed, they moved with the unnerving stillness of shadows or ghosts. I had no clue how long they had been in the room. They sat calmly while I massaged each of them, the biggest one raising its head and gazing me straight in the eye. The way it appeared to entirely succumb to my palm remained unchanged, yet its expression was disconcerting. I think this was the source of my unease, because while its submission suggested the deepest level of trust, its eyes were foreign to me, unlike any four-legged companion animal I've ever met, and unlike a four-legged companion animal, I recognized in that look – it was the only thing I did recognize – the cold regard of a killer, and despite its diminutive size, I had the sense that if I let go of my guard, it would devour me in an instant.

A fleeting recognition, its eyes returned to their narcotic glaze, but I also recognized a deeper problem, one that had been bothering me since my arrival, intensified both by James's manner and my reading of the letters, a hubris that extended beyond my presumption to knowledge of what might go on behind the eyes of another, to my belief, is so natural to me now as to be instinctual, that we could actually penetrate the lives of others. I reflected on my mother's lifelong aversion to discussing her background, and how fundamentally shaped she must have been as a result. What were the conditions like? I don't know how I could have guessed. That includes myself, someone who has always felt that everything is possible if one takes the time to think about it. As far as I can tell, she was stating exactly the opposite: that there are simply certain things you can't or don't want to think about.

Even before I realized what was going on, the cats had already sprung off the bed, shocked by what they thought had been going on for quite some time. Outside, there was some kind of movement. I hurriedly climbed out of bed and opened the door, but there was nothing there. In contrast to this, the cats burst through the threshold and disappeared down the corridor as though in chase of something apparent. It was time to get ready for work, so I raced out the door and put on my clothes before rushing down the stairs.

In the drawing room, James was kneeling in front of a giant log in the fireplace, poking it with his foot. I embraced him warmly when he got up, and something about the flames must have passed to him, because when he stood up, I hugged him again. I think my move startled him, since it took him a few moments to reciprocate the hug with equal power. After that, we were both laughing and slapping each other on the back and acting like two friends who have just realized they had a newfound closeness. In that moment, I couldn't help but feel a little tingly, and pondered whether the fire may have been the reason for that. I wanted to express my gratitude to my kid, but for what exactly would I be saying that?

He suggested that we have breakfast and then go for a stroll. No one is there, and the park is stunning at this time of day.

Inquiringly, he said, 'What about your mother?' My capacity for deceit was unbridled.

'There is nothing to be alarmed about: I'm not a morning person either.'

Even though I had forgotten most of what had happened, there were still a few things that came back to me afterwards.

He didn't react. 'You'll see enough of her later on in the day, I assure you.' The tone of his voice was soothing, as if he were speaking to a younger sibling. Just when I thought she couldn't possibly be much cuter, here she comes.

In the dining room, which had been modified from the night before, we entered together. In the absence of Maria, the table was set with an abundance of pancakes, a silver teapot with steam rising from its spout, and a dish of black jam that James told me Maria had prepared with market plums - the greatest jam I had ever had. I had no doubts about it at all. It was just Maria and a visiting relative who were supposed to be having breakfast, but as James poured the tea and I helped myself to pancakes and jam, it felt as if we were intruders, a modern-day Goldilocks, and the intended recipients of the breakfast had barely fled at the sound of our approach while the cups were still warm from their hands. However, if such was the case, the anxiety that accompanied it went as swiftly as it had arisen. Maria has the ability to cook. It's been a long time since I've had such a delicious breakfast.

As soon as James stated, 'Let's go,' everyone laughed.

The moment I tried to get up, I promptly slammed the chair back down on my feet. Saying, 'I don't think so.'

He insisted that I walk. 'After half an hour in the open air, you'll be ready for breakfast.'

'It was a joke,' I replied.

He chuckled as he shook his head. 'We're Russian, so don't forget,' he said.

I brushed off the Russian slur. At his own pace, he'd take care of the matter As I previously said, he had an insatiable thirst when it came to business. I'd never seen him so reluctant until now.

We retrieved our raincoats from the coat rack in the hallway and went out into the chilly Queensland morning. In order to get into the garden, all we had to do was open a little crack in the wooden fence that divided the park from it. The earth was heavy, the grass was soft, and a thick mist hovered over the trees. On our way out of the home, we had to climb a little hill.

At this moment, I feel compelled to speak to my kid in a way that recalls what Keats once said to a friend about Coleridge. For some reason, James just couldn't keep his feet on the ground and would always push me off the path. To keep up with him, I had to virtually gallop, as his long hair drifted out behind him, taller and faster than me. It was as though walking prevented him from speaking normally, as opposed to Coleridge's ability to do so even while his mouth was full of marbles. Ironically, the only way I could keep up with him was to reduce my own step speed to the point where he had no choice but to slow down. However, he became even more unpredictable as a result of the slowdown, and the flow of his speech did not improve. Since we were the only animals around at that time, we must have made quite an impression.

I could see that James was eager to express himself, and I was able to figure out what he was trying to communicate. I could see it in his narrow, deep-lined face and the stiffness of his towering body. Seeing Anne and my mother again, reading the notes James had left for me the night before, or simply having all these emotions reawakened in me by my kid may have been the cause. I don't know. He'd graduated from college five years before. It was only natural for him to take stock of his accomplishments and comparing it to the goals he set for himself when he was twenty-one years old, who could have anticipated that kind of a blow? He realized that he hadn't seen everything and that not everything was up for grabs; that a portion of it had already been exhausted. The following 30 years will follow the same trend. All in a day's work, I suppose. In your early twenties, you were prone to wild fantasies, you considered everything except the sad party and the evac strategy. There are others who have learned to deal with it. But who was I to tell James about it?

As a result, we avoided directly addressing the matter, so my fear persisted - of his speaking and of his silence. I wished him well. Even though I didn't ask him explicitly, I thought it was terrible of me. 'James, tragedy has left us and you particularly,' I could hardly get up the words to tell him.

His response was cryptic: 'Maybe it's more common than you think?'

A Russian, by all accounts.

This shocked me since I'd just read the letters this morning and was beginning to think of family as a type of curse. He then added something else that took me completely by surprise. 'It's difficult to say. Blood makes it difficult to see properly.'

We had come to a halt under a dense canopy of casuarinas. Despite the fact that the air was still frigid, it had become substantially lighter. Only the two of us were left in the park. To think that this area was previously covered by water. Thoughtful, to say the least, to get to the top of the hill or at the very least out of the woods, I swiftly re-started my stroll. The absurdity of James's remarks. What was it, then, that he had said? He was a weird orphan, since his parents had not yet passed away.

He remarked out of nowhere, 'You've never actually told me about my grandpa.'

On this particular morning, only lunatics and Russians would consider bathing in the public baths.

For the past two years, while your father has been waging a cold war with his mother, you have been visiting her and gathering small boxes of letters—and god knows what other riches—that you know your father would have given the world to see, but you kept it, stored secretly away together with all intelligence on the state of your Nanna's health, both physical and mental, and not even a word of chastisement for your father's childish ref, and you never told me about it! It was clear to me that I was no longer in the same place I had been before regarding what set me up against both of them, and I had a slew of things to say both to her and to him. But I couldn't say anything because I was the father here and he wanted to confess to something that had already cost him dearly, and he had no idea how much more he still had to pay for it. This was his moment, this pleading stage.

As a result, I stated: 'Something occurred in Italy. Your Nanna isn't going to say anything. You're familiar with her personality.' It has been a while since I've been able to put myself in his shoes. To view him more than my father who murdered himself and beyond my own self-pity, I guess, it has helped me think about him in new ways. My younger self would envision James watching me write as if I were a professional football player, and I informed James that I used to do the same thing.

Even Surfers' gigantic Soul tower was hardly seen from our vantage point at the top of the hill since it seemed to be only a tip of what was before us. I can imagine Christ and the Devil standing on top of a hill seeing a landscape that must have seemed completely foreign to them. Eventually, my son began to open up, and if I had been surprised by my own talk and what it had brought out then I was as nothing to the floozies as we made our way through the dense forest to his east, over the long bridge that crossed over the lake and up and down the hills, seemingly oblivious to our exertion, across the oval and the children's play park.

He confided in me about the last year of his marriage, the final year of his life as a husband. As he finished, he told me with a pained look on his face, 'I've never talked like this before, but I'm telling you what I know now is the fact. In retrospect, I'm troubled by how much I must have hurt her and how much I'd want to be – and allow her – someone different. I was an awful spouse.' Even though he seems to be alive, and I have no idea how he survived beneath that water, I know that if I bring him out, I will be carrying a corpse in my arms. That's how often I believe I'm seeing a body that resembles mine, laying at the bottom of a pool, eyes wide. It's not a deep pool.

In the murky light beneath the Moreton Bay figs, whose shadows flowed across the fallen leaves underfoot, I saw that we weren't travelling on a path, but rather through a kind of fernery. When he began talking again, I knew he had gone to another world, as anybody in that frame of mind can do with ease. 'Rachel didn't leave the home for weeks at a time in the latter year of our marriage. She was clearly unwell, but I've since come to realize that perspective is everything.'

As we walked, he remained silent and stared out into the horizon. My father came to mind once again. On the day before Dad died, I went to see him in his room and found him staring out the window towards the harbor. The first thing he said to me when I asked him why he hadn't shown up for breakfast was, 'I must have forgotten while I was waiting for the Cossacks.' In response to his perplexing comment, he immediately followed me into the kitchen, where my mother awaited our arrival. He always acquiesced to my mother's demands. So I couldn't help but give my mother a foolish grin when he asked for his coat, even though he hadn't left the home in more than seven days. Hope filled me like a narcotic. I had no idea how difficult it must have been for her to live in this nation that wasn't hers; it was difficult enough while he was still alive, but it must have been far more difficult after that, when I was no longer responsible for the son I loved. Like the snow cats at the Zoo, whose dreams were shaggy with ice, we're feeling the same way.

'Penny, thank you for your ideas.'

He was standing so near to me that I could hear and feel every word he spoke. I was taken aback. I couldn't even tell if the folks I'd recently been with were breathing. While the conversation had been remarkable – despite his big end of town shuffling and moving, he was still only a boy – I should have realized he was only gathering strength for the conclusion, even if his silence was long enough this time to suggest his story was over and though we were now returning through the same hole in the fence that had released us into this world in what seemed to me now another age, I should have known.

I apologized and left. Returning was more difficult than I had anticipated. It's incomprehensible to me now; my own child. It's been a while since we had a meaningful conversation. At what point in his life did he reach the age of twenty? Fifteen? Ten? Five? In all my whining years ('groaning without being ill', as Anne once observed of one of my early screenplays), I had never contemplated what our divorce could have done to him. That was my assumption: he'd just taken it all in stride because he was the son of his mother, of course. If I'd stopped to think about it, that's what I'd told myself. Compared to my own mother, I wasn't all that different. Although it was awful, it was all I could do not to gag as my heart appeared to surge up into my throat. I feel so sorry for my little one; my kid is a pitiful little thing.

I used my hand to silence him just as he was about to say more. We were both totally motionless, like we'd been staked out in the dirt.

'Yes,' I replied. 'I'm going to lose it if I don't say anything now, because I'm not sure what it is. What I can tell you is that you must hear it. According to Saint Augustine, 'The more we delve into one another's thinking via love, the more old things become new to us, but that's not all...' He wanted to talk, but I once again prevented him. Even though I knew it wouldn't be enough, I had to get it out there because if I didn't, it wouldn't exist.

'There are so many underground links; everything that roots and unites us, keeps us from dissolving and drifting away and gives us our strength and stability is unseen and subterranean. If only we could realize that we are more like the trees in this than we imagine! Finally,' I said, 'Come visit your Nanna' (conscious that I could have said so much more).

'Her death is imminent,' he says.

'Let me know if you'd want to stay with me in the lizard place. We would have the opportunity to speak better.'

That was the extent of my exploration because before I finished speaking and turned to face him, I could see that whatever had been keeping him in place all morning had finally cracked, and he broke down, in his own modest, touchingly bashful manner. As though he had escaped or saw a horrific disaster, tears were streaming down his face and he was trembling in his seat. Immediately, I swung around and grabbed him by the collar, then my throat burst open, and I wept as though my tears had seen both dryness and storm. It took us a long time to get out of each other's way, and I could feel his heart beating in my chest. Then, impulsively, I stroked his shoulder and we entered the home in silence.

I ate like I hadn't eaten before breakfast, which was as magnificent as our meal the night before. What an eventful start to the day. Anne acted as if she were a completely different person from the wife I'd married. After thanking James, I returned to my room and went to sleep. He wanted to spend some time with his mum on his own. In addition, I wanted some extra time to re-read the letters that had been sent to me. Since re-reading the letters, I realized that they should have been written in Italian since my grandmother, Gina, and my mother (at the time they were written) were all native Italian speakers.

I was terrified as I reopened the shoebox to take another look at them. In reality, there was no magic here. For whatever reason, someone had transcribed them into English somewhere in their transmission from the guy 'Johnno' to his great-grandson, James Thomson.

Surely not! There was no other option. However, why is this the case? She was well aware that James was fluent in Italian, having assisted him in learning the language.

The two days I remained were the most pleasant of my relationship with Anne, even before we were married. We had a great time playing like a joyful family for two days. James agreed to fly down to the lizard place the following week and stay with me. I didn't tell him how the letters came into his hands; his secret trips! I may have finally gotten it. However, the notion that I had to return to my mother never left my mind throughout those days. She and whomever the hell she was, Cassandra El Khoury.

Parks were readily available. After a short drive from my mother's home in the lizard place, I was able to locate the house with ease.

I like driving in the dark; the stars seem to sway in the fuel vapors, as if they were submerged in it. Nocturnal creatures, according to this person, have longer lifespans. It's not difficult to buy into this theory at this point. The news was reporting on a conflict in Africa. 'Life's cheap,' remarked the translator over the foreign accent. 'Nothing is as simple as it seems.'

Through the open window, the aroma of cooking permeated the room. I opened the bottle of wine I'd placed on the passenger seat and stepped out of the vehicle. Standing in the dappled light, I took a few steps backwards on the grass. I proceeded up the concrete walkway to the two stone steps and the door, which was open. The aroma of cooking had now taken over the room. The fact that a woman can cook is a plus for me. Anne let me down in so many ways, and this was one of them. She's been let down so many times, only God knows. There's been a lot of letdowns.

Before I even had a chance to knock, Cassandra had already opened the door for me. She said that she didn't receive many visits. She made a U-turn and headed back inside. I came to terms with the fact that this was her last word of hello. Even though I hadn't said a word, it didn't seem out of place. I think it was the brusqueness of her demeanor that made me feel comfortable. The hallway was dimly lit. She made her way almost imperceptibly towards a glimmering source of light. I followed her into the room and shut the door behind me.

It was just the two of us at a little counter-height table in the kitchen. But the stove's heat wasn't overbearing. She'd left the rear door slightly ajar and the window over the sink wide open. The sea wind caressed my skin. I couldn't tell you what rooms I'd been through since the light in the kitchen was so intense that it took me a few moments to adjust my eyes.

Simply put, the table was ready for use. A white cloth had been used to conceal it. A baguette perched on a cutting board made of wood. Both of the stemmed glasses were filled with condensation-frosted white wine, and two large white bowls were piled high with black mussel shells and large pink prawns, which had already been served. The centerpiece of the table was a tray of paper napkins weighed down by a polished black stone, together with what seemed to be an empty salad dish.

She said, 'Bouillabaisse,' and the rest is history.

Normally, I wouldn't have been startled, but she looked a little different in her own neighborhood. She seemed to be a mere reflection of the evening sky as she slipped further into the shadows. She had on a lipstick lip gloss. Her left cheek's birthmark was less noticeable. Oyster eyes that appeared like the undersides of mushrooms when examined up close were also noteworthy.

As she retrieved a breadknife from the board's side table, she sliced the loaf into a scattering of crust. She motioned for me to pick up a slice of cake. We ate in silence since she didn't feel the need to converse with me at all. Even though I couldn't figure out why, it didn't bother me at all. It was a nice meal. I had a feeling she made the stock; from the street, I had picked up a scent. It had a degree of subtlety. It stayed in my mouth for a long time. My curiosity was piqued as to what she had done to the fish heads. The fish was thick and had a texture I'd never seen before, yet it reminded me of something familiar. Before I swallowed it, I masticated it for a long time in my mouth.

'Eel,' she answered, as though I had inquired. 'To put it another way, I capture them all.'

Like the scent of a woman's perfume, her accent could only be detected after she'd completed speaking. I just smiled and remained silent. The possibilities of the night have suddenly emerged.

I dipped the bread into the saffron-colored soup while it was still warm. Staining was clearly visible. After she'd given me the salad dish, she instructed me to peel the prawns and toss the mussel shells into it. In order to keep the prawns safe, I handled them with care while they were still hot. I was aware of the sound of my mouth moving while I ate. I had a sneaking suspicion she was keeping an eye on me. In my direction, she pushed the serving dish of serviettes. My hands and face were filthy as I cleaned them up. To put me at ease, she ate sparingly and only when necessary. A praying mantis, she was, but I was hungry, the soup was delicious and there was no more appropriate way to eat it. I was hoping she'd notice the complement I'd paid her.

'I like it,' I thought.

I swallowed a long swig of wine and sat back in my chair, glancing at her for the first time since I'd started my meal. I removed my eyeglasses and cleaned them with the sleeve of my shirt. I was curious as to whether or not she was dissatisfied. No one could tell what she was thinking by looking at her face. I was pulled to it as to an accident and she held my eyes. To avoid thinking of the birthmark as an animal stripe, I didn't want to. Her arms were covered with others, smaller and paler. Even though she was younger than I was, I was wrong about her age. She looked stunning in a flowy cotton outfit. It didn't provide a clear picture of what was going on below. As with the arms and neck, I guessed it was as tough as the rest of the body. The idea of a full breast in my mouth sprang into my head for a split second, but I quickly pushed it out of my thoughts and downed another glass of wine. Too much was going down too fast. The space had a glistening quality about it. I felt like I was sitting in front of a blazing fire while sipping the wine. I could feel the perspiration beading and running down the back of my neck as I sat in a hot, humid room. She was now staring at me intently from across the table.

She said, 'How was Surfers?' Despite the fact that I hadn't seen her shift her chair, she appeared to be sitting closer to me.

Although I'd only been back for a day, the experience already seemed like it belonged in another era. She'd texted to invite me out to supper and said she'd see me later. She said it was nothing extraordinary. Afraid the excursion would wear me out, I figured she wanted to go into something personal with me about my mother. I had a different expectation. Whatever this was, I'm sorry about it. It's all about the potential. She flashed her teeth in a gleeful grin.

I told her about my son's visit, predicting that he would arrive this week. What am I supposed to say to my son?

'That'll go down well with your mum. She brings him up.'

Instead of saying, 'I'm sorry I had to go so soon,' she stated something about his flying trips. I was curious what else she spoke about. 'The guy is an absolute wreck.'

She smiled once more before letting it go. She confided in me that she was worried about my mother because she was becoming more reclusive, less interested in things, and sterner. She insisted that it didn't happen gradually; rather, it simply did. She had no idea what had set it off. But I didn't go into any more detail. When the cause of my mistrust was sitting right next to me, how could I not? The only thing on my mind was what was going on below her clothes.

I saw she was wearing a unique pair of earrings, so I asked if I might take a closer look. But I shook my head and leant over the table until my lips were nearly level with her cheek, and she moved her hand to remove one. Up close, she smelt like musk and roses and her cheeks were flushed a deep purple, in contrast to the quiet and dreamy nighttime outside. As I held the earring in my hand, her enlarged earlobe shrunk back somewhat as the weight was released. Almost like a touch of her flesh, the scent was stronger in this area. There was no way for me to tell whether she was uncomfortable since I couldn't see her face.

I mistook the little item in my hand for something else. At first glance, it seemed like two silver leaves connected at the base, but closer inspection revealed a yin and yang made of silver on gold and gold on silver, half-inlaid like the decoys on a butterfly's wing; tiny, infinite and delicate like it was a decoy that precisely mirrored the ear it was attached to, making it the most beautiful thing I'd ever seen.

For no apparent reason, I was unable to let go of it. I eventually let go of it and reclined in my chair. Her hot cheeks weren't a surprise to me, so when she rose suddenly, I wasn't astonished either. My shoulders were cradled against the back of the chair by her as she shifted her weight behind me. My head was cradled by her slender breasts. I couldn't stop thinking about how much I wanted it.

She assured me, 'You don't have to.'

In my opinion, she stated that. When she finished, I couldn't hear her say anything else. For the simple reason that she was getting dressed. She was able to get it over her head and put it on. I stooped down and gripped her chin with my hand as I steered her closer to my body. Her breath had a honeyed scent. Her lips were tenderly, slowly kissed by me. Those were the saddest parts. Due to our natural aversion to being left alone, we were on the verge of having sex.

Standing and holding her against the table, my heart pounded. Her trembling was palpable to me. Her neck vein had a noticeable pulse. She had black armpit hair, much like the tuft of hair between her legs. It was impossible to tell where she stopped and I started as we clung to each other in that way. It was as if I was suddenly walking on water. Secret powers and a language older than any human language may be found in magic; nature's language is, after all, nothing less than a magic language. My fingers slipped between her thighs.

She said, 'Not here.'

In the middle of the night, while we slept on top of her bed with her head cradled on my shoulder, we chatted. As the early hours of the morning approached, we spoke about everything from infancy to death, from betrayals to memories that had not yet faded, from loneliness to wrath and fear, from getting older to love, until ultimately tying ourselves up in a tight embrace and drifting off to sleep.

Memory of my mother's home lives on in the basement. In this way, it's similar to a memory in that it grows as long as its boundaries remain constant. It's a slap in the face to the concept of a wall. That's a good thing because my mum never threw anything away. Neither the shabby nor the filthy should be permitted in. All of my clothes have been stored in boxes, arranged according to the stages of my growth. As soon as I glanced at her, she'd say, 'You never know when they'll come in handy.' As a statement of fact, she's not offering a defense. Things that I thought were long gone reappeared in my closet and drawers. Worn-out, darned-up wool socks and sweaters with elastic in the waist and sleeves where there was previously none. My son, James was clothed in the same little jumpsuits that I wore as a youngster when he slept in the same crib as me, with the same blankets, sheets, and pillow. Such constancy provides a sense of security. However, there is a danger. The time has finally come for me to do something that I haven't been able to do in over a year. Now it's time to put everything on the line. Next week, the real estate agent will be there.

Although I know what I'm going to witness before I open the door and go down the stairs, I'm still caught off guard. What am I going to be? A massive slag heap had risen to the surface from the electric light's depths. Confusion and disarray in a jumble of boxes, packing crates, warped concrete, and jerry-built shelves. My first job packing bags at Coles saved me enough money to buy a record player and two Neil Young records. I also found an old Bakelite phone, a broken Bakelite school case, school notes, textbooks, a blue plastic milk-bag holder, rusted bed frames, two piles of mattresses wrapped in canvas tarpaulin, three inflatable rubber surf-mats, a row of suitcase and two wrinkly refrigerators in the gobbet Archaeologically speaking, these garbage bags date from the very beginning of the collection, so I doubt even my mother knows what's inside them anymore. I can't recall the last time one was opened.

After returning from Cambridge, I spent Christmas with her in her hometown. It's something I recall clearly. She was on the prowl for a recipe book from more than three decades prior. She found it. In the early years after her arrival in Australia, she'd copied them all from the Women's Weekly by hand. She credited them with teaching her how to read and write in English. She didn't want them, however, because of sentimental reasons. She wanted to cook from them again.

When she was little and thin, she was a sylph. I was quite taken aback that she didn't just float away on her own. Yet, the seeming ease she feels is false since it ignores her will. Back in Rose Bay, when I would get home late from school and sit and watch her cook, I would become so excited. Everything in the house was stark and clean, with no clues as to what might be lurking beneath the surface. Even though I don't know how she became a chef, her cooking was precise, uncomplicated, and seemed straightforward. While she was cooking, she spoke a lot. The language of instruction is Italian. It's like I'm speaking a shadow language in my brain, hundreds of lines that I can repeat word for word and that I can hear myself saying just before I wake up, with no other significance beyond the sound they make and their subconscious imprint.

I believe she didn't realize she was speaking Italian at times. I believe she spoke without even realizing she was doing so at times. It was a language used only by the speaker and no one else.

55

The
exclusion
didn't bother me at
all. It didn't bother me since
I was accustomed to it.
Having access to
what seemed
like a hidden
intimacy was
a treat, and I
appreciated the privacy
it afforded me (and the
confusion of never quite knowing whether I was out or
in). Like a vehicle that won't stop, she'd catch me off guard
and talk to me in the same terms over and over again, only to
realize when she returned that I hadn't comprehended a
word she said.

The eyes of the hypogeal may be
seen in the highchair's glowing eyes
under the overhead light. Red Laminex
surfaces may be seen through the
sand and grit. The stairwell's uneven
wall serves as a resting place for its rear
two legs. I'd guess it's been that way
for the last two decades. First, it was
my highchair, and later that of my kid.
Simmered apple spoonfuls were lifted out
of a bowl and pushed into James's mouth
by my mother in a halo of grey hair. It was
not an easy job and there were a lot of misses,
but my mother is a strong-willed lady and she
picks up everything that falls and gives it to
my kid again. She does this every day.

Here, the air is devoid of smells
and as sterile as one could find in a
tomb. Only when I walk does the
dust stir, and it settles soon. My
fingertips are tingling; dirt
makes me feel uneasy. Even
though I was wearing shoes
and socks, my mother insisted
that I wash my feet in the
washing tub
before

entering the home. She washed them for me until I was eight years old, aggressively massaging them between her hands. Later, I'd raise them to be checked while I stood at the doorway for the same period of time. If they didn't pass inspection (which happened frequently), she'd have me come back out and do them again because she had a better eye for dirt than I did. There was a much deeper ritual going on in my mother's house, one dedicated to the fragile (and capricious) gods guarding the threshold between inside and outside. The house was empty except for the modern, functional, and new furnishings. My father's absence from the house was evident in the absence of photographs, artwork, or knick-knacks of any kind, except for the flowers, which were in vases in every room, mainly roses, reds, yellows and creams but also gardenias, camellias and irises; my mother loved gardening and she made the barky. I've never seen a single dropped petal despite the abundance of flowers; the carpet looks just as fresh today as it did when it was first laid down twenty years ago. That has not changed for me, and I'll continue to do so.

My friends' childhood homes were filled with the stories of their families. They lived surrounded by meaningful items, heirlooms that came before them. All our furniture was new. When I go to the basement I know before I start that I'm entering a universe where nothing exists beyond myself.

I used to believe that my mother's obsession with her Australian history was a way for her to make up for the loss of her European roots, which she had long since accepted was unrecoverable. This is no longer the case, in my opinion. Those memories are all too easily accessible. Her recollection of the event is a painful one. As a result of the seemingly random nature of her collection, we may deduce that she has been trying hard (but ultimately unsuccessfully) to forget.

As a result, unlike the majority of hoarders, she shows little enthusiasm for the items in her collection. Each and every item in the basement can only be defined as a 'refuse' and that's it. Even if I don't throw anything out, it's not enough. Her favorite pastime is scouring garage sales for bargains;

lampshades, linoleum off-cuts, rubber bathmats, blinds, paint jars, screen doors, magazines, photos etc. I see it all before me. Because she understands it has no practical use, unlike the other people who purchase it, she wants it more than they do. It's as though she can't take the sight of a thing being left behind. If not redeemed by her hoarding, at least given somewhere to call home are the unwanted, unloved, broken and superseded items of the world. They're a part of this. Furthermore, there is an infinite supply.

When I discovered the shoebox hidden behind an old iron bed that had been pushed up against the wall to the right of the stairwell, it came as no surprise. Even though they were untranslated, I recognized the letters that James had given me in Surfers and had them in the same box (now on the table upstairs). I was reminded of the cold Venetian morning when my grandfather, the guy, discovered a similar box on the desk of his deceased father (about whom I had just read). The afternoon after my father's burial, my mother retreated to the basement of our Rose Bay home and stayed there for an unknown amount of time until I went down to fetch her back, something I had forgotten about for over fifty years. In the basement, she knelt down and prayed. There she was. i observed her. She was surrounded by all of her boxes. As soon as I got her back up the stairs, she whispered something to me that stayed with me. Though I couldn't comprehend a word of it, the lyrics stayed with me like music on a cassette for some reason. If she had talked in this manner, I still don't think she did.

'Polar cold dropped from the sky one clear night.' She was talking to herself, but she acted as though she was talking to me. She was telling me about how my father had made it through the Holocaust. Looking up from the kitchen table she said, 'People suffering from a loss of identity can sink into a torpor and think only about how to shed the burden of time.' She had just cleared the table. 'They often harbor a naive belief that they will one day be able to return to their former selves. As a result, their entire existence revolves around anticipating the first glimpse of a promised land, such as a gleaming coastline in the distance. Even though no such creature has ever been in this world, and never will, they have eyes for nothing else. It is a kind of waiting sickness.'

For the first time in my life, I think, though it shames me to say, as I carried the box back up the stairs and closed the door behind me, I was pierced by the thought of what it must have been like for her - her life, I mean. Is there any love more selfish than a child's? Even at the age of fifty-five, that child is still a child. I wiped my eyes with the back of my palm because I couldn't stop the tears, but it was better not to know which of us I was sobbing for.

The letters in that shoebox provide the bulk of the material for the rest of the tale. To begin, The guy Johnno, mother's father, arrives to the Hand Palace just before the outbreak of The main war of the 20th century and discovers a mysterious message while making arrangements for his father's burial in Venetian.

Memory, to me, has always seemed to be nothing more than a way of carrying on with the past in a different form. I'd like to believe that in creating the character of my mother (along with the father she never met) in the pages that follow, I've gotten closer to love than I anticipated.

The man makes his way through the mist. There is no fog in the past when he looks back to assess the people of the past. Their route seemed to be crystal apparent to him from his current perspective, which was thousands of years in the future. While looking back, he can make out the route, the people walking down it, and their errors, but he can't make out anything in the fog.

– Sam Lieblich

A letter written by a lady on an ordinary piece of paper caught my eye. 'Yes, the concierge may take care of the money; he's the most reticent person I've ever met. Tomorrow is the day I go. I won't be returning to your side any time soon.' Even though he hadn't seen it in twenty-four years, he was familiar with it.

The message had been hidden in a little sandalwood box on the desk. His father was dead, slumped over the desk. What was the purpose of his father's inaction and what was the point of her letter to him? How much money do you have? That's not to say it wasn't obvious to him when he began to ask questions that he had previously answered. An uncomfortable sensation similar to what the little boat had felt that morning as it moaned against its own inertia, its propellers reversing away from the beach as it drifted in, seemingly stretched between arrival and taking leave, on the grey darkness of the Grand Canal. He began to feel sick even before he stepped on dry land, as if he had somehow absorbed the movement of the ocean.

In the early morning light, the painted street names appeared strangely translucent, as if they were floating on water. He remembered walking through the narrow streets, as if on water, and taking refuge in the square, whose grotesque bell tower's face, though barely visible in the mist, he found oddly compelling. Two grey four-legged companion animals that were scarcely affected by his presence snored softly and periodically opened their eyes to look at him with little more interest in him than the stone on which he sat, for the whole hour he had been there.

His trance was broken by the sight of a moth. Looking down at the bag that had once held his father, he felt a sense of loss. Blaming himself had always made more sense. However, might the elderly guy have bribed her to leave the house?? Even if he had offered her the chance to satisfy him, she would have been too stubborn to accept. That's the one. She seemed to enjoy his father's dislike at times, he thought. However, the time was impeccable: November of 1915; it's been nearly exactly a century and a half since that fateful month. Why, therefore, is this the case? Isn't it possible that she might have succumbed two years earlier, on the night when he carried her back from the Girlboss's salon and the old man had acted so abominably at the Place? He figured it couldn't be the money. She was well aware that my mother had taken care of things for me and that I didn't have to rely on him for it. Nothing was off-limits to me. I was ordered to make her work a bit easy, despite the fact that she had urged me to. It's hard to imagine what I knew back then. What was the state of affairs when it came to trade between men and women? Is this a business? Had the elderly guy really said that?

Turned his attention away from a little but still drooping corpse. Opened it again, this time in a little armchair in the living room where he had taken the box from the desk. Scanning up and down, he could see paint flaking off of the ceiling, as if that was the normal condition of this home and had been for a hundred years or more. As he reached inside the box, he became aware of the tremor in his hands. So it seemed to him that secrets grew under the surface of the actual world, just as roots thrived in a subterranean environment. He was most taken aback by the loudness. As many as twenty letters, all written by the same person, were all on the same monogrammed paper: Do you know how many of these letters he has hidden away in his desk?

Despite the fact that it was still gloomy, the light had become brighter, and he could now hear the faint clamor of the street as it sprang to life. An unmistakable dampness permeated the space, making it seem chilly and uninviting. When his father first brought him here in the late spring, he was just five years old and he recalled the flowers in the window boxes from his childhood. He had always connected red geraniums with a wet scent. After looking down, he glanced up at his hand. One of the letters from the box may be found in it. He opened the book to the first page and started reading.

Who is his biological father? What about him? His dizziness was like that of falling in a dream, and he couldn't be sure for a split second. Despite the understanding that it couldn't be him, he wished it would never stop.

'What you ask will never be. I'm aware of what the Girlboss has told you. If I tell you it's not true, you better believe me. There is always a way to characterize things that might make what truly occurred look false. There is absolutely no need for her to poison me. Not only did she bring me to the big city three years ago when I performed at the Theater, she also transported me to the bigger city when I sang at the Theater three years ago. No, I don't recall seeing you. She adored me back then, urged me to come back to the city founded by those wolf babies after seeing me speak, and then this happened. She is an Agrippina, a politician. What is it that she has her eyes on? Not your son, I hope. You've got a lot of clout. That's what she said to me. But if you believe I know nothing about the world, you're kidding yourself. Do you understand what I'm saying? My apologies for writing to you in my own tongue, but Girlboss claims that you have lived in The Italian canal city for a long time and have a greater understanding of our customs than I do. That's possible. Such an enquiry from a woman would be inappropriate, and it would be inappropriate for us to respond with such an assumption. I'm hoping you'll view this as a sign that the only obstacle to our future communication is your own.

As your humble servant, I will continue to serve you in this capacity.'

As he read, he found himself falling again. It was the start of the week-long festivities marking the 300th year of the reign of the now famously deposed royal family, and he was sitting in his father's box at the Place, listening to the voice of a lady he had yet to meet – who is as yet just a name – but what an amazing name! In this moment, the shape that will give it life and never be seen without it has already attached itself like the robe of she who baked her sons in a pie and is growing like live skin, Gina da Rinehart — a voice that draws from the air surrounding it and everything that is in that air. The expectancy it carries in the Girlboss 's salon that night, the same skin he will feel against his own when they sneak out to the kitchen, and she will laugh and her eyes will sparkle when he says that a kissed mouth does not lose its freshness, but like the moon, it returns to its original state after a while.

The guy squinted at the skylight above him. Intensely focused on something neither near nor distant, his face was flushed and his eyes wide open. His jacket pocket was full of cigarettes, so he pulled one out and lighted it. Imagining the smoke sliding into his veins, he inhaled it. That time in one's life when one sees nothing but loss in front of him, he wondered, could anybody genuinely identify?

My first impression was that she had just had a shower, based on the dampness of her hair. Then I realized that I hadn't seen her walk since my return. I knew she must.

I greeted my mother with a cheery, 'Good morning, Mom.'

In response, she snarled back. Her toothpaste had a peppermint scent to it, and I recognized it. As a result, she was reduced to a featureless shape with no way to tell how she was feeling on the inside. This was not the first time that I was grateful for the anonymity of the conversation.

'What did you bring me?' She inquired.

It wasn't long before I realized what was going on and turned to see a guy in a wheelchair that seemed to be moving on its own, as if he were a slide in a projector.

Although I had no clue what she was talking about, 'I detest it when people hide secrets from me,' she repeated, dragging me back to her. Her voice was harsh and hurtful.

I took a step closer to the bed, lowered my shoulders, and offered her what I thought was an embrace, but she made no attempt to reciprocate the hug I had given. Her upper arms were hidden from view by the bedclothes. Her hair was scented with baby shampoo, and I could smell it. She smelled like a baby, and I smelled her baby smell.

Whatever was in front of her, she said, 'I liked the gardenias the most.'

I could hear a vehicle starting up and a few drowsy birds tweeting in the tree next to the balcony from my window. It was otherwise quiet in the neighborhood. A whisper seemed to be enough to spook the tranquility.

I said, 'Are you ready?'

I placed the Dictaphone on the nightstand next to her bed after taking it out of my pocket. Neither of us noticed as she swiveled around to look at it and then at me. It seemed that way for some reason, just as I was going to remind her of what we had agreed upon the previous time I went, she answered the question I hadn't asked.

'We left the mountain town of Piedmont with my mother when I was around four or five years old. On the back of a military vehicle, there were also other youngsters. At my mind's eye, I can still see the teacher who taught us in the school, the empty rooms of our home, the goose-necked geese, and the sweltering people resting around the railed-off stove in the waiting area at Torino Porta Nuova. There was a ship in port. To make ourselves at home, we tried our best. The issue is that life is too lengthy. As long as it was just a matter of a few years, and we knew it was coming...'

It was a well-crafted monologue that sounded like it had been rehearsed and was still being rehearsed, though she may have gotten stuck on a few details. None of this made sense to me. She seemed to be a regular person at times. She informed me about a recurring dream in which she gave birth to individuals who were already deceased instead of having children of her own. She described the sensation as being like a big weight placed on her chest.

There must be a better way to describe this story, I thought.

'You may believe anything you want,' she said.

When I heard her voice and heard the challenge, she had issued twenty or perhaps fifty years before, I felt a pang of remembrance.

'When you say that, I know that you're not talking about making a choice. Instead of slithering away, you might admit you were wrong and apologize to your mother.'

'There is absolutely no excuse for my actions.'

As I declared, 'I am not righteous,' I did so with considerable force. 'I'm OK,' I reply. But I wasn't. In and out of focus at the same time. Pain that is both physical and unique.

'I saw it in The Italian canal city, guys walking on water,' he recalled. Was she even paying attention? 'I believe that, as long as I'm alive, I can dream of anything. After the war, that's how I imagined we'd live, I thought. Killing isn't what God intended for us to do. He created us out of love. Everyone was in awe of me. I was filled with fervor and excitement, but I didn't know that I'd always wanted to have a family My... was all I had.'

It hurt my heart to hear her speak in this way, as if in her mind I was dead (I didn't even know the half of it). Just when I thought she'd gone silent, she turned and stared at me, her eyes wide and attentive. She was able to tell who I was right away. I Shuddered and my hand was quickly dropped when she yanked her arm out from under the covers and grasped it. It was now time for her to say something. 'So long as she's still your mother, that is. While her eyes are fixed on you. Everything you need to know will be revealed to you by me. If you agree to help me die, I'll accept.'
Then I had a feeling I would.

In his father's office, he sat with the sandalwood box open in front of him. When he realized he had to open the box and read the messages, he was unable to do it. He was certain of what he would discover there, regardless of the circumstances. He had no doubts after reading the letter. The whole time, he'd been thinking it was his own father. Almost as if he'd already died, he'd known. An unwillingness to know is a refusal to know.

Though he had hoped the anguish would lessen with time, the void left by her absence remained startling even after twenty-five years. Suddenly, she vanished. In his father's box, he found her - the same monogrammed paper, the same exquisite hand – and her loss filled him up once again. He felt like he was running out of oxygen, as if his lungs were constricted.

He had no notion what time it was. the mist had lifted, and daylight had begun even though it was still chilly, he could tell by the brightness. The bustle of the city. He could sense his father's body behind him as if it were a tsunami crashing on a rocky shore. Perfume and talc fill the air with their distinct scents. It's imperative that he be reduced to ash as quickly as possible. There was nothing except waiting until that moment.

The letters were pulled out of the box by his right hand and placed on the desk without his noticing. So close to his face that he couldn't even see the text on the first page. His thoughts turned to the hand that had written the words one after the other and the mind that had travelled through it, and how they had come to be there. It's so near, it's almost unbearable. Twenty-six years have passed since that fateful night. Almost as if his body had detected a shift in the atmosphere, he'd felt her presence before he ever saw her. In the drawing room of Girlboss, she had walked in. It looked as if she was seeking for something in his face with her dark violet eyes, which were made darker by her long, thick lashes, and then returning to the hostess, who was speaking urgently to her. He took just enough of a look at her to observe the constrained expression on her face and the barely detectable grin that curled her red lips was reserved just for him.

His attention was drawn to a large mirror behind which sat a table with a vase of the most stunning lilies stretching their long necks as if they were about to take flight. He had moved aside, careful not to look too eager, and in that turn saw her again in one of the long mirrors.

Her last words to him before he turned around were: 'I'm pleased you didn't go to the Ambassador's,' she added. A song-like voice came to him in the mirror, as if it were coming from the reflection of her face. Even her breath had a distinct sourness to it. 'Isn't it a great evening?'

As though embarrassed by the situation, she escorted him down the kitchen passageway by his arm. As soon as he saw the gesture and movement, he appeared to calm himself and begin speaking to her in a near whisper. While they waited for them to complete, two servers stood with trays of food and drink, seeming to understand but without showing it, while they listened to their Italian conversation.

'It has been said that the ball will be quite excellent.' Her conversation was centered on the upcoming festivities in the grand house where they live in winter, which were scheduled to go until the early hours of the morning. What if we go there some other time?' There are going to be a lot of gorgeous ladies there, according to the Girlboss.'

He took a drink from the waiter and handed it to her, 'Not all,' he relied, laughing now. He lowered his arm for a long time after she had taken the drink, as if he was pleading with her. Either way, no one could tell.

She retreated a bit, but still smiled, and turned to face the busy room. Her voice was loud and tremulous, yet firm and commanding when she finally spoke. He was already a fan of the radicalism. She had fashion sense and the power of her natural beauty – and skill – but she didn't have the social hierarchy on her side.

'I know,' he said, 'but you already know that.'

She grinned. There was a lot going on today. 'Even your monarch who for hundreds of years now has named himself after the proto-emperor of the Romans would not let me off the hook.' Almost as if she wasn't sure what she was about to say, she took a few breaths to make it apparent that she didn't want it to be taken that way, and then continued. It was followed by a reference to 'your father.'

He didn't say anything in response. Of course, she was correct — there was a pause. He was setting himself up for failure by sleeping with her. Why? In contrast to his disbelief, he had no clue how to cope with the overwhelming intensity of his feelings for her. This was compounded by the fact that she presented herself to him as if they were just stage props. He had to break the trance to get out of it. He grabbed her by the arm and dragged her through the door with him. He was taken aback when she didn't fight back, instead gliding along as though on ice. In the passageway that connects the kitchen to the drawing room, he remarked, 'You know?' There were servants all over the place, but this was the type of home where, even if strange things happened on a regular basis, they understood how to ignore their eccentric owners' antics. In other words, 'I don't give a damn.' He spoke as if he'd just climbed a flight of steps to get to her, as if he was out of breath. A passionate kiss on the lips sealed the deal. It was the same flowing ease he had in the process of pulling her out that he felt in kissing her again.

There was no censure in her eyes as she drew away from him. She took a note out of the sleeve of her dress and tucked it in her pocket. When she gave him the message, she told him that he may be interested in it.

As soon as he saw the hand, he had a premonition of what the message would be. She wished he could see her thoughts. She wanted to pit him against his father, which was understandable. Nevertheless, who was she testing, and how did she want him to behave?

At this point, she was laughing as naturally as he had ever seen her do before. When she acted this time, you could see it: a little tremble in her lips as the laugh faded and changed into something else, a flutter in her eyelids, and an intake of air that came with an agonizing need. With one hand on his shoulders, she drew him down towards her while simultaneously raising her own to kiss him on the lips. She kissed him passionately.

In the weeks and months that followed, the Gina he envisioned at that time, this mysterious and shadowy person who had risen so ripe with languor from the black backdrop that was everything beyond the halo of her voice, became a very different Gina from the Gina he conjured at that moment. The following morning, as he stumbled out of her apartment after a night of drinking, he realized he had already planted in the depths of those eyes, without any memory of the past, a hint of an already glamorous and genuine future, like an opera itself without the final act. His mind was ringing with Boccaccio, and he was reciting, whispering to her ecstatic eyes, 'Bocca basciato non perde ventura, anzi rinnuova come fa la luna,' and she was laughing, with her eyes sparkling and he kissed the new moon of her lips again where still in his mind the warmth of their reflected light remained.

So many good times! He grudgingly awoke from his trance and saw the letter he'd been holding in his hand. It was 26 years ago today! As soon as she had brought him to bed, she began to wonder about this!

'I'm hoping you'll recognize that the only thing standing between us in the future is you.'

He pictured his father, who had arrived late to the soirée and was now huddled with the Girlboss, his face crimson with excitement. Gina was right behind him as he emerged from the kitchen. His carriage was waiting outside, and he'd whirled around just in time to take hold of her arm, rushed her back through the kitchen, down a set of snowy stairs, and out into a gorgeous Big city night and his carriage, which would whisk them away to the Hotel Belmont and everything that would follow. As soon as he saw her in the mirror and read what she had just said, she must have handed him his father's message, and she must have responded while he was still sleeping comfortably in her bed and they're all the same, too.

For almost a year, he had no idea that anything was amiss. Putting the letter aside was all he could manage.

He turned and looked around the room, but he didn't see the dead corpse in the corner. His father had been an avid collector of paintings, particularly impressionists like Cezanne, Monet, and Degas, as well as some moderns like Matisse and Picasso, but he had progressively removed them from the walls and sold them off over the years. Surely, it wasn't because of the money. Before the Revolution, he had realized that the wealth was secure in Italy. Only their city home and the vacation house and whatever money he had in national accounts were taken from them. As for the guy's personal riches, it had been carefully stored away in banks in well-known tax havens at some important time or another.

'The last letter I wrote to you may have been a little confusing to you. There can be no repeat of what occurred in Paris. You request that I keep your son's contact information a secret. You're just five rows behind him in the crowd, so how is it possible? In my dressing room, he's there every day. He asks for my hand in marriage. There's no good reason for me to turn you down. You claim that if he marries against his mother's desires, he won't receive anything. In other words, she's set everything up and he's off the table already. 'What's up?' I have no interest in this. I believe Johnno when he says he is free to act. Obviously, you're married, so I don't need to remind you. You are not permitted to write to The Guy anymore. In my dressing room, they leave them behind. I can't promise that he won't come across them. Even though I have given him no reason to be suspicious (as you well know), he has recently become more pessimistic. There is nothing else you can do except tell him the truth if you keep behaving this way. I can only hope that you and I both hope that doesn't happen. I will always be your obedient servant.'

That may not be totally true, but the old goat had undoubtedly traced her across the continent. Regardless. This is all completely unknown to Gina. His doubts were also poked fun at. The fact that males like being jealous makes it hard for them to fall in love without suspicion, as she had opined. That wasn't how he felt, however. Even while she protested, the truth had found him, but how could he have known?

This pain pierced the guy's left shoulder as well as the soles of his feet. If he didn't do anything different, his heart was going to stop beating. A rock-solid foundation, Tiana and Briana returned to his mind as he recalled his two years spent in Europe during the main war of the 20th century sleeping in opera houses and sharing his bed with them. Her voice followed no rules other than the laws of the night and honey and her eyes reflected his own stupid, blind, passionate yearning for happiness. For this reason, she had her sights set on riches, whether they came from gambling or love. It had also been a case of love at first sight. It had to be a question of love, at the very least.

'It is clear from the tone of your letter that you interpret much into our encounter from last night. Nonetheless, I write to assure you that it was nothing more than an attempt to achieve in person what I had previously failed in writing – that I respect you as a man of rank and intelligence but that I cannot have relations with you in the manner of your preference. Because of you and your son's uncontrollable envy, my health is starting to suffer. I can't keep doing things in this manner. What you don't know is how bad my situation really is! Dude, I assure you that I am not deluded. I'm a musician who also happens to be a vocalist. I'll keep singing until they discover someone who's more popular with the general people. This has to come to an end right now. Otherwise, I have no option but to accept your offer. I think I've explained myself well.

I will always be your obedient servant.'

What a joy to read, but she must have been in so much suffering. He had thought that to the lover, the loved one must always appear as solitary. However, he had left her all by herself. He couldn't be forgiven for what he had done. Still, this letter clearly demonstrated that his resentment had been well-founded. She'd finally given in, hadn't she? In what other contexts may the word 'encounter' be used? Despite this, she had assured him it was all in his brain earlier in the conversation. That he was driving her crazy. Is that what happened? Had her life been devastated by his pitiful dejection? Her career was ruined. Away from me? No. He'd been deceived by her for a long time. She was well aware of his mistrust, but she chose not to express it. It was as if she had never spoken the truth despite the fact that she was well aware that one phrase would put an end to his suffering.

His father's only responsibility was to raise him. Is it possible that he didn't know? Did she really say that? That he was responsible for it? There was no chance for her if he had known and not taken action. This could never happen to a guy. He was a kid when it came to love, and she had to have known it. What son ever thinks of his father in this way? But how could he ever have predicted the extremes to which the old goat would go? What kind of a state of rage may his envy push him to? Is that all it came down to? Surely, he's a liar. She, on the other hand, was fully aware of everything. Is there a reason she didn't tell him? She was able to see his blindness and the pain he was going through, what's the point of vanishing without a word? Her singing career was over. He looked for her for almost a year. What happened to her? How on earth did she manage to make it? The whole ordeal seemed unjust. How long had he been her lover? If it were the case, she would not have gone in such a manner. There is no way she could have gone on with his father in this manner and not said anything to him. If only he had access to his father's correspondence, too. Nothing would have changed for him, he was sure. What could it possibly do? But he would have done everything to find out.

When his father wrote to tell him he was dying, he refused to come. Forgiveness on the deathbed was out of the question because of the inability to reach an agreement at the eleventh hour. Without the need to dispose of the deceased, he would not be here right now. Unless, of course, he was able to see the letters. If not for him, then why were they left on the desk by the elderly man? There is nothing wrong with his expressing his remorse in the message he wrote, but he may have been trying to make a last confession before his death, The Guy reasoned. If he'd been there on time as requested, he may have discovered the truth instead of being subjected to these fabrications.

'I'm writing to let you know that I am indeed pregnant, as you had guessed. I haven't told your child yet. I'm not sure how long I'll be able to hide it, but soon I'll be unable to sing at all. Please excuse my harshness from the other night. In the last several days, I haven't felt like myself. If your proposal is genuine – as you assure me it is – I urge you to disregard the remarks of a sleep-deprived woman and allow me some time to think about it before making a decision. My response to your enquiry will be sent to you by tomorrow. Before then, I will not speak to Johnno.

I will be your obedient slave.'

Yes, a child? It's hard to imagine what was going through her head. However, when he read the lines and picked up the last sheet (the message he had read when he first came but had not comprehended until this moment), all he could think about was whether or not she was carrying his father's or his own kid.

'Yes, you may leave the cash with the concierge; he maintains the highest level of secrecy. Tomorrow, I'll be on my way. I won't be returning to your side any time soon.'

Surely we haven't begun yet? Good.

First day.

On the table are four blank cassettes. Nurses were not to be disturbed by us, and so I closed the door. Cassandra was taking the week off, so everything worked out well. Whatever the reason, I got the distinct impression she would disapprove. I didn't know what to expect at all. My mother was still being evasive and guarded, but I could sense she was ready to open up now. She wanted to put it out of her mind. It was a massive whirlwind of activity, it didn't need any help from me. I was nothing more than a passive observer. I sat behind her at the windowsill, tape recorder in hand, listening intently to what she had to say. With her eyes closed, she was drenched in the winter sun. She had forgotten about me. She had returned to her world, the only one she had ever known. I was curious to know what she was seeing through her eyes, and how she felt about the situation. In my imagination, her memories lay there before her, frozen like a stream.

'They claimed to have eaten all the cats and four-legged companion animals during the siege, and I believe them. Magnificent birds of prey, even rats and mice, somehow, were all cooked. Bird cherry plants may be seen scattered across the woods. Snowdrops in blue and blue blooms fill a whole field. O, to die in the midst of such beauty! I used to be a foolish little girl. In my imagination, that's how dying would be. I can't tell you how breathtakingly lovely the sunrises were. It was so peaceful; the air and the light - I'm talking about the nurses here, and one community had us sleep in a castle for the night. There were many chambers and corridors to explore. There was a surplus of clothing in the dorm rooms' closets. There are no other outfits like them. We each picked out an outfit of our

own. I really loved the yellow one, as well as the dressing robe. There aren't enough words to describe how lovely the dressing robe was—long and airy: it was like fluff. We were drained. We changed into our nightgowns and slept out immediately. I was still wearing my dress and a dressing robe as I laid there. We awoke each morning, took a last look in the mirror, then changed into our school clothes; not a single item was taken.

'My apologies: I don't know how to organize it. Many things have slipped my mind. I have no idea how it's on my mind almost nonstop. Although I had hoped I wouldn't forget, I have no idea how it's there.

'It was the first fight that was the most horrendous, and I should have begun there. I had no idea what was going on. I was terrified to death. Nevertheless, I was compelled to see it for myself. That's where I come from. I kept my head up to take in everything even as the police continued pushing me back. How could I have been slain so soon after arriving at the front? I had no idea how commonplace death was. It's impossible to persuade or plead with it.

'Faces were not to be looked at after an assault since they were different from the ones people generally had; it's better to avoid it. My sleep was disrupted by recurring visions of … It is common for men to murmur something as they die; that's scarier than their screams. I recall seeing a young man being brought to his death. You could see by the look in his eyes that he didn't believe it, and he didn't until the very end. He took a stand in front of the rifles. He hid his face with his hands just as he was about to speak. All over again: how the dead lay - their lips gaping, their screams audible; their guts torn apart. When I first began stammering, it lasted for days. Is it clear to you? Please, tell me how I should feel when I think about it.'

Slowly but surely, she made her way down the winding road, huffing and puffing her way into the solitude. Out in the quiet of the icy plains she had left the mountains and battlefronts behind, the living and the dead. The wind carved sand-like patterns in the snow while Skylarks circled above. The road came to an end at the crest of a hill, where bricks and stone had crumbled into dust. In a valley, a walkway dipped. Wildflowers such as Queen Anne's lace, poppies, chamomile, and margaritas, buttercups, and clover would cover its slopes in another season. There was nothing except ancient poplar and oak trees blowing in the wind when she came to the top of the hill.

She was completely lost. In the hills around, ruins of different shapes and sizes might be seen. In the distance, she could still hear the rushing of the stream, but the hills were no longer visible. Astonishingly, she had no idea what she was thinking. In the countryside outside Arezzo, where they had stopped for a few days of recuperation, she recalled taking a stroll with her mother years before. To get over the creek, they needed a spot to land. In contrast, a derelict vineyard was seen on the opposite side, with its poles sagging with undone gnarled vines. Her mother was reminiscing about her early years with her daughter. When she talked, she opened a chink into her inner world, only to close it back up at immediately as if she was hiding it from her, but at the same time, she wanted her to get a glimpse of it .

On that day, it was snowing as well. Small flakes of snow started to fall as her mother spoke of her father selling flowers in the city founded by those wolf babies's market and her acceptance to the Conservatory. Pulling it up, she swaddled herself. The snowflakes whirled in the air like tiny seedpods, despite the fact that the wind had calmed down. She remembers stopping in the grounds of a ruined building with a collapsing tower. A whole wall had fallen, exposing the inside. Only the holes in the walls remained as evidence of the once-strenuous inner stairs, but only one of the outer stone stairs survived, buried in weeds. The snow continued to fall, so they sought refuge in the barn when the weather became worse. The major beam in the hayloft had decayed, split in two, and fallen. Fungi had taken over the house, growing out of control and entangling everything in its path. They remained silent as they surveyed the valley below. Nothing changed.

She awoke from her trance amid a hushed, chilly silence. Alone. The snow had ceased, but the vast, snow-covered plains were in front of her. After hearing the sound of a Central European country that was unified in the 19th century and was famously geopolitically aggressive in the 20th century convoy approaching, she had followed the route north, hiding in the ditches and gullies whenever she heard one coming.

Walking for what seemed like an eternity, she finally came to a windmill. Scraps of canvas dangled from its blades after the tower's top was blasted off. Not a single person or animal could be found. The gate was in ruins, and the stables were little more than a heap of wreckage. The area seemed to be empty for quite some time. In the open barn, she noticed two individuals. A man and a woman (husband and wife?) dangling from the roof; their clothes striped by the stray light that filtered through the crevices. Salt ringed the black woman's headscarf, while the man's crotch was dripping wet. Their eyes were red with tears. They'd only just passed away, if at all. The wire used to bind their wrists behind their backs had sliced into their bloated flesh so deeply that it was scarcely visible. In addition to their fingernails breaking, they had tight nooses around their necks. The grain loft, which was deserted at the time of year, resonated with the cooing of doves as the ropes were draped from a beam there. Underneath them were two swiveling stools.

Even after so much death, she had vomited where she stood. The notion of using a knife to kill them crossed her mind, but she decided against it in the end. What would happen if they returned? No matter how much noise you make, she reasoned, it will all be over eventually.

The doves had all but stopped talking. Floating down from the loft, a mix of light grey and white feathers caught the wind and twirled back up. The sound of gunfire could be heard in the hills. She could see the inmates walking down the road behind her in their tattered uniforms as she stood in the barn. It seemed as if a goat trail meandered its way across the fields to the west as she exited the barn by a rear door. The landscape stretched as far as the eye could see. People and livestock were nowhere to be seen, but under the snow and the burned-out or dilapidated homes along the route were fields that had been tilled.

A little village of five rusted-metal clapboard cottages had appeared before her. An Italian soldier was dangling from an oak tree near the bridge. He had ice on his face and a large bandage on his hand. She could see beak markings on his face, which almost brushed his shoulder.

A black cloud of smoke formed on the horizon as smoke pillars soared into the sky. Her feet vibrated as shells exploded; the knot on a tree limb groaned whenever a gust of wind disturbed the hanging guy. She wandered back to the nearest cottage and passed out on the floor inside her coat for more than an hour. Before continuing on her journey through the narrow path through the thorny woods, she ate some bread and cheese that she had brought along in her coat's sleeve pocket.

The length of the shadows expanded. It had become considerably colder out. Rain was in the air. She took a cobblestone road after leaving the field. Ash trees lined the road as it headed towards a little town. The settlement was deserted save for a cemetery whose fence had collapsed at its western end. Another abandoned home became her new safe haven. Despite the door being locked, she could still see the moonlight rims of clouds through the gaps in the ceiling. Afterward, she drank from her flask, listened to the night, and fell asleep.

Rain began to fall in the early hours of the morning, pounding on the roof and trickling down the walls. Initially, she assumed the shaking was coming from her own body, but then she felt the ground itself quivering. She could make out the shadows of troop carriers and tanks through the shattered glass; vast columns moving fast in her way, against the reddish tinge of the morning. Even in their winter disguise, Central European country that was unified in the 19th century and was famously geopolitically aggressive in the 20th century troopers clung to the trucks' surfaces, sitting or standing and grabbing on securely wherever they could. As the morning light began to shine on the battlefield, those who had been injured stood out more plainly. There were several who drew eagerly on their cigarettes, the little embers twinkling like night eyes as they did so.

The fact is, it was either yesterday, the day before, or perhaps the day before that. She could now see a little settlement out in the distance. Throughout the night, snow had been falling from a sky that was the color of rising veins and sank through the orange light of a distant fire. The snow eventually stopped around daybreak.

Her clothes were drenched from head to toe. she enveloped herself in her coat but knew that if she didn't keep moving, her life would be over. She didn't feel a decent amount of warmth. Both her left and right arms were numb and probably definitely fractured at the elbow and her right ankle was swelled and jammed against the side of her boot from the force of a fall, down an embankment. However, even though she was covered in blood from fallen branches, she had managed to escape injury thanks to her quick dash through the forest.

After the mortars had exploded, there was a lot of debris on the ground. To support her weight, it was simple to locate a staff sturdy enough. The sword that slashed into her leg with each stride had nowhere to go.

Even when the wind became stronger, she could see a trail of prints in the snow, shadow pairs of unequal depth, as if in nature's endless grotesquery there were creatures grown in half, gigantic and dwarf at the same time, that she might follow. She had fled to the top of a small slope, where a stand of beechwood loomed over the path that ran back at least a half-mile. Birds are already haggling in the trees' canopy. In spite of being so far away, she could still pick up on a tinny molecular rumble coming from the woods.

The length of time she'd been limping in the snow or how long she'd been comatose on that ragged patch of woodland floor escaped her. She walked even more slowly than the night's paleness, but she couldn't tell when the sun came out.

She walked on the edge of a field, where she could see a route in the snow that was clean and unmarked. In the early morning light, a hilltop seemed to like a whaleback. She could see the lights of the town below her as she staggered towards it. Underfoot, the dry snow snatched and held on tight. The tiny, red, dog-like animal that some liken to a sexy woman or whose nature they use as a metaphor for cunning, darted across the lawn. A dazzling hawthorn hedge covered with snow petals. Everything, even the quiet, was magnified by the snow. Knowing that she couldn't enter the settlement by the route was a relief.

Her first hints of trouble emerged when she walked across the field, which had seemed perfect from the walkway. The traces of birds and animals were imprinted in the snow, creating a magnificent ledger of the unseen. There were rune-like letters stretching out from her over the field, their shadow ink spilling out and vanishing into the shadows or a hedge; her own, a rough well in the uneven drifts, was one of them and this suffering engulfed her like a raging subterranean inferno that had already decimated the trees under her feet.

When she saw the footprints of a tiny, red, dog-like animal that some liken to a sexy woman or whose nature they use as a metaphor for cunning, in the field, she opted to follow a clue that zigzagged across a corner of the field, it was as though the animal was attempting to cover up its tracks. A blackthorn hedge was used as a passageway in the mystery. After snagging her way to it, she fell into a trance. For almost a mile in front of her, the earth sloped gently downward. As she approached, she noticed the settlement she had been attracted to in the middle of a field with snow-covered trees; cypress and pine trees strewn over a landscape dotted with unexpected dips and troughs. Even in the midst of such tragedy, she couldn't help but believe that a civilization may still be salvaged despite the ruins proclaiming an ultimate disaster.

In the snow, the fields glowed like jewels, reflecting the sun's rays back into the sky. Snow began to fall as a bird flew through a tall pine. A stone road emerged from an arbor of cypresses and proceeded through an enormous triumphal arch at the foot of the hill, making it seem as if she had been going for many miles or hours until she finally arrived at the site. She was confronted with charred trees, demolished buildings, and a metallic taste in her lips. In the snow, rabbit tracks resembled death masks.

As the smoke cleared and human forms emerged from the ruins, she sat on a shattered slab under the arch. It was still quite early in the morning, based on the rising light.

***

The banging on the door had awoken him. How long had he been snoozing on the desk, five minutes? That's a long time. Exactly how long would it take? He knew he'd had a dream, but he couldn't remember anything about it.

He was taken aback by the brightness and had to strain to make out the outlines. Despite the commotion outside, he hadn't noticed anything from the inside. They were two men; the long boat propelled and steered by a standing man in a striped shirt drivers. They had the same physique and wore the same mourning attire. Standing as though joined at the hip, they were a perfect mirror image of one another, their motions flawless and even. They were elderly but clean-shaven, with just a few patches of grey hair peeking out of their caps. These two figures reminded him of two pantomimes. That made him chuckle. His father deserved nothing less than the best for his son.

Inviting them inside the home, he exchanged pleasantries. The guy was relieved to have the conversation put on hold. It became clear to him that for them, death was not a significant event. They had a lot of work to do before they could go back to their lives. What is the daily average number of such visits?

Regardless of what they anticipated; it didn't show. He found himself wishing he could reply, 'You should have been here fifty years ago.' He was ashamed by the urge. He reflected that it was an odd morning.

Extending from the table where it had been stretched on a stretcher, his father's hands were resting on it. Until now, the guy hadn't noticed, but he hadn't given the old man any attention since his arrival. All of this would have been better done without him being present. He was, however, there in front of me. As a result of the legislation, but also for other reasons.

His father, who had formerly been a substantial figure, had shrunk to the size of a tea leaf. The guy hadn't visited him in a while, although being aware of the illness. No less difficult to love while dying.

The guy nodded in response to the men's attention. In the end, they divided, one to the man's head and one to his feet. They seemed to hoist the stretcher with ease, gripping the grips with both hands. The guy guessed that they were accustomed to considerably heavier loads. He drew a picture in his mind of the muscles behind their knuckles. The cloth bulged under his father as he moved slightly. The stench of perfume and powder disgusted him, he held his nose with the handkerchief he pulled from his pocket. Though he felt no remorse, he guessed that guys saw this kind of thing all the time.

They all agreed that the long boat propelled and steered by a standing man in a striped shirt was exactly what his father had wanted, albeit he couldn't be sure which one. Already, he'd made a U-turn and was making his way to the open entrance. He was in desperate need of chilly air. Coins on his father's eyes were the last thing he saw before turning away. For a brief time, he wished they'd disappear, that his father's eyelids would drop, and he could say, 'Look, Johnno, here I am. I outlived you.'

His gaze was drawn back to the door as he stood outside, watching it open and shut. He could just make out the two guys approaching him like air passing through a curtain in the pitch-black interior. Paper shreds blew in his direction as a little wind blew off the ocean. The idea that objects that had been inert may suddenly move without any apparent reason had surprised him as a child; the beginning of life as we know it.

The air outside was quite chilly. Through the stone he could feel it rising up. The days were becoming shorter, yet the frost lingered, lurking under the bridges as though from a legend. In the canal, a carved saint soared over the embankment on the prow of a black, long boat propelled and steered by a standing man in a striped shirt in what seemed to be the most incredible levitation.

When the guys passed him, he took a step back. He followed them to the canal, closing the door behind him. He was already clad in his coat due to the fact that he had forgotten to turn on the heater in the room where he had been sitting.

Even though he was accustomed to the long boat propelled and steered by a standing man in a striped shirt being an odd vehicle, the scene that met him as he reached the embankment's edge still shocked him. To his dismay, the long boat propelled and steered by a standing man in a striped shirt was totally black save for the gilded saint on the prow, which made him wonder why the notion had occurred to him as unusual. It seemed like a floating graveyard. Stable on the boat were two guys dressed exactly like the two men who were carrying his father on the stretcher. The handles of the stretcher were put on the velvet-covered bench seats that their legs rested on when they sat down. Black velvet covered every inch of the inside. He could see his reflection in the long boat propelled and steered by a standing man in a striped shirt's prow as clearly as if he were standing in front of a mirror.

Words were not required by the four guys. They acted as though they were a single entity.

While waiting for his father to board, another long boat propelled and steered by a standing man in a striped shirt approached and parked behind him. Prior to its sudden arrival, he hadn't paid attention to its approach. Flower boxes in the fifth gondolier's possession were transferred forward by him and his companions, who in turn carried them down to his father's coffin, where they were spilt over him like a pall, leaving just his head visible. The two men on the embankment held the guy's arms and steadied him as they handed him down to their colleague, who in a single accomplished movement took him and sat him as simply as a doll in the second long boat propelled and steered by a standing man in a striped shirt. When the coffin arrived, the two guys on the embankment trailed after him, agile as mountain goats and the two long boats propelled and steered by standing men in striped shirts began their parade. It seemed weird, but not unpleasant, to be back on the sea.

The long boat propelled and steered by a standing man in a striped shirt swayed like a cradle in the throngs of bustle on the canal. The canal was bordered with two-storey buildings, tiny motorboats and enormous ferries, all transporting vegetables and garbage. In spite of it all, The Guy was a little self-conscious because of all the attention he received. His limbs were starting to hurt. He wanted to get up and stretch his legs, but he was afraid he'd fall over. Only admiration could be expressed for the complacence of the gondoliers, their motions were as fluid as the water they were responding to.

The long boat carrying his father which was propelled and steered by a standing man in a striped shirt, was a few minutes ahead of his own. As it rose and topped a wave, the guy would get a glimpse of his father, like a dusted moth just emerging from its cocoon. The Guy had no idea from whence he had awoken in this other planet. The shadow of the school chilled him to the bone, even in the dim light. He smelled the salt and weed, felt the chilly water on his face, and saw the trash heaps that bordered the slope.

While approaching the church, it seemed as if the banks were being pushed apart by the water, increasing imperceptibly. In an instant, they were surrounded by an azure sea as the city finally opened out to the horizon. The lagoon spread out in front of him, and the shimmering sails of the barges floating out with the tide seemed to stand still in clusters of canvas sharply peaked in the dimly bright emptiness. The low coastlines that extended out to sea in diminishing flatness were shrouded in a thick cloud.

The long boat propelled and steered by a standing man in a striped shirt, moved like they were alive from inside when they were caught in the retreating tide, with the gondoliers' poles serving just as helms. He could see little fish leaping ahead of him, as the murky water underneath him boiled. 'All that life,' he thought, 'that's not apparent. It's not only about life.'

As they made their way around the island of the one they call Saint George in their language, the number of boats in the water started to decrease. People around The Guy were acting differently. However, though the mist had cleared away, there was no separation between sea and sky due to the tightly packed clouds. Slowing down in front of him, his own glided up alongside the long boat propelled and steered by a standing man in a striped shirt in front of him.

When he was a kid, he wanted to throw his father in the canal outside their house with the rest of the garbage. It was too late to undo the foolishness that the old man had planned in the last week before his death, and The Guy had no desire to do anything about it. In any event, he was interested by the ritual. Those Venetian burghers of the past who felt it as their right to give themselves such operatic ends, were no viler than his father. The bodies of powerful men, who had dedicated their whole lives to the study of wickedness, were lowered into water coffins and let to float to the point where the sky met the sea, where they were destined to meet their last fate.

Slowly, The Guy emerged from his reverie. He could hear the folks across the water conversing in their native tongue, but he didn't pay attention and simply nodded when it was asked of him. Even though he could feel the river rushing past him, they managed to keep the two boats afloat by exchanging magic words.

In his mind, he was able to reach out and touch his father's corpse, but only with disgust. He felt he looked like a goat despite the fact that this was neither a sacrifice or an altar worthy of the term. Through the flowers, he saw for the first time the straw piled between the two seats that held up the stretcher's weight. The long boat propelled and steered by a standing man in a striped shirt who had taken his father to this conclusion seemed to be watching him. They may have thought he was capable of such knowledge. He nodded again, and the two guys retrieved little tapers from underneath their jackets, lit them and placed them on the straw. They then sat back down and continued their conversation.

A sound like someone taking a breath sounded, and little flame tongues started to emerge from underneath the body. For a few moment, nothing occurred, as if the fire was deep in meditation. Someone or something shifted in his father's eyeball. It didn't open all the way, but it did rise just enough to let him peer out through the lashes and see his reflection. After all, he'd just been fooled into thinking it was the eye of the serpent, The Guy reflected. He knew it was macabre fantasy, yet he still felt the judgement.

While they could, they had to act fast after the blaze had started. In order to save his father, they jumped from one boat to the next, then pushed the blazing vessel back into the stream with their poles, which appeared to come alive with the deed and carried his father dashing out to sea.

It began with flowers, then the velvet lining, and eventually his father's face. He couldn't resist the allure of the blazing fire and the enticing aroma of sizzling meat. Last seen as it faded from view was the gilded saint on the prow catching fire like the martyrs of old as the boat succumbed to the flames. This floating fire, going out to sea, felt appropriate to him even though he knew fire and water couldn't be together. He prayed that it would continue to burn for all eternity.

Five guys stood motionless behind him; their gazes focused solemnly on the blazing embers. There wasn't much room in the boat, yet it didn't seem overcrowded as he floated on the ocean. He didn't know why the plane was so quiet, but he took advantage of the opportunity to get up and stretch his legs for the first time since boarding. For all the world seemed, he was getting ready to take flight. When he lowered his arms and seemed to return to himself and smiled genuinely at them, the guys relaxed their guard and stopped staring at him like he was some odd bug. After an explosion, they seemed as though they had been waiting for a signal; the same acoustically silent cohesion. They all took out their pocket bags of tobacco and started rolling their own cigarettes. An older gentleman who was believed to be The Guy in charge then presented the guy his bag, and he was gratefully welcomed by the young fella. He smoked a lot less these days, but it felt like the right moment to make a show of affection. Having done rolling, he took the taper the guy had offered him and smoked it in private, just him and the stranger.

After he had finished his cigarette and thrown the end over the edge into the lecherous water, he finally said, 'So it's going to be war?'

His only remarks since he'd left the home, the guys didn't need to say anything back. The long boat propelled and steered by a standing man in a striped shirt swung about and returned to the tranquil city; a melancholy under an overcast sky, like the miniature paper boats he had once sailed with his father in another lifetime.

***

'... I recall once when we were surrounded by other people, we had nothing but our own hands to work with, so we dug into the dirt ourselves; there were no shovels here. Nothing was going on. We were squeezing in from every angle. That night, we had already resolved that we were either going to break through or die. I'm not

sure whether it's appropriate for me to bring this up right now.

'The troops, myself, and the two other nurses who'd been stranded there all wore camouflage clothing. We awaited the arrival of darkness so that we might make some kind of breakthrough and the twenty-year-old lieutenant taking the place of the injured commander started to recollect how much he enjoyed dancing and playing the guitar; so inexperienced. I felt we were going to die that night. Is it possible that we slept in shallow trenches or by a campfire for months while wearing heavy boots and overcoats then went about our daily routines without laughing or dancing? No matter what, we were all going to perish. You need to get it; thoughts of death haunted us throughout the ordeal.

'I wouldn't have made it through this ordeal without the love I found in the form of my boyfriend. There were so

77

many wonderful memories to be made. We had the time of our lives! We enjoyed a full life in the few weeks before his death. To this day, nobody has ever understood why I do what I do. Things move faster over there.

'I was dragged out of the wreckage of an ancient farmhouse and placed on the floor, where I was draped in rags. Neither tables nor chairs were available. If it was the doctor, he draped the windows with parachute silk, something I'd never seen before. Soldiers on both sides of the entrance kept guard. One person held the doctor's flashlight. I was scarcely able to contain my groaning. I was in a lot of agony, and I couldn't move. As the doctor expressed his concern about the loudness, he begged me again, 'Bear with it, signorina. The only thing you can do is not to weep. Stay with it.' It was a realm of no return. The People from the

European country that was unified in the 19th century and was famously geopolitically aggressive in the 20th century would murder us all if they saw us. Nevertheless, as soon as the troops learned of the baby's birth, I named her Erica. Erica. It's barely audible, like a whisper. They had water with them. There was nowhere to heat it, so I used cold water to wash the infant. My foot wraps swaddled her tightly since the only item in the home was the rags on which I was sleeping.'

In the process of this narration, I learned that I had a sibling.

***

79

Things moved really quickly. It was impossible for the villagers to know who she was, where she had come from, or why she was here. Despite this, they risked their own safety to aid her, perhaps out of a sense of generosity.

A little automobile pulled up and it was a doctor. In what way did he know this information? A big bear-like figure, with grizzled hair and an enormous frame, appeared on the doorway. Afterward, he lifted his shoulders, uttered something that sounded like 'urgh' and proceeded to meet with two elderly guys who stood nearby, watching intently. He inspected her elbow and ankle, which were significantly more painful now that she had stopped.

A small army of women and children descended on the barn where she had been concealed and crowded around her stall as the men spoke. There was wine, bread, cheese, fruit and eggs, canned meat, and cigarettes left behind by the People from the European country that was unified in the 19th century and was famously geopolitically aggressive in the 20th century as they fled. She savored every morsel. They were both hefty, corduroy-style bottoms, which she discovered in her closet. When they departed, she fought to get into her pants, draping her jacket over her like a cloak. She didn't have a mirror, but she wondered whether tucking her hair behind a hat would make her seem more masculine.

The doctor reappeared later that afternoon, huge, authoritative, and uncommunicative. After he injected her with what she hoped was a strong painkiller, he set her ankle in plaster of Paris (her elbow was badly bruised but not broken), and then went away while she fell asleep beneath clean blankets and sheets like a great cosseted baby. She had not felt safe in a long time, lying on her makeshift mattress of straw.

She laughed out loud the next morning when she woke up. She'd been sleeping on the run for months, wishing for the companionship of her own people and thinking about food nonstop. Then, all at once, everything happened. The worst-case scenario is that it was all a dream and she had gone insane. Or it might have been the painkilling injection she received from the doctor.

Whatever the reason, she was rudely awakened from her slumber by a deafening droning. For some reason, she could see two enormous cargo aircraft circling above the settlement, and as they passed overhead, they released what seemed to be vast flocks of white birds that swarmed down to the ground. A few minutes later, a girl came into the barn with one of the pamphlets her father had grabbed from the street outside, saying that her father had found it. On a single piece of paper, the booklet was printed in Italian. Anyone who takes the time to read it will have no doubts about how the People from the European country that was unified in the 19th century and was famously geopolitically aggressive in the 20th century feel or what they want. After being betrayed, they were enraged, ready to fight, and God help anybody who helped partisans or traitors.

She was unable to remain. Already, she had endangered them. Until she was able to walk again, she had no choice but to leave.

Later in the day, the girl's father, who seemed to be the town mayor or some other official, came to her. He would not allow her to leave the house. To keep her entertained, he brought her a radio. The People from the European country that was unified in the 19th century and was famously geopolitically aggressive in the 20th century had taken the community, but they refused to bow to them, and they would not submit now. However, the situation deteriorated steadily over time. On Radio Roma, these People were mounting a tremendous counterattack on the beachhead at Salerno, where they had been rescuing Mussolini. All Italian officers,

NCOs, and cadets above the age of 18 were ordered to report to the closest Central European country's military headquarters immediately. Such an order would only be carried out by a madman. Her worst fear had been realized when she learned the next day of the impending imposition of martial rule on anybody caught with the assistance of partisans or fugitives. In her mind's eye, she saw the girl and her father before a firing squad. The SS Commandant in The city founded by those wolf babies then made a statement in response. Amid horrific bonhomie, Mussolini congratulated the populace and Fascists in particular and then predicted an era of wealth for the Italians. He then announced that a curfew will go into effect at ten o'clock that night as a result of his irrational proclamation. Those who ignored it would be put to death.

She had to leave the village as soon as possible. She inquired about the partisans from the man. He tried to persuade her to return to Switzerland when her health improved, but she refused, so he said he'd look into it and come back to her with more information. He was able to persuade her to agree not to go until the doctor had removed the plaster from her ankle.

When she saw how reckless he was with his own life and the lives of others around him, she reluctantly consented to what she had first refused to do. When she was satisfied that everyone was fast asleep, she used a shoeing hammer she found in the barn to remove the plaster from her ankle. To avoid further injury, she re-laced her boots despite the agonizing pain they had caused her, she staggered over the path and past the hedge onto the vast stubble field where a magnificent moon was rising. The croaking of frogs and the chirping of insects was deafeningly loud in the blazing sun.

She was well aware that the partisans would have discovered her existence by now and that she would be discovered by either the partisans or the People from the European country Despite the excruciating agony she felt in her foot, she sped through the stubble as swiftly as she could, blinding herself to a hidden ditch into which she fell up to her waist in black muck. After a while, she came upon a rutted road leading northward. To get to the intersection, she followed it for a half-mile or more, past the farm home with a yard full of barking four-legged companion animals. At the intersection, there was a vehicle surrounded by two guys who waited expectantly. When she saw one of the individuals she recognized, she decided to halt her plans to flee. She couldn't run since they'd spotted her and she couldn't move her ankle. It was then that she realized the guy waving at her was the doctor. It was the other man's first time seeing her. The doctor addressed him as Captain because of his greying hair.

It was a wonder to her how any of the men had known she had left the hamlet, much alone travelled this far, so she decided to leave it unanswered. She couldn't even see them because she was so relieved. The captain had a perpetually raised brow and stern look. She wanted to ask him so many things, but even without his look, she could see that now was not the time with the People from the European country watching from a nearby crossroads in the moonlight.

'I am sorry,' she apologized. It sounded weak, but she had nothing more to say.

When the doctor told the patient to 'come in,' he was joking. 'Don't simply stand there,' he said. In his demeanor, it was as if he'd been summoned in the middle of the night to attend to some little grievance. No one noticed her unusual look, despite the fact that she was coated in grime. The doctor's eyes did go to her foot, but he remained mute about this and only replied, 'You're fortunate my buddy here heard about your escapades in Salerno. Please, do not let him down.' Captain grinned, but the seriousness in his eyes did not dim.

She initially spotted the painted Red Cross on the door panel of the backseat as she climbed into the vehicle. Even though the curfew was in effect, the doctor was able to travel throughout the countryside without being shot. It was now almost certain that she would be shot if they were stopped and caught travelling with them.

They started out on a narrow, curving, and elevated embankment with deep ditches on each side of the road. It was a dark and spooky night. The moon had hardly risen above the vines when long plumes of mist began to drift across the fields like a searchlight. Nobody else could be seen. Between two steep, grass-covered embankments, they crossed a tiny brook on a makeshift bridge. She could see the mountains ahead of them against the night sky, but they were so far away that she couldn't tell whether they were travelling north or south. She couldn't help but wonder where they were headed, so she asked the doctor for the names of the locations they went through, names she promptly forgot.

The automobile came to a fork in the road after rounding a steep curve and driving over an irrigation canal on a bridge. She could hear the unusual whining sound made by cross-country tyre treads on a rough surface above the abrupt increase in road traffic noise; vehicles belonging to the armed forces. There were quite a few. They took a left here and headed east, away from the main highway.

They'd been driving for at least thirty minutes without seeing anybody when they arrived at a hamlet that was bigger than the one she'd left, complete with a church towering above it.

It came out of the blue: 'Police,' the captain remarked. In other words, 'Keep it on the DL!'

In front of them, two people emerged, one of whom was shining a torch in their direction. The doctor's bag took up a portion of the car's undercarriage on one side. Her feet lifted in the air and Captain grabbed them, lowering them and covering her with a blanket as she sought to crawl beneath the seat head-first. The agony was so terrible that for a second she passed out. He was able to complete these tasks only in time for the automobile to come to a halt.

As the carabinieri's torch was flashed into the vehicle, she could hear the doctor unlock the side window and saw the blaze of his flashlight through the blanket. A voice said, 'Doctor, where are you going?' before she heard the words 'Ah, doctor.' Although the tone was cordial, the man's eyes betrayed his curiosity. She was curious to know what he was thinking about the other person in the vehicle.

'It's an emergency,' stated the doctor calmly and matter-of-factly. 'At the elementary school. My buddy from Milan, who is visiting from up north, was curious to see what I was up to at work. I advised him to remain in front of the fire with a drink of chianti, but he insisted on going with me.' A few seconds later, she heard, 'You must hurry then.' She pictured the two guys beaming up at each other, and it worked. 'Go! Go! Finally, goodbye.' She thought.

The captain signaled for her to come out of concealment after they had left the hamlet and were on the main road. As she repositioned herself in the back, her elbow was hurting more than her ankle, but she said nothing. It seemed as though they had entered a maze of little roads. A thick layer of low-lying fog blanketed most of the nation, and the air was frigid. Over the low area on each side, they drove along the top of a dyke for quite some time. For the next twenty minutes, they followed a long, straight road past poplar groves down a ramp. Frogs all appeared to be singing at the same time, until they finally slowed down. This time, she was given new boots by the doctor and a small bag, and Captain gave her a full change of clothing, which included a black jacket and dark felt pants and instructed her to put them on. As she dressed, he and the doctor turned away and waited expectantly. She received a knife from the captain as well, which he said was just for cutting meals and not as a defensive weapon. The doctor handed her a bottle of medicine in a little container.

He grimaced and added, 'You may need this. Even with the frogs, there are a lot of mosquitoes. Apply it on your hands and face. Tomorrow morning, a guy will arrive. His whistle will sound like he is whistling to his four-legged companion animal, and he will do it three times.' He mimicked the sound of a whistle with a low, hushed tone. 'The guy, who seems to be in his forties, has a large moustache. Giovanni is a proper name for him. He'll take you to the partisans if it's safe. In the event he doesn't arrive, you still have enough water in your bag to last. The water in the ditches is not fit to drink.'

They exchanged handshakes with each other. She didn't initiate the handshake, but she was happy when they offered it. It was at this point that they got back into their automobile and drove up the track until the doctor discovered a spot big enough for them to turn the vehicle. If Giovanni, the mustachioed guy, did not show up, she recalled to ask him where she was, which was vital to her in the event that he did not show up.

'A half-mile from the Po,' he told her. He drew his finger up and pointed beyond the tree. 'If Giovanni doesn't arrive, don't attempt to cross the river, no matter what you do,' he said. 'Head for the hills.'

She walked down into the woods once they were gone. The moon shone brightly through the trees, revealing the absence of any kind of comfort. It was very cold, and the tiny canals that watered it kept it perpetually soggy. The frogs were drowned out by the buzzing of insects, which reminded her of the sound of bombers. The bottle of citronella she had left was enough to keep her safe. She was exhausted from the night's excitement and strain. In order to get some rest, she lay out the blanket Captain had given her, put on her sleeping bag from the pack, bathed her arms, hands, and face with the citronella, and buried her head in the pack to screen it from the insects before falling asleep.

'I am unable to get a message out to Russia. Were you fortunate enough to have survived this conflict in the same home where I made my debut, like me? If so, I can only hope that you did so in the place where I have so many pleasant memories. What a whirlwind it is. Are you still of the opinion that our meeting was not preordained? You used to taunt me about my superstitious tendencies, and I remember that. As a result, you'd become grave as you asserted that our character determines our destiny. That has stayed with me to this day. You may have been correct in more ways than you could have ever imagined.'

'If you're still here, I'm sure you've learned to listen to spirits as I have. Because of this, I need to tell you why this spirit came back to you after so long. What I should have told you a long time ago is what I'm going to tell you now: The only way out of the curse I've been living under is to die, if that's any comfort.

'Even after 28 years, the way in which I left you still makes my skin numb. Not for the sake of sympathy, I say this. I have no idea what you've been up to. I've heard nothing from your father. I pray that you were able to forget me fast and get married, and that you were able to live long enough to watch your children grow up in a world like this.

'No one has the right to beg for your pardon. It's not the purpose of my writing though. Although I've confessed my sins to God, I don't believe that death can be controlled.

'But no matter how hard I try, I can never quite get everything out of my head and leave myself with nothing.

'Despite my best efforts, I am afraid that your eyes have already closed as you read this message in light of the recent events in your nation. Even if you can only see my words in my thoughts, I write for you. In order to say what has to be said, a dead lady must talk to the dead.

'Why now, after so many years of waiting? My lips are sealed. You know, I've tried writing to you a million times, but every time, something came up.

'He may still be alive, or he may not. I don't know what you learnt from him or if he really exists. I had the impression that he was the kind of guy who, if for no other reason, could live indefinitely. Even if your father was a bad person, I will not criticize him. To declare that I'm not a decent lady is all that justifies my utterances.

'My professional life was finished before I left you, despite your best efforts to pretend otherwise (you were always a kid). I didn't need to hear it from anybody else to know it. You don't need to be reminded that climbing the stairs is more difficult. Violets don't need to be declared dead after they have wilted.

'So, let's get to the bottom of things. It wasn't until we returned to Russia that your father made a proposal to me. I subsequently learned that it was an act of retribution for something your father had not done for his kid. At this point, I must tell you, despite the fact that I can only offer you my word, that I did not once give in to your father's advances, and for the period that we were together, while I cannot call it joyful, I was faithful to you. In the end, I could have married you (I was grateful for your loyalty), but I didn't love you. It seems that marrying you would have been an even more treacherous act of betrayal.

'So, I betrayed you by vanishing from your life. And I deprived you of something I had no right to withhold. You've had a daughter, congratulations. This is what I told your father. I didn't tell you, and I'm sorry about that. Even though I don't want anything in return from my revelation, I want you to know that I'd do it all over again if I could. However, I believe this is simply another manner in which I have fooled myself into believing that my actions were more damaging to me than they were to you.

'When your father found out I was pregnant, he gave me money and the promise of my support in exchange for my disappearance and ceasing any contact with you. I don't know why he did this, but I can tell you what I did.

'I did not love you, as I had previously said, my job was over and I was pregnant. In my opinion, accepting your father's offer was preferable than the alternative. While it would have been nobler (or simply human) of me to share this with you at the time, it still seems to me that I have no choice – that I am doomed regardless – and even though I have lived with the guilt and regret for what I have done to you, after all these years, I still have not thought otherwise. It's funny how time passes and how little we change.

'In the absence of a husband, I raised our daughter on my own. My mother's maiden name is Dualipa Warehouseparty, therefore that's what she goes by. A little convent in The Italian canal city set up by your father for me gave birth to her on January 8, 1916. It was simple to get the package delivered. I wish I could say the same for the rest of the day.

'I'm not going to bore you with all the gory details right now. Because of the war and your revolution, I was unable to return to Russia, no matter how much I wanted to. After my mother's death, we lived in Naples for a while, then moved to Milan, where we stayed for a while before settling in The city founded by those wolf babies. While my singing career had come to an end, I had the happiest time of my life raising my kid. She was a stunning young lady.

'In the years after the big war of the 1930s and 1940s, we made sporadic journeys to The Italian canal city. In the end, I'm not sure what I was expecting. To be with you? Perhaps. Even though we went by your home on the vaporetto every day, I didn't tell Dualipa about you or the fact that the house belonged to her father. When I don't know what you were doing throughout those years, I've never seen you or your father while we were visiting the city. As I sat in the café, telling Dualipa about my time there, I couldn't help but imagine you next to me, sipping champagne with a flushed face. What a time!

'I know I should have anticipated her to enquire about you as she became older, but I still didn't anticipate it. We were living in an apartment in The city founded by those wolf babies in 1931 with a fifteen-year-old daughter and wouldn't have had anything if it weren't for your father's generosity. As you may be aware, I've never been great with money, but the money wasn't the only factor.

'Alternatively, I might have informed Dualipa about you and your father would have never known. It still baffles me that he placed such a high value on my opinion of him. Because I was embarrassed of the life we had led and of the dishonesty that had been its basis, I couldn't tell my daughter who her father was; I also didn't want to lose her. In my mind, it was only a matter of time until she found out about you and rushed to your aid. In this regard, you must realize that I had lost everything and that she was the only thing I had left. I persuaded myself it was to keep you safe. Rather than finding out fifteen years later that you had a kid you were completely unaware of, it was preferable to remain ignorant.

'In the end, I had to give up on her since she was already gone. But by that point, I'd sunk my heels so far that I couldn't pull them out. I have no idea why I failed to inform her that you had died. How simple it would have been considering the number of men who perished in those years. Compounding one lie with another didn't seem right - morality has an odd way of working, as I've learned – so I declined to answer her enquiry. After that, it was the only time that I said 'no' to her. The last three years have been spent in an unofficial state of war. That's how long it's been since we last saw each other before the outbreak of this new conflict. When she eventually returned, she was twenty-four years old. She's a lady!

'I thought she'd arrived to settle things. Her willpower had slipped my mind for some reason. When I informed her that I couldn't tell her who her father was, she announced that she was joining the military and that I would never see her again. The reason her father had departed, she said, was now clear to her. With a lady like me, who could possibly stay together? It is possible that the truth is closer to us than we think. Death, for example, is never far away from the one who fears him the most.

'She kept her promise and hasn't let anybody down. She hasn't gotten back to me since then. Six months ago, I made the move to Paris. I'm living with a guy who used to hang out with me while I was singing. To date, he's managed to learn as much as possible. She went missing at Salerno one week ago, and he informed me about it the other day. He is considered deceased after going missing.

'At the same time as I am taking her away, I am sad to have given you a daughter. I've run out of things to live for. In spite of the fact that I know it would have been better for me not to have made contact, I believe you deserve to know the truth. When I say I do this for you, I hope you believe me, even if you don't think it was the same for you when I left you. The last thing I'd want to do is beg for your forgiveness.

'I had feared I would never be able to speak those words again in my life. I've cursed you so much. I placed you in every hell I could find. However, I've already lived for much too long. The flames have died out. And I've figured it all out. Everything.'

***

'Dear Gina, I'd want to repeat what I've just said.

'Please, accept my apologies for the extended delay in my response (as you once left me). This was not a result of any deliberate effort on the part of the author. I no longer have the urge to inflict further suffering on someone else. Although I'm an Italian citizen, I still have to keep my distance from the city of The Italian canal city, which is still under the control of the occupying forces. Not long ago, I returned from a trip to Geneva.

'However, this is not the cause for the delay in the project's completion. The fact is, I've had your letter for the last three weeks. I'm sorry. Throughout the day, I've read it. I've been affected by it. I've been unable to formulate coherent thoughts. In a blur, the days have flown by.

'I had to get up early this morning since the last of my obstinate geraniums had perished and the wind had picked up a lot, sweeping yellow leaves into the canal. As if the sky were made of lead, the clouds sped over the horizon. To keep warm, I hunkered down in the living room with an enormous fire, while the naked branches of Ivy shivered against the glass. The experience had the feel of a recollection, even though I was right in the middle of it, as though The Italian canal city, too, had vanished and only existed in this dream.

'My reaction to your letter was not that of astonishment as you would have expected. I discovered the letters you sent to my father when he passed away four years ago. This is what he left for me: I don't know why he did this. After you left me, I spent an indeterminable amount of time looking for you. After reading those letters, I was tempted to give it another

go. How could I locate you if I couldn't find you in the midst of peacetime?

'Before he died, my father and I lived in this house as if we were spirits. For years, I couldn't experience the many aspects of my personality. With the money my mother gave me, I purchased a smaller, more practical apartment near the Rialto. When I was living with him, I couldn't spend a night in the same room. He was responsible for Mother's demise. In the end, her lovely face seemed to ooze and collect like dried wax under its own weight. Her death came only two years after you went missing. However, he's the one who gave me the money. He made certain that everything was out of there well in advance of the Revolution. He died as an Italian. I'll do the same, as well. He made no admissions of guilt.

'I had no idea you were pregnant. That was the biggest surprise of them

all. You can't give up on your dreams. She is your daughter, after all; her departure does not require death. As you may guess, there is a lot of talk around here. Many troops were taken prisoner or surrendered to an enemy they intended to join despite the fierce combat in Salerno, I've heard. People in this area have no allegiance to the People from the European country that was unified in the 19th century and was famously geopolitically aggressive in the 20th century except dread, which will fade when the Americans arrive.

'In the past, you were perplexed as to how I could see anything with my eyes so firmly planted in the clouds. Lo and behold, it was I who had predicted your reappearance. Our daughter will have the same experience. It's a certainty.

'My curiosity is piqued. Describe her to me. Please, accept my apologies, Father. To say you didn't tell me about

her would be an understatement. If that's the case, then I no longer need to know her. In fact, I'd want to meet her more than anything in the world. I know it's hard for you to believe, but your letter has given me a new lease on life. Since we were together, I haven't woken up as eager about a new day as I do now. I intend to do all in my power to locate her. This is a turning point. Soon, this conflict will be ended. The world as we know it will be transformed. We may possibly be able to form a family.

'And that leads me to the point I've been meaning to make since I first sat down to write; I'd love to see you in Paris sometime. I'll be able to depart today if I want. I've come to the realization that life is meaningless without the possibility of redemption, that I'm not quite a ghost yet, at least not in the traditional sense.

'I'm happy for you to call me Misha. Happier than you might ever imagine.'

***

'Even after all these years, I still have no trouble remembering your name. Time is a cruel mistress, forcing us to experience things in a linear fashion. Everything would be perfect if it could all happen at once. It would be an amazing experience to live that way.

'Although it snowed lightly this evening, it didn't make it to the sidewalks or monuments before melting. Pity. I have yet to see Paris covered in snow. I'm not a city explorer. The people from the European country that was unified in the 19th century and was famously geopolitically aggressive in the 20th century are masters of anxiety. I seldom go outside of my one-bedroom apartment unless absolutely necessary.

'You have no business being in Paris. Inquiring minds want to know. You wouldn't stand a chance if you were a Russian in the conquered territory. Watched it. Why then? Nostalgia?

'My situation is fragile at the moment. Ask yourself how a lady like me is able to make it in this world. Do you want me to go into detail? In the event that you continue with your plan, you will never see or hear from me again.

'To be able to explain myself to you and to know that you don't hold anything against me is enough for me. In the end, our daughter is dead, the past no longer exists, and time itself is impenetrable. You can't do it any other way around it.

'Remember me kindly.'

***

'I'm sorry for causing you so much pain with my message. It wasn't my intention. I was completely unaware of my own existence until a little respite - I choose to call it bliss - came into my life. I'd lost track of where I was and why I'd come to this place. Forget about the bloodshed and the battle. Your letter was the only thing I remembered.

'I'm sorry, but I'm unable to follow your advice. For all these years, I've been searching for you, only to discover your existence and then choose to keep my distance? It's not even possible. As a matter of fact, you might just as well ask me to go to the skies.

'You claim that your own existence is in jeopardy. Think about me. If you can't come to me, I'll come to you. When it comes to living together, we don't have to. I'm still living in the same neighborhood as before. The fact that you are here and safe will be enough for me. You don't need anything else.

'I'm not buying your story that our daughter is no longer with us. It's impossible to believe. What evidence do you have? Even though I've been unable to uncover any information on her absence, I'm filled with both optimism and despair. Isn't this obvious to you? Tomorrow, I'll be on my way to Salerno. I'll track her down if she's there. It's possible that we'll become what we've always wanted to be. Still, there's no news after two months.

'Surely, I won't be able to get my hands on you again. You wrote for a reason. Was it just for my own amusement? To find out how strong you really are? What's the point? You should know by now that there is and never will be anything else. All my life, I've been by myself. All of my hopes and dreams have been shattered by this ordeal because there was only hope for so long. It was important in my survival. Then, as if by magic, your letter came.

'I had not wasted a single day of my life. I came back to you because of you. My scars slipped my mind; even lunacy can't compare to what you've done. You leave behind nothing except the deepest slumber. That's not right.

'Misha here. How can I help you?'

***

When she eventually finished telling me the tale, we were seated in her kitchen. While the tea steeped, she sat down with her cookies and a package of Monte Carlo's. When I peeked out the window, I saw a pair of magpies perched on the clothesline. In her mind, they were calling her.

She responded, 'Don't be concerned about them.'

'They're the worst of the worst,' I said.

'Later, I'll give them something to eat. When we first came in Parramatta, as a child, they'd jump down to take the four-legged companion animal food from the dish and eat it themselves. I'd stay inside and keep an eye on everything. I believe I was afraid of them.'

She then smiled at me, giving me the once-in-a-lifetime chance to see a smile that had the character of perpetual reassurance. For a brief moment, it seemed to confront the whole of eternity before narrowing down on you with an unwavering bias in your favor. In the way you wanted to be understood, it believed in you, and it reassured you that it had the image of you that you sought to express at your best. It understood you in the way that you wanted to be believed.

The last time we had seen each other was three days ago, since I had been so occupied with my mother. And she was eager to learn everything she could. Is it possible that I did not get enough sleep? Do you eat three meals a day on a regular basis? Was I able to go swimming? What was going on with my mother? Then, she wasn't really listening to what I was saying. She had a look of enthusiasm on her face. Her speech was rambling, tumultuous, and vertigo-inducing. Though that wasn't the foreplay I'd hoped for, I got the sense it was a precursor to something. Despite this, we maintained lengthy and unwavering eye contact with her throughout her speech. While refilling the teapot, I caught her glancing at me as if to assess how well we'd grown to know each other, or to see whether the space between us was enough to allow me the strength to endure whatever she was thinking and emerge even closer on the other side. To say I was awed by the avalanche would be an understatement.

When I inquired about it last week, she responded, 'I need to tell you what happened,' and she did. 'We need to be an item if we're going to be together,' she said in a tone of more gravity, like a bubble rising slowly through honey, and she smiled like a loon as she asked me to stay, 'if what's happening here is serious,' in her voice now. 'If we want to be together, there are certain issues that need to be discussed openly, not buried away like a beast in the basement.'

'I can't believe you're so tense. I'm sure you're eager to learn. I can't believe it's been so long because it's been there so long, my recollection of it seems like it's older than me. It's heartbreaking. Because of that, I still get choked up thinking about it

Getting to it seemed like a needle pointing towards the unseeable. I remained as quiet as the tomb. When we first met, she had been reluctant, and I didn't want that to go by unnoticed. Even though I was afraid of what she might say, my curiosity much outweighed my apprehension, like tidelines glossed by the moon, there were thin lines of sweat on her forehead and under her eyes. She was bathed in a beam of early morning light.

'My father and I moved into my uncle's home in Granville about a year after my mother died.'

'How do you know?' he inquired.

'His religion was pretty strong, to say the least, when he was younger. Then, one night, I woke up and found him staring at me from a doorway in the hallway. That would be my uncle. At first, I thought he had just woken up, but when he saw that I was awake, it made me doubt whether he had been there at all. However, he had. Because it occurred once more, I'm not sure how many nights or how long he stood there, but every time I woke up in the middle of the night, the hall light would be on and he'd be staring at me as if he was terrified of something. I didn't wake up every night.

'When she was still living, he had a deep affection for my mother. He'd murmur something and then go every time I woke up. If I had any inkling, it was that he was concerned about my well-being. My mother died when I was fourteen, so I was probably fifteen at the time. In a bizarre way, none of us mentioned it. Even though we both knew the other was aware of it, it seemed like a private matter we couldn't discuss.

'There you have it. I didn't tell my father anything. During the day, everything went on as usual. My family and friends left to go to work, but I stayed home to go to school. When I was getting ready in the morning, he came into my room and sat down next to me. Because we didn't have any locks on the doors, he was able to access it without knocking even if the door was closed. That was something that not even my father had ever done before. For school, I was still in my pajamas and pulling up my stockings. However, instead of walking away, he stayed there and stared at me like he was watching my dreams. This time, on the other hand, he wasn't so fast to flee. He was my uncle, and that made me feel better. He was a well-liked figure in the neighborhood. It belonged to him; I mean the sentence, "You've got a way with words."

'After then, it occurred again. I didn't do it every morning, but I did it every time I got ready for class. His response was to apologize as if it were a mistake, then enquire about my breakfast preferences before shutting the door. I was in the bathroom when he did it again, although, he seemed ashamed at that point. He often expressed his regret. "I didn't believe anybody was in here," he said, despite the fact that we only closed the door while someone was in the room. He seemed to be in a state of agitation, like he did during my mother's memorial service.

'I doubt he intended me to witness him in such a state of emotional distress. After a long day at work, I decided to take a bath before supper one day. That was something I did quite a bit. It had claw-footed tubs, just like in the ancient days. I was washing myself in the sink when I saw you. It was probably approximately 5 p.m. at the time. In spite of the darkness, there was still a fair amount of light. Then I heard footsteps and realized it was him. The footfall in the corridor seemed lighter than usual when I heard them. Alternatively, it's possible that's how I recall it. Outside the bathroom door, they waited. He seemed to be watching me from afar. It was as though it were about to rain. He then walked up to the door and turned to face me. I am the whole package. He was aware that I was present. This time, it wasn't a mistake. And I believe he was aware of it. The way he looked at me that day was different from how he looked at me in the past. The flannel was the only thing I could find to wrap myself with.

'I had no idea how long it went on for. It didn't feel like long, but I'm sure it wasn't. I'd never heard him say that before: "Excuse me." It seemed like he was disappointed in me somehow, or he was furious with me but wouldn't explain why. I could hear him return down the hall to the kitchen through the open door he'd left ajar. I went to my room, changed into my pajamas, and didn't come out till the next morning.

'My father didn't specify whether he was concerned about my skipping supper; he must have heard something from my uncle. To my chagrin, he left me alone and didn't come in to wish me goodnight, as he normally did. Everything seemed normal when I awoke in the morning and went to the kitchen. Despite the fact that I was sure it had, I questioned if it had really occurred. Having gone to work, my uncle prepared me a typical breakfast, as he always did. The local Arabic newspaper had been delivered to him; he was reading it. Then he came up behind me and grasped my shoulder as I was ready to leave for school. I'm sure I flinched when he touched me for the first time. The sound of his voice still reverberates in my ears. "Cassandra, I'm sorry," he said. When he said that, I thought to myself, "I wish he hadn't said that." I knew he was sorry, but until he said it, I believed I could still pretend it was all some sort of accident or mistake since he was my uncle, my father's brother. I assured him that everything would be OK, although my tone sounded a little strained. I was ready for it to be done. To leave the home and be free of his presence.

'When I went home from school that afternoon, I had no idea what would happen or what dad would say. I was hoping he wouldn't say anything. However, as it grew dark and neither he nor my father had returned, I started to become worried. None of this made sense to me. Friends of theirs played cards at a local cafe on the weekends, but they never went out during business hours. My father returned alone. When I saw him, his face had a look on it I had never seen before; stern seems intent on causing harm. He insisted that I join him at the dinner table. When I asked him whether he'd spoken to my uncle, he responded, 'Yes.' It seemed as though he didn't even notice that I was there. I could feel my body trembling, but I couldn't put my finger on it; nothing was wrong with me.

'"No one here can take care of you. It's about time you tied the knot." That was all there was to it. I was so taken aback that I couldn't come up with a response. I'd seen a shift in his demeanor after my mother's death, but I knew it wasn't him, my uncle, of course. I told him everything back then, and I'll tell you everything today as well. In a flash, it all poured out. When I turned to look at him, he was like a statue. If anything, he had a more serious look on his face. "Is this your way of saying thank you to your uncle for taking us in?" He also mentioned other, horrifying things. His brother had confided in him, so he was aware of the reality. Without a mother, I was morphing into this new kind of woman; in a land where there is no God. I was on the market for a spouse. If my uncle could, he'd take care of it. That was the end of it.

'In all honesty, I've never divulged this information to anybody else. At first, I was skeptical. I assumed we'd wake up one day and find ourselves just where we left off, that we'd return to our home in Parramatta and forget about all of this. With the help of my uncle, he began attending the mosque with him on Sundays. He'd never gone to church in such a fervent way. In my mind, I didn't believe it was about me at all. The truth is that I didn't want to accept it was about my father even back then, despite the fact that my comprehension of the situation has improved much since then. It was neither mine nor his fault; he was raising me all by himself after my mother's death. His brother was the individual in question. Does that make any sense to you?

'Back then, I didn't get it. I was outraged. In the company of my uncle, but mostly my uncle. There were no lies in my story that I'd ever told him. My father had a daughter, and I was his child. In Lebanon, he showed me pictures of a guy. His appearance resembled that of an elderly relative of mine. He identified the man as being his wife's spouse.

'That weekend, he was travelling to Sydney. I was just sixteen at the time. I don't know what occurred at that point in time. I didn't beg him to take me seriously. I refrained from crying. Nothing came out of my mouth. I would have turned much harder if he had turned to stone. As a good daughter should, I lowered my head and made my way to my room. I gathered my belongings and put them in a bag. I went down to the kitchen with my stuff that night and waited until they were both fast asleep before entering. I made off with whatever they had stashed away in the desk drawer. They had a lot since banks were a pet peeve of theirs. The fact that I had no idea where I was heading was irrelevant; I wasn't even thinking about it. All I could think about was getting out of here. It was the last time I saw any of them.

'For the first time since she began speaking, she looked me straight in the eyes, her eyes as intense as those of a hunting bird. Never in my life have they ever looked so tattered. Almost if she had just emerged from deep water and was still waiting for what she'd seen there to follow her back up to the surface. I nodded my head in agreement.

'I never expected such a sense of relief. Because I've spoken to you in this manner, I hope you don't assume that I don't feel terrible for him. I do, every day. If there's a fault, it's in the way we're created. What I mean is that you need to move outside of it... Has making you listen to all this not humiliated you?'

I flatly refused.

'You know, this is all completely foreign to me.' What's going on with you? 'It's not like me to...'

I rose and made my way around the table to where she was seated and nodded once again. And now this woman's life, into which I'd swooped so suddenly. Is it really so unusual to be able to move that quickly? It was clear that the journey that brought us here had been unusual. Inhaling her beautiful scent, I kissed her on the head and thought about how tragedy accumulates like a storm, and how we have no control over it.

Instead of abandoning her, I should have remained with her. I was able to see the price tag. But for reasons I can't understand (as if I wanted to fail), I was unable to face her at the time. Apologies were exchanged immediately. I informed her that there was a buyer for Mom's property who needed access (as if I'd never heard of estate agents) and that I'd be back in the evening. Untruths abound, of course. What's more, how could I possibly tell her the truth if I didn't know it for myself? And I now have a sibling I didn't even know about until just now! During the time she was still sitting in her chair, I kissed her and vowed to make it up the following evening when she was able to get out of her chair.

I remember my mum telling me that happiness is beyond the mountains, but pain is just around the corner....

Because of my prior nursing knowledge, the detachment commanders moved me around a lot. They were quite kind to me. I was the only female in the group, as you may have seen. There were no two squadrons that were alike. Variations in size were caused by the terrain and local assistance. In the Po River flatland, my final squadron engaged in sabotage. Ex-soldiers provided us with rifles, Berettas, revolvers, potato-masher grenades, and subsequently machine guns and submachine guns that the People from the European country that was unified in the 19th century and was famously geopolitically aggressive in the 20th century had acquired. The situation was dire. A person's ability to move freely was very essential. Donkeys utilized by the peasants in the fields by day were commonly used to haul equipment at night. Those kids have incredible guts.

To our detachment, we were informed that the commander's wife, two little girls and his elderly mother had been kidnapped by the Gestapo. If the commander didn't surrender, his family would be executed by hanging. His two days of contemplation were up. The People from the European country that was unified in the 19th century and was famously geopolitically aggressive in the 20th century spread the rumor that the partisans didn't care for their own children as they marched from town to hamlet. Were they monsters? They revered nothing. The aircraft dropped leaflets over the woodland... The general wanted to give up the fight. We kept a close eye on him. As far as we were concerned, he had the ability to murder himself. We immediately contacted our embassy in Washington, D.C., and informed them of the situation. We were given specific directions, which we've followed. They told us to resist Central European country that was unified in the 19th century and was famously geopolitically aggressive in the 20th century aggression... We found out two days later that the whole family had been executed. The next morning, he set out on his own on a mission. Our report said that he was accidently killed... When we arrived at the scene, we saw him hanging from the tree...

We could hear screams from the farmhouse across the river one spring night when all was silent in the forest. It sent a shiver down my spine. I was unable to look someone in the eye because of the trauma I had experienced. When we returned the next morning, I was reminded of how we had crossed the river. The body of an elderly man was being laid to rest. In the middle of the night, he had been shot and died. Wheat seeding. Because of the force with which he held on to the grain, we were unable to straighten his fingers. It was used to bury him...

I despised them... I was aided by my contempt... On every operation, I wanted to murder as many people as I could. One by one, I wanted to sink my teeth into each and every Central European country that was unified in the 19th century and was famously geopolitically aggressive in the 20th century National Socialist prisoner I saw. Strangulation is the only way to deal with this situation. With my hands, I could suffocate them; with my teeth, I could hack them to pieces.

We were deceived by someone... The People from the European country that was unified in the 19th century and was famously geopolitically aggressive in the 20th century discovered the camp. The marshes came to our rescue. We sat there for days on end. Water and mud. The infant was in need of nourishment... It had no idea... The People from the European country that was unified in the 19th century and was famously geopolitically aggressive in the 20th century came very near... This canine chorus was audible. The four-legged companion animals could have heard it...? What was my age at the time? I was out of milk. I was starving, too. A group of thirty of us gathered for the event. Nobody was able to look at me... No one is able to... You've got the gist...

***

When she awoke, the woods were very cold, and the fog obscured everything. There were said to be extensive brackish water enclosures at the mouth of the river in the delta, where they might seek sanctuary if the People from the European country that was unified in the 19th century and was famously geopolitically aggressive in the 20th century ever found their camp. She had been informed this. Her kid was two months old and she had been with the partisans for half a year. In order to keep the baby safe, she had made her own baby sling out of a flour bag. Her appearance was unnoticed by anybody. There was a glimmer of optimism in the freshness of life. Many of them were superstitious. It was as if the baby was a charm.

At dawn and dark in winter, migratory birds like duck and geese flocked to the valley, which was inhabited by people who were obsessed with shooting and would wait for the birds to fly past or stalk them using their punts, a man who knew the valley well informed her. Great swarms of eels passed through in November on their way to the Sargasso Sea, where they would give birth to their young in the frigid waters of the Atlantic, never to be seen again. Nobody had any idea what had become of those who had ventured forwards. He spoke about the river's other inhabitants, such as the carp, pike, and occasionally-appearing large sturgeon. He demonstrated the operation of the big net, the source of the majority of the food they consumed.

Despite their disparate backgrounds, they were all drawn to the river, and when she came with Giovanni, they welcomed her as if she had been part of the family for years. There was a mellow rhythm to their days, interrupted only by the frantic sabotage or the tense searching out of Central European country that was unified in the 19th century and was famously geopolitically aggressive in the 20th century positions, which she adapted to with a kind of family ease she'd never had with her mother. She didn't expect it, but the peace and quiet helped her recover. Their treatment of her was compassionate, even though she had been through so much and

96

showed no desire to be carried. They adored her kid to the point that she was never alone with her. In fact, he'd never held any of his own six children, according to Salvatore, one of the elder guys. Because he didn't want her to see his tears, he would look away from her. His thoughts may have been drawn to his own children. There was plenty of time to ponder these things.

Before the birth of her baby, they would transport her to a little hideaway they had built near the station, which was only a bark cover at the edge of the woodland and completely obscured from view by the tracks. They made it clear to her what she needed to retain. While hiding in the shelter, she would count the number of trains that came and went. She had a mental list of everything they hauled: weaponry, tanks, and troops. Although it appeared like they were shooting for no cause, it still startled her two or three times a day.

She recalled a certain morning vividly in her mind. Her early arrival was due to a lot of activity the night before, which was seen as a forerunner to something significant. The pylons and radio tower above the rails seemed to be moving or melting in the shimmering air. The station's sweeping arches were devoid of glass, and the roof was supported only by spruce tree stumps in a few spots. Nearly every wall was shattered. He could see the platform from where they were standing, but as they drew away she saw something that would stay with her forever: around twenty soldiers, still in uniform, lined up head to toe on stretchers along the platform. They were obviously malnourished, as seen by the thin looks on their faces.

She sang a lullaby to herself to lift her spirits.

This was something she figured out in her first year at the head of the class. When the injured were taken inside the tents at night. Even if 'learnt' was not the correct term, she was aware of this. Putting one's hand on a hot plate was more like this. The drawing away was as compelling as the singeing. Because she wasn't able to look away or divert her gaze away. Once a week, she'd come out of her medical tent in her nurse's outfit and follow the troops as they retreated from an enemy onslaught. Men stabbing one other and killing each other occurred right in front of her eyes. It was the most harrowing experience of my life... Such guys weren't familiar to her. These were guys she'd never seen before.

The breeze from the woods swept over to them in the twilight. The night sky was very chilly. A musician was among those who were hurt. He picked up his violin and began to play. The rest of the group took a seat, leaning on anything they could find for support. With that distant expression violinists often have, he played while sitting in a chair. When he started playing folk songs everyone hummed along, then stopped when he finished. Still, the violin was there. It sounded like it was cold in the night. It'd be better in a room, I'd wager. It broke her heart to hear it walking about on its own out here.

She watched a guy being dragged away, his back ripped open and his lung throbbing. For the first time, she watched guys carry on living without the top of their heads being attached to their bodies. She saw troops continue sprinting after having one or both of their feet blasted away. For a half-mile, one guy crawled on his hands and knees, dragging his legs behind him. With his stomach pouring out of his hands, he made it to a dressing station. She saw troops with their mouths gone, their lower jaws missing, and their cheeks disappearing; she saw a guy who had grasped the major artery in his arm between his teeth, so he didn't bleed to death.

She would sometimes ride along with the paramedics in the ambulance. They'd take a leisurely drive around the deserted battlefield. The sun's rays faded the green of the dead warriors' cut heads. The faces of the deceased had a bright green-yellow color. It looked like a field of potatoes had been ploughed. Birds ripped their eyeballs out, pecked their cheeks, and even their hands. In time, she began to think that when a man dies, he always looks towards the sky.

Some form of disbelief can be seen on his face while lying dead, like the thought, 'How can I be dead?' Is it possible that I've passed away?'

A dead guy weighs more than a live one. Much more weight. She soon picked up on it. As soon as the combat was ended, the allocated troops rushed to bury their comrades. They bury them under a layer of dirt. Dry sand is also an option. The sand seemed to move when she gazed at it for a long time. To tremble, as though in fear. These guys had only just begun to exist. She caught a glimpse of them giggling. With them, she mingled. She was stunned that they had vanished.

One of the nurses was abducted in a hamlet whose name she couldn't recall at the time. Dead horses, motorbikes, and armored vehicles littered the settlement the following day when it was retaken. They discovered the nurse impaled on a stick with her eyes gouged out and her breasts hacked off. It was very cold, and she was as white as a sheet with silver strands in her hair. She had just turned the big 5-0. They discovered messages from her family as well as a green rubber bird in her bag. Toy for children.

She had seen the deaths of numerous nurses throughout her time as a nurse. In sludge; in a puddle. A death like that was not something she wished upon her own death for. Even when she couldn't hide from the shelling, she'd shield herself from it with her hands—not to make herself invisible like a kid, but to protect her face. She was taken aback by how rapidly she transformed. She first feared death. Then astonishment and intrigue seemed to coexist in her. Then they were gone. When she pushed her body to the maximum, she did so for years on end! Finally, and this was the most shocking part, there was only one dread left: the fear of being ugly in the hereafter.

As she sat in the underground shelter, keeping an eye out for trains and contemplating the kid developing within her, she smiled to herself. Her skin had solidified into an armor, and she was no longer vulnerable to the elements. As a result, she had ceased to be a nurse. After all, she was a mum. She had transformed into a railway track partisan. She was now solely interested in killing.

They were duped by someone. It was never made apparent who the perpetrators were. In any case, how could they evaluate the villagers? It was clear to her that the People from the European country that was unified in the 19th century and was famously geopolitically aggressive in the 20th century were not beyond murdering women and children in retaliation and torturing them to get information. The fact that they persisted for so long was quite unexpected. To make things simpler for everyone, they moved camp often. But this time, the People from the European country that was unified in the 19th century and was famously geopolitically aggressive in the 20th century pounced on them with little or no notice. The wetlands were the only thing that could have rescued them.

Their limbs were numb from the cold after standing in muck and water for three hours. Only fifty feet away, the raging river sounded like the wind among the trees. It was impossible to cross. The spot where they were hiding was bordered by dense woodland and trees that had fallen into the water. The muck was foul-smelling, and the water's passage had left no traces. There were a lot of Central European country that was unified in the 19th century and was famously geopolitically aggressive in the 20th century four-legged companion animals all over the place. Four-legged companion animals barking, snapping orders, the crack of undergrowth, and their lathering and snuffling could all be heard in the distance. They were well aware that the end was near.

The baby's stomach growled in protest. Once it was out of its sling and above the water, her arms were sore, and it started to cry every time she gave it off to a man. It had no idea. It was starving. Then then, she was hungry and only had a little amount of milk. In any event, her breasts were submerged under the surface, and she was unable to extract them from the muddy bottom of the water. Thirty of them were standing neck-to-neck, lips locked. Even when she brought the infant to her face and murmured to it, the baby would not stop wailing. She could hear the barking of the four-legged companion animals.

Nobody paid attention to her despite the fact there were thirty of them. You get it, they're not staring at you. She'd known for a long time that this was what she needed to do. The human intellect, on the other hand, is not built to deal with challenges of this magnitude. It was only the new commander who would give her a second glance. He was the weakest, tiniest member of the group. Then then, he was in charge of all of them.

Despite her best efforts, she was unable to identify the baby's father. Despite that, she was still enamored with the object. Her thoughts and feelings were with it. Added to the sense of desperation. It has no way of knowing. She would have murdered them right then and then if they had informed her that should have made it simpler. She was overwhelmed by the weight of her responsibilities. I, too, felt the child's confusion. It's the absence of the incorrect. In spite of the fact that it was still sobbing, thirty guys stood up to their necks next to her and refused to raise their heads. When the baby began to cry, she kept hustling. She could hear the barking of four-legged companion animals and the shouting of men as they stumbled into the forest. They were tense as a result. Because they were running late, they had no time to waste. They were in a rush to get out of there.

She kissed the small creature on the forehead, which was now so wrinkled that it resembled a prune. If it could only keep sucking long enough, the baby's mouth would become a breast out of air, and its milk would flow out of it. It was a terrible experience. She pushed off a mosquito that had coiled up like a small cigar when it was put against her ear. She dipped its little body beneath the water and felt its tiny life thrash against her hands and stomach as if all the unlived life to come gathered in that minute before death and erupted. She continued to stare into its eyes, frantic with desire.

When there was no longer any effort on her part and her body was limp, she knew it was finished.

Indeed, the remembrance of Gina had faded like a faded mural over the years. In the midst of the guy's own country's civil war, Central European country that was unified in the 19th century and was famously geopolitically aggressive in the 20th century negotiated an Armistice with the Allies. To put it simply, the Treaty of Versailles was the last nail in the coffin of an already-suffering nation. Final session of Paris Peace Conference ended with the first General Assembly of the League of Nations. The Reaper's journey around cathedral clocks at noon was a constant reminder of the passage of time. Last remaining white troops in Siberia were crushed by the Bolsheviks in Siberia. Benito Mussolini, the dictator of the Fascist regime in Italy, was named prime minister. Ottoman sultanate was dissolved by the Grand National Assembly of Turkey. Many currencies were decimated by the massive inflation. The Soviet leader was assassinated. The Central European country that was unified in the 19th century and was famously geopolitically aggressive in the 20th century people chose Hindenburg as their new president. This agreement was made between Central European country that was unified in the 19th century and was famously geopolitically aggressive in the 20th century and the Soviet Union and Central European country that was unified in the 19th century and was famously geopolitically aggressive in the 20th century became a full member of the League of Nations. During the reign of Hirohito, Japan's Emperor, so started the conflict that would eventually lead to Chinese unification. After the signing of the Kellogg-Briand Pact in Paris, a ban on offensive combat was put into place worldwide. Invasion of Manchuria by Japanese Russia unveiled the first five-year plan of its planning process Millions of Ukrainians perished of starvation. Central European country that was unified in the 19th century and was famously geopolitically aggressive in the 20th century's new chancellor, The main guy from WW2, was sworn in. The Reichstag was set ablaze. The Gestapo was created, and labor unions were abolished as a result. James Szilard came up with the notion of a chain reaction in a nuclear reactor. Stalin's Great Purge resulted in the deaths of many people. Mother-in-law of the guy of Wales died alone at the holiday residence The Nuremberg Laws were ratified by the Reichstag. Italy occupied Ethiopia. There was a Central European country that was unified in the 19th century and was famously geopolitically aggressive in the 20th century seizure of Rhineland. Spanish Civil War was sparked by the Nationalist coup that failed. Italy withdrew from the League of Nations. Austria was absorbed into the Central European country that was unified in the 19th century and was famously geopolitically aggressive in the 20th century empire. Neither the United States nor Great Britain would admit any more Jewish refugees. Central European country that was unified in the 19th century and was famously geopolitically aggressive in the 20th century annexation of the Czechoslovak Sudetenland was made possible by the Munich Agreement, which was signed by Central European country that was unified in the 19th century and was famously geopolitically aggressive in the 20th century, France, the United Kingdom, and Italy in return for world peace. Numerous Jewish businesses and synagogues were destroyed, plundered, or set ablaze across Central European country that was unified in the 19th century and was famously geopolitically aggressive in the 20th century during the Holocaust. atomic fusion at Columbia University resulted in the first ever atom splitting of uranium. Molotov and Ribbentrop signed the pact. Central European country that was unified in the 19th century and was famously geopolitically aggressive in the 20th century seized control of Poland and occupied it. Sowing and harvesting were the primary activities of farmers. There were mills that grind, butchers butchered and factories that smoked, doctors who treated and buried, and miners that dug for ore. Time passed as it usually does, slowly in the present yet quickly in the past, and it seemed as if the guy had been left behind on an island where time had slowed down.

But the two letters from Paris – the sound of her voice in the words – had been like a restoration and she had returned to him as vividly as that morning almost thirty years earlier when he realized she had gone.

Then there was also his daughter. He'd neglected his own well-being for so long that he'd forgotten what it was like to be concerned. Have a cause for being. Again, there was a sense of majesty. And there's also dread. A sea of People from the European country that was unified in the 19th century and was famously geopolitically aggressive in the 20th century whirled across the countryside, nervous as a pack of wolves. However, it was as if his daughter had never been. There wasn't any evidence that she enlisted; he assumed a wounded soldier he talked to at the field hospital in Salerno recalled her. It was as if she'd vanished into thin air the instant she'd left her mother's side. Finally, he returned to The Italian canal city after two months of unsuccessful seeking. He was unable to get out of bed for days at a time.

The idea for the letters occurred to him strangely, like an act of grace, given the weight of his depression. All of the things he had previously held to be true and immutable vanished in a flash. Only this time, he believed he could have gone in a different direction had he viewed the world in a different manner earlier. He felt that if he had seen the world in this way, he would have taken a different route. To put it another way, it's unavoidable. He had the power to bring his daughter back to life and give her to her mother because of his ultimate act of devotion for her. Gina's yearning would take care of the rest if he only signed the letters with her name.

'Dear Mother,

'I know you'll be surprised to hear this, but I'm still grieving the end of your singing career. In an instant, you flung it away. It's such a shame. I know, even if you won't admit it, that it was all my fault. The sacrifices you made as a child were something I didn't fully comprehend until I was an adult. Forgiveness, even if it delivers nothing back, is all I can ask for from you.

'First and foremost, allow me to assuage your concerns; my health and safety are not in jeopardy. I can't tell you anything about my personal situation or how I came to discover you and send this letter, but I'm doing something that I think you'd consider significant.

'You're going to have a tough time in this battle. However, the tide has changed, and we will soon be victorious. However, I cannot risk attracting the evil eye. A lot of work has to be done.

Every bullet, it is said, comes from the future. Even if there is no one named after me, who am I to judge?

I'm still baffled as to why you withheld information regarding my father from me. It's a puzzle that, I think, I'll never be able to solve. The conflict, on the other hand, has changed my perspective. Alternatively, maybe I've simply matured. Whatsoever the situation may be, I now see that the harm I inflicted on you much surpasses the harm you inflicted on me. In my opinion, you didn't deserve the way you were treated by me. I couldn't bear the sorrow you must have felt. I hope you can take this as a sign of the selfishness of youth, which you may have already known. Fighting with people we care about is a waste of time.

'Even if I don't understand your decision, I

want you to know that I respect it. To expect people to act in the same manner as they were born is a violation of human nature. I've had to learn this on my own.

'I'm sorry, Mama, but I don't know how you can respond. However, it is the only way for me to hear your voice and know that you are safe. My heart aches for you, my dear, and I wish I could tell you how much you mean to me. My apologies for the way things have played out so far. The guys here can't believe I'm your daughter, so know that my thoughts are always with you. The Lord willing, I'll be back with you sooner than we think.

Her mother's heartfelt daughter

Dualipa'

It had been a long day for The Guy, and his pen had finally run out of ink. No, it wasn't quite right. Her personality? Her perspective? What gave him the right to make such a judgement? He'd conjured her from thin air. Using such poor language bothered him; it came out as cruel. The man must have been crazy if he thought Gina would fall for it. It was a complete waste of time. She could relate to her daughter. I'd been following her development for a long time. She had a complete picture of her childhood, as her daughter had come to know and love her before she passed away. He had nothing compared to her. A year ago, he didn't even know she existed. She was a fabrication of his imagination. But in composing this letter, he made her alive to him, and he felt like he knew her better than anybody he had ever known. And the thrill he felt as a result was unlike anything he had experienced since he first met her mother.

To view it through Gina's eyes, he read the letter again. Do you think that was his intention? Something human, definitely, that expressed his love clearly yet ethereally; everything he was experiencing right then and there. He was certain of its lunacy. He couldn't help but see his daughter's face wherever he turned. Whenever he sat quiet, the air seemed as though it were warmed by her almost-real form.

It was then that he started writing letters every day, lengthy ones that might cover up to twenty pages of the handmade paper that he purchased from a tiny store on the Rialto in The Italian canal city. He had found that it was possible to quietly send letters to Paris if you were willing to pay for it, but it was hard to tell whether Gina was still living at the same place. A reply was not anything that bothered him. Only a mental picture of her reading the words was required. To picture the way her fingers may flutter over the table in the quiet after reading, and the strands of wetness on her neck.

After a while, the intrigue began to diminish, inexplicably. It was like the dawning of a new day. He was exhausted. He had no idea that the letter he sat down to write on that last November morning would be his last. It was as if his daughter had vanished into thin air, like a board thrown over a gaping hole. Despite this, he still loved her and everything about her, but his affection was tinged with the sad sweetness of an unattainable love that could never be realized. When Gina entered the chamber at the Girlboss Juggalo, he couldn't recall anything about the guy he had been before her arrival. Only Gina could be seen reading the last paragraphs of his letter.

> 'Dear Mother,
>
> 'After a little snowfall this morning in Naples, the snow melted quickly before it had a chance to reach the sidewalks and monuments. Sadly, I've yet to see Naples covered with snow. I'm not a city explorer. There is nothing to see here after three weeks. When I'm not at work, I spend my days cooped up in this little room. This is the room I'm assigned to train a student from Genoa who arrived a week ago. Bread, milk, veggies, and a cup of black coffee are the staples of our two daily meals.
>
> Your life in Paris has been difficult since you were forced to evacuate. You never mentioned loneliness to me, but everything you said reeked of it. As far as I can remember, you were always a woman apart; whether you were stitching or spending time alone in your room daydreaming. Over the years, I've tried to get you to open up about yourself, but you've always shifted the conversation to something else, like Tosca, Carmen, or the process of dying silk. I guess my aim was that I might get you to open up a little more. However, the shell is an integral aspect of your identity.
>
> 'Your Frenchman or Central European country is probably a sickly, capricious fusspot, a Rumpelstiltskin or a Bluebeard who keeps you locked up all day and

wants you to dote on him in the evening because he's been gracious enough to let you reside in his home. This is how I see your existence; in a gloomy, decaying basement. As far as I know, the fall in Paris may be pretty chilly, so I hope you have adequate clothing.

'For a while there, I had hoped that you might marry someone else, someone you could love and be loved by. When I was eleven or twelve years old in The city founded by those wolf babies, I recall a guy paying a surprise visit to you. He struck me as the most polar opposite of anybody I've ever met. This isn't always a negative thing. There is nothing wrong with being who you are, and he was obnoxious and nasty. You'd be stitching away, and he'd be chatting nonstop across from you, as if he didn't need to take a breath. Once again, by nine o'clock in the evening, you were drowsy and ready to go to your room, but he insisted on dragging you out into town to visit the movies, coffee shops, and the river to have a stroll. I figured over time he'd elicit the emergence of yet another Mama from inside you, one who was less reclusive and more animated. Perhaps.

'What's going on? Did you get into a fight? Did he insist on living together, and you refused? Was he interested in you as a wife? Alternatively, maybe you wanted to end things and return to your lonesome solitude? At this point, it doesn't matter to me. Memory is a squandered resource. You are who you are, and that's all that matters. Nonetheless, if this were to happen today, I'd be happy to support you. My father has lost all meaning to me. Because of that, I've seen too many dads die in front of my eyes.

'When I was around eleven or twelve, you and I boarded a train to The Italian canal city and spent the weekend there. While I was wearing the hat you had me wear due to the heat, I saw the swarm of blackbirds you described as looking like an opening in the sky. Because you moved so close to the wall, I saw your lengthy shadow on the walls. Such a dreary, quiet, aloof mother. Your response when I inquired about whether or not you liked to have a window seat on the train was, "What difference does it make?" Your ideas were so private that you didn't want to tell me about them. You didn't want anybody else to know about them.

'As we sat on the train, I told you that you should be a lot more thrilled about this weekend in The Italian canal city: it's your first time there! There were several options open to us. What was your favorite? Is it the long boat propelled and steered by a standing man in a striped shirt trip something you'd want to do? Visiting Murano to see the glassblowing process? What about a vacation to the Lido? Going up St. Mark's tower? When I offered a proposal, you always said "Yes, wonderful." As soon as I asked you to make a decision, you said, "It doesn't really matter."

'That ache in your heart. In spite of the fact that at times you may speak for hours, endlessly, sing with a type of intense delight, but only in one direction, and never as part of a dialogue.

'Unlike you, I'm not the same. I've always had at least two or three female companions. I had a boyfriend in The city founded by those wolf babies. And then there was Ricardo, who was my third. Do you remember who he was? Youth pastor? Here in Naples, I've got someone who I met in the mountains; we've been dating for a while now. Giovanni is a literary translator who was born and reared in Milan. He's not a youngster at all; he's a thirty-four-year-old divorced guy, making him six years my senior. Elena, his eight-year-old daughter, is now more in touch with me than her own mother is with her. Her mother, who lives in Bologna, is distant from her. Mama is the only name Lena will call me. My face is rubbed with one hand, while her father's is rubbed with the other.

'We can only meet on weekends since Giovanni is busy during the day, and as I've already said, I must work evenings and it would be unsafe for us to be seen together in any situation.

He resides in the city's northernmost reaches. Saturday night is the only time I go to his house, and I spend the rest of the weekend there. Cooking for the two of them for the whole week begins at four a.m. on Sundays. You'd never have guessed it, would you? If it is a nice day, we ride our bikes out of town and have a picnic in a pine forest, under the shadow of an old ruin, with his family.

'Giovanni is aware of the fact that I must rely only on my income. His translation doesn't pay him much, but it doesn't stop him from offering to assist me financially. I flat-out declined each and every time, and I was becoming irritated with him by the end of it. I'm not sure why I said no. Even now, I'm not sure why I was so irritated. He was hurt by my refusal, but he didn't say anything about it. Exactly like you. His benevolence is something I admire. Generosity, in my opinion, is the most appealing attribute in a guy and the most macho one.

'Couldn't you, Mama, get a job as a singer or teach privately? Why did you give up everything? Who or what prompted you to abruptly turn your back on it? What if it wasn't entirely my fault?

'Were it not for this war and my lack of funds, I would leave Naples right now and go to Paris to rouse you from the tomb you have dug for yourself, shake you mercilessly, and compel you to live again. It's not too late. It's easy for me to recall the day we spent wandering the streets of The Italian canal city as a group of eleven or twelve-year-olds. We passed shop windows with barely a glance and were soon dripping wet from the heat. We consumed soda twice and ice cream once, and we watched a silent film in the middle of the movie theatre, content to be lost because we couldn't find anything specific. Mama, maybe it's time to quit searching for things that don't exist and begin enjoying your own life.

'It's possible that there is something in you that craves a sense of punishment. However, why are you doing this to yourself?

'I'd love to hear about your daily activities in Paris and how you're feeling in a letter. It's a lengthy one. There is just too much at stake for us to jeopardies now. Keep in mind how much I care about you and how much I want to reunite with you after the conflict is over. The two of us have a unique perspective. We could sail to Australia, which is as far away from Europe as you can go and start over there. If I've learned anything, it's that you can start again, just as trees do every spring when new leaves and blossoms appear.

'You once begged for forgiveness from me, but I refused. I'd give it to you right now if I could, but I don't want to forgive you; I want to be forgiven. It has always been like this. Mama, can you find the strength to forgive your one and only daughter? She's loved you more than you could ever imagine.'

True enough. He did, in fact, accept her forgiveness. He didn't do it with his mind; he did it with all of his heart. Gina might turn those little brown daubs into horses in all of his previous messages, he had maintained the details as impressionist as a Degas racecourse. This final letter, on the other hand, included recollections that were so exact that only by some miracle did they match the reality. He didn't know why he had decided to write this way, but he knew it was critical for Gina to recognize the lie and yet be tricked at the same time. To me, it was the determining factor. Despite the fact that he had no idea what she had gone through with her daughter, he was certain that she would accept the letter as the truth, since it wasn't in men or women to see just what was the bare truth.

The guy was up and dressed in a matter of minutes. A tiny leather bag was waiting for him on his desk when he emerged from his bedroom. Before he went to sleep the night before, he'd stuffed the sandalwood box with the letters he'd received from his father. That courier, who had previously picked it up from the hotel, had been sent once again. He was costly, but trustworthy and discreet. Every time The Guy needed him, he would call the bar and leave a message for him since he didn't recognize him. That was OK with him. He was the only one who could get the letters to Gina.

The door was locked and he departed the property. He was taking his time as he made his way through the labyrinth of lanes that led to some other street. It's possible the trail he took was one he'd carved into the rock himself. Pigeons were pecking at the droplets that trickled from the bronze tap of a well in the square. 'What if,' as he pondered, 'existence was nothing more than the faint buzz of death's looming presence?'

A huge window provided a view of the opera house, so he settled into his normal spot by the window, where he ordered his usual pastry and pot of tea. What's the purpose of doing that right now? When he grabbed a newspaper, he didn't bother to look at it; even if it was brighter than the light outside, it was still dull. For a brief while, he had the unsettling feeling that this was the final time he would see her. Despite this, the world would continue to function normally. Regardless of whether or not the war was over, it was not the end of warfare. The heart was little more than a blood-filled organ.

He hadn't seen the server set the tea and a pastry in the form of a pig's ear on the table. As he filled the cup, the steam coming from the little blue flowers painted around it smelled like a perfume. Scooping out a tiny bit of apricot jam from the white dish adjacent to the pot on the black lacquered tray, he elevated the teaspoon. As soon as he licked the jam off the spoon, he lifted up the cup and sipped the hot beverage from it. Eventually, he slid his eyes shut. It seemed to him that there were things he couldn't alter. The fact that he had spent the most of his life in Italy did not make him Italian. His routine continued as he snatched another lozenge of jam from his knapsack. He closed his eyes once again and succumbed to a blush that was more than physical, allowing himself to be overcome by the sensation. It wasn't until he opened his eyes again that he saw his reflection in the glass, sitting at a table much like this one, looking out into the square, with a look of despair on its face that he couldn't explain; sixty-two years old.

He recalled how Gina had been charmed by the way he sipped his tea when he initially arrived with her. That's exactly how she attempted to drink it too, but she coughed and sputtered and fell to laughing in wonderful operatic manner that made even the simplest motion appear spectacular and packed with life. He'd been madly in love with her back then, and he believed she felt the same way. The fact that she was leaving him made him realize that, at least in this one way, her predicament was similar to his own, his own mind had continued to gnaw on like a piece of meat it couldn't swallow since she had returned.

Only by escaping reality did he find fulfilment. As long as he lives, he can imagine that one night at dusk she'll walk through the door with a smile on her face, older than he remembers, with softer skin around the middle and more wrinkles, but she'll be all together as she was those first nights here in the bar with the triumph of her performance, having just woken up and immediately begun the journey back to where she'd gone off on that long trip. As they sit in the candlelight darkness of the hotel bar, they contemplate a stroll up the stairs to his bedroom, which they imagine would be a bizarre thrill as they contemplate it. They hug and weep as they eat dinner together. They suddenly burst out of it — even in a dream, he can't get beyond this moment. They laugh a bit but grow separated and impatient as they realize there isn't enough language to cover the void of years, so at a little after midnight, she passes through the door to oblivion with the other not-quite-dead. They're both humiliated.

As soon as he wakes up and gets out of the dream, the realization sinks in that even though he hasn't stopped loving her (and still does, even as he is pondering this concept), he has never forgiven her and never will. He can't accomplish it since he lacks the stamina. If not the ability to not be bound by the past (which is distinct from forgetting it), then what is forgiveness? All along, we've known the answer was simple. His solitude in The Italian canal city has made him acutely aware of this fact. The fact remains, however, that something has always existed. His eyes had always been able to see things that weren't there. That, though, was not noteworthy. It was now clear to him that he was no different from the rest of those people who were looking for a better life, but he realized that he had already given up on it.

His attention was diverted from the task at hand by a nibble of the pastry. He left the tea in the cup since he didn't want to reheat it. It was customary for him to leave the bar without saying a word after he had pulled some bank notes from his wallet and placed them on the tray. The concierge at the lobby received the bag from him. His eyes gradually adjusted to the tenebrous light as if he were a hypogeal creature, or more likely, a submarine, considering the position. He returned to the dreary late-spring morning.

He had so much to say, but no one was there to hear him, not even an apology.

***

After the discovery of the previous morning, I was unable to think about anything else for more than a day. There was nothing more to say to my mother regarding the events that took place in the swamp and thereafter, even though I pressured her fiercely. Asked why she had never informed me, she simply said, 'What difference would it have made?'

And it's possible that she was correct. What happened? At the very least, didn't I have the right to make a choice? What do you want to know? Why? Because I had no idea. That was just not possible for me. Her anguish was palpable. I believed it was me at first, but it wasn't. That I had somehow disappointed her. However, she'd never reveal what it was. It was somber and chilling at the same time. She responded, 'You think that knowledge would erase it?' It seemed as though she would purposefully misinterpret what I was attempting to express at any costs, because she was well aware that I knew for a fact that you cannot just erase the past. Couldn't she meet me halfway once in a while? All I truly wanted to know was why she did what she did. Her inability to comprehend what it was like for me was baffling to me; not showing up at all, her being the way she was and to think I was the one doing all the work. She was correct, I had no clue what she was talking about. How could I, when she hadn't spoken to me for the better part of my life? Concerning my sister. My thoughts about my dad. Her affliction. That was the gist. In my heart, I felt remorseful for what I had done because I'd mistakenly assumed she was the one; her, that she was the monster. Everything she'd been and nothing she'd ever be, all at the same time. In the course of whatever she had or hadn't said Initially, I believed it may have been her. But it wasn't the case at all. That much was clear to me at this point. It all made sense now. After what she'd done, how does one go on with one's life?

It wasn't too late for me to tell her that I got it, and that I was there for her. Even though I spoke her language, it was as if she hadn't heard me before. None of it sat well with her. None of it, if that is what it was. She was disgusted by my sympathy, to say the least. Then she snarled, 'It was you. It's just the two of us. She was not your sister at all. She had nothing to do with your situation at all.'

It was clear to me that she was joking. James, Anne, her and I might have had such different outcomes if she had informed me otherwise. I had the opportunity to assist her. 'What's the big deal?' Yesterday's recording had her final words archived.

'That was your doing. There are so many unanswered questions. It makes no difference. John, I did what I had to do. Do you think I'd be happy with another child? Sorry again.

You'll learn more than you ever thought possible. Nullification. Keep your mouth shut. Now go out of here, I'm exhausted. Please don't bother me. What more would you want to know from me? You know everything I've said.'

That's not entirely true. In the last few days, she had an amazing ability to remember. Who knows how much that will cost? It was only then that she warned me that if I even mentioned my sister, she would never speak to me again. There was no way I could have doubted it. She felt drained and agitated, and she needed to rest. I should have just let it go. However, there was so much more to learn.

***

'Where did you receive the letters from?'

'In The city founded by those wolf babies.'

I reconnected with Mama. When I walked through the door, there she was, seated at the dining room table. It seemed as though she didn't recognize me. Sobbing so hard, we were unable to talk for a long time. I haven't shed a tear since. It was not after your father died that you had to deal with this. Misha, you weren't even born at the time of your birth. Sorry again. She begged for my forgiveness, and I obliged. The problem was, I'd already done it. Other than that, what else were they? To my surprise, she agreed. However, it was too late at this point. Of course, we knew. Life had come to an end. I was a twenty-nine-year-old woman at the time.

Who wrote those?

***

Her mother had lately returned from Paris, where she had spent the latter years of the big war of the 1930s and 1940s, to the spacious apartment in The city founded by those wolf babies where she had grown up. However, neither of them was in the mood for a celebration at this homecoming event. The nostalgia that Dualipa felt was more like a non-feeling. There was an end to the conflict. However, they were only words. A faucet-like control would not work with such devices. This remained a point of contention between them. Invisible yet as real as the apricot jam in the teapot, the white linen on the table, and the cups of tea. Both of them yearned for the story to come to a conclusion.

An epilogue or coda seemed to be in the air. All of this was revealed to her by her mother, of course. It was as if she had never concealed anything from her daughter, and thus there was no regret or sorrow in the conversation, but rather, as if they were two women awaiting execution, as though, if there was ever a tomorrow, it was no business of theirs to discuss. Nothing was uttered; it was all sensed. She held her mother's hands and stroked the hair off the girl's forehead, kissing her there so delicately that it amounted to little more than a puff of air. They sat with their knees touching. And they sobbed for hours; you wouldn't expect such long tears of silent wailing to allow for words to be salted into the otherwise simple and unadorned language. But these were tears of silence. Nothing else mattered to her. She didn't want any unnecessary fuss, she was devoid of feeling or drama. They'd ended up here, at this point, because of their feelings. The mother and daughter are shown here; this conflict has lasted much too long. She admired her mother's beauty in the early morning rays, and she smiled. She was going to invite her to sing later on. One track. Having that would suffice. But only if she chose to do so.

In her life, she had never consumed so much tea. Mother stated her father had instilled the habit in her by placing a jam-covered lozenge on her tongue as she drank it. It was as if a bird that had been extinct for a long time had suddenly reappeared in the midst of the bustling streets. There will be no more fighting.

When her mother returned to the room, she had a bag full of letters. When she flipped the bag over, the letters tumbled out onto the table. The night before she left Paris, a guy delivered them to her, she said. She'd read them all night, on the train, and every day since she got back to her apartment in The city founded by those wolf babies, she claimed to have read them all. Repeatedly. She made a similar gesture to her daughter. Then, Dualipa screamed in terror as she watched, because they had to do with her father. She was engrossed in a book about her father. Mother-daughter letters that were sent from her to her father (and his father). The writing was really terrible. She went through each and every one of them. That was followed by another round of reading. She was horrified by what she saw. She couldn't help but look at it. Is it possible for her mother to have behaved in this way towards her father? However, there was a preamble to that enquiry; who was she to say what was right or wrong in her own eyes? Isn't it right that her mother was made aware of what she'd been up to?

As soon as she observed her daughter's silence, her mother told her, 'She acted poorly.' However, she hadn't really grasped what it must have been like for him until she saw the things she had written. The quality of this paper is superb. I really like the simplicity of these monogramed sheets. Her mother told her that she may relate the story as she wanted to. That's something I shouldn't have done, but I ended up doing it anyhow. And a little part of me has never ceased wanting I could go back in time to that time. I, on the other hand, am unable to. There's no going back. There is no such thing as a single step on the journey of a lifetime.

Because there could be nothing left unsaid, she told her daughter then that she didn't love the guy or that she didn't love him enough and that she was pregnant and her career was in jeopardy because she had told her daughter then that she didn't love the guy or that she didn't love him enough and that they had fallen in love in St. Big city and had spent years travelling around Europe and staying in grand hotels and opera houses. You should put yourself in my position because she realized what it must sound like and she had no explanation for why she had left him in that way, without saying a word, on that frigid Big city morning and would never see him again. Even if none of it was written down, it was still there. Who else could have sent them to her? There was no message or even a postmark on the package.

Her daughter inquired, 'Why would he do this?' What's the point of asking this question right now?

She stayed mute, despite the fact that there was only one possible explanation. Despite the fact that the tea cups on the table were still full and cold, she got up and brewed more. There was no way she could be doing nothing. The expression in her daughter's eyes broke her heart. It was never going to happen now that they were finally together and there was reality in the air. Truth or a near approximation to it. When the battle and all it had cost them ended, they could finally have each other and create what shouldn't have needed to be created in the first place. History, on the other hand, had been formed and could not be reversed. She wasn't only an enemy to her kid; she was an adversary to everyone she came into contact with. The guy and his father had nothing to do with it. A loveless life is like a life free of strife or fight or blood; there is no fire and, thus, there can be no love. But how can you tell your daughter this, Mom? It's too early for guns, so no. Despite the fact that what hurt was usually good in her or blood, her daughter drove her crazy as a youngster. Even though her daughter had suffered, she could see it, since she had grown up into a lady and they would now communicate as women, Dualipa would read her letters and she would know. After a moment's reflection, she realized that they were a gift, even if she was aware that such a gift was also a curse because she had felt her young self again in the cruel letters, frigid phrases, and she knew that her daughter must have felt the same.

Then there was the issue of who had sent them. And the devastation that comes with it because he had come to life in a way he had never come to life before in her daughter. She had just given her daughter a father when she had to take him away from her. The only possible explanation is if they were sent by someone who had passed away and whose mind was now on the other side of the grave. She paid great attention to her daughter, who was still absorbed in her book. The striking likeness between the two of them. It was her father, of course. Bafflement's sweetness, so near to anguish. What a wonder it is. Those restless illusions in a picture book she had once seen, duck or rabbit depending on how you looked, but never both at once, were like the lines on his face that might be masculine and feminine at the same time.

Dualipa realized her mother had left the room after a few seconds. This time, she saw that she was sobbing when she returned, clutching a hefty letter. She retrieved the sheets from the envelope while remaining silent (her mother had said nothing when she gave it to her). In a hand she'd never seen before, and surely not her mother's, she received letters once again from her mother. She heard her mother remark, 'They were the only things that kept me alive.' When she flipped the first letter over, she was shocked to see her own name at the end. It seemed as though she was breaking apart within. As she sped through each chapter, she acted the same way on each page. It's hard to imagine who might have done this. It was illogical. No, they didn't believe her. Dualipa, however, could tell that she had, as she hovered over her mother as she read, tears flowing down her cheeks. Her mother's reaction to her daughter's skepticism was to see it as the fulfilment of a prayer, and she realized that it wasn't that outlandish after all. Belief would always win out over facts in the end. That a mother who had assumed her kid was dead would only notice that she was no longer four years old when she was two and a half.

Dualipa was at a loss for words. She was aware that she had the ability to fabricate stories. Make it clear to her mother that the letters belong to her. Even if she couldn't physically see her mother in Paris, she could at least do something better than nothing by writing a letter to let her know she was still alive, loved, and missed, and that she longed to be with her once again. She could have told her this. She would not have to pay for it. However, she had run out of place in her heart for such sentiments any longer, not after reading the letters her mother had written to her father and his father's father only minutes before, she didn't think so. And not after everything she had endured and accomplished. As a result, she informed her mother that, despite the fact that the documents were signed with her name, they were not authored by her.

'How could I?' she said. 'You must have known that, didn't you?

It occurred to her at that point as to who had written them and for what purpose. She also knew that if her mother hadn't been such a sentimentalist, it would have happened to her as well. That's what she said; 'He must have been responsible,' she murmured, pointing to the man she thought was her father. So, this was his response to the letters that sat on the table in front of them like the intestines of some unlucky beast. As a response to adversity, love.

He left her and her husband because he was afraid of having children, she claimed. 'However, he never knew.'

'You didn't tell him.' That's what she was about to say, but she held her tongue and was forever grateful to whoever her guardian angel was that day, because not saying something is different from telling a lie, and the truth as she knew it then and did not say was that she hated her mother more than she had ever hated anyone else. Not because of what her mother had done to keep him hidden from her, but because she had betrayed her father by keeping her existence hidden from him and making her think it was her father who had betrayed her.

As her fingers became claws, she wanted nothing more than to stab and strike out. Only the desire to cause pain was expressed. She was filled with malice by the hateful comments that were being hurled at her. However, when she glanced at her mother and saw the realization that the guy had written these letters signed with his daughter's name (such lovely letters), even though Dualipa hated her then as she had never hated her in all the years they had lived in quiet hatred, she was defused. A light went on within her, like if she had a bigger heart than the one she was familiar with. Her mother, whose face was etched with anguish, was mourning herself because he had loved her and she had not rescued him, despite everything she had done. Seeing her mother's face confirmed that she had known all along what the satchel signified, but it was only until she glanced up and saw her mother's face that she was able to truly comprehend what it meant.

Even if there were words to say, there was no need for them. The two of them went to their separate rooms, like they had done so many times after previous conflicts, and only emerged when they were quite confident the other wouldn't see them. Neither of them was able to get any rest. The night wore on, and each sat alone in her thoughts. In another galaxy, the noises of celebration could be heard from the street.

The following morning, they set out for The Italian canal city. It was common for the trains to halt often and seemingly for no cause, allowing the demobilized troops on board to step down onto the tracks where they could stand and smoke. Sometimes there would be little brawls. They'd also sometimes burst into song without warning. What a wonderful feeling. It's unbearable. There's a lot of numbness going on. There are a lot of ghosts.

To get there, we had to drive two days. She recognized the home as soon as they arrived. Her mother had taken her there many times when she was a child. They'd walk by it and admire it, but her mother would only tell her the palace's name when they did. It's hard to imagine a better moniker. It was her mother's key. Despite this, Dualipa resisted entering. The clock was ticking. Eventually it was too late. They were turned away by the cops. They couldn't find anything that tied them to him. After discovering that her mother was a famous opera singer, they confessed to her that he had opened his wrists while taking a bath. Her mother compared her to Seneca. And that's all.

'It's not clear what happened to the home. Phew! I didn't exist in the eyes of the law, so to speak. Mama's identity was unknown to everyone. It was taken care of by his father. It's possible, if he was certain I was still alive. I'm at a loss for words in this regard. That's when she sent him a letter informing him of my existence. In the midst of the conflict, I learned that she had finally completed the task. It didn't matter how hard she tried; she was never the same. She held a grudge because she was unhappy with herself. She was, in fact, accurate.

'A month after we arrived back in The city founded by those wolf babies, my mother succumbed to her illness. All the while, I was right there at her side. Seeing that brought tears to my eyes. Even though she was older at the time, she wasn't quite old enough to be considered frail. A spectacular welcome awaited her when she arrived in The city founded by those wolf babies. Maybe something like that. People were stranded on the street as a result. It was covered in every newspaper. For a while, it provided a break from the violence. I couldn't make it. No, that's incorrect, too. I wasn't sincere in any way. She had no money at the time. That's exactly what I was thinking. To be honest, I had no interest in anything at all. You're wasting your time if you're trying to reclaim what you've lost. To put it simply, all I wanted to do was end it, all I wanted was for it to be over with. I wish I had died sooner rather than later, what a waste of time. In what capacity, if any, did you first meet your father? I'm not interested in talking about it. That dude was fantastic.

'Like my father, I am a native Russian speaker. He was the one who woke me up because he would have returned on his own. He knew who I was. I'm unable to do anything, I'm sorry. I don't want to be reminded of it. I made it through... Quiet! Don't spill the beans. Yes, I was there. You're still too young for this. I was twenty-nine years old when the war ended. Of course, getting married was the farthest thing from my mind. I was exhausted and much older than the other gals who remained. Fun was had at the dances they attended. I could not. I stared at them as if I had seen them before from another galaxy. It's an elderly lady!

'I was being pursued by a number of young males. In reality, they couldn't see what was in me. When you're in battle, your spirit aged. Do you know what we were thinking about when we were fighting? We daydreamed: If only we could make it... People are going to be overjoyed! It's going to be a wonderful, wonderful life. People who have gone through a lot will sympathies with each other; they'll be madly in love. Afterwards, they'll be completely different individuals. There was never any question in our minds, not at all. They yearned for and feared returning to their homes. They had no idea what to expect when they arrived.

'What about your father?'

'Everything was taken from me. I was a guy for two years. My body had stopped breathing. It's difficult to re-learn how to love after having learned to hate. To bring back memories of the past. Unremembered words in order to be molded by anything other than conflict, one must be exposed to it.

'"The war is finished," your father remarked when he proposed to me in Naples. "We're still here, thanks be to God. The time has come for us to tie the knot." I was itching to smack him. What does 'married' mean to you? Now? What's the point now?

'"Look at me," I commanded. I could tell he'd witnessed something horrific since one half of his face was a deep shade of purple. I can't believe I'm telling him, "Yes, I'll marry you," as he's weeping. What makes Australia so special? Take a look at the location on the map. Why is he so pleased? I didn't want to have children, as a result of... yes, she. Keeping it from you was a mistake. I should have kept my mouth shut. Is he aware of this? Everything was on the table for him. Who am I now? Is this a blunder? Every time he glanced at me he saw it. he was just too excellent. Instead of taking responsibility for his actions, he laid the burden squarely on his own shoulders. You're aware of what transpired.'

'If you imply that he committed suicide, I am aware of it, but there's nothing you've ever told me. When I was a kid, dad suddenly vanished. Even after I should have figured it out, I still didn't know.'

'After the events of your father's death. I'm sure you can imagine what I went through.'

***

'Why?'

'John, for the love of God, stop acting like a child. Suppose your poor luck is there to save you from something worse. That's all there is to it. I think it would be better if we were each given just one word at birth, and we had to use it whenever we spoke it. The curse of language... Every time I recall the conversation, it brings up a strange and unsettling memory.'

For some reason, she seemed to be completely isolated from everyone else in the world. Even while it seems as though the responses are still there in the words like fading features in an old image, all I have left of that discussion is my own voice. Like one does with the dead (although she was still very much alive), I felt like I'd left something undone, and I was continuing on that dialogue, addressing myself to her. For as long as I'm moving my lips, I know that the dead are listening (or not listening, just as when they were living).

'Why are you in this place?' I put it to her. 'In Nelson Bay, to be precise.'

We were on our way to Fingal Bay at that time. In the morning, the sky was clear, and the sun was warming the automobile as though from afar. After two days, I was still attempting to make up for her revelation. On the phone, she had been very kind when I phoned to apologize.

'For a vacation while my mother was still living, a train and a bus took me to Wollongong. In Soldiers Point, I found a room in a boarding house, there were no inquiries. Remember when I had money? I did not re-enter education. What made me think that? A professor at Wollongong University was one of the persons I cleaned for. She was kind and helpful when I spoke with her. There were bridging courses, she informed me. That I would be able to get into college this way. So I completed a nursing degree. She suggested it to me, but I decided to specialize on geriatric care because I felt it to be a good fit for me.'

She sounded as if she was waiting for it to reassemble, as if it had vanished when she turned around. Memory is like the crumbs Hansel and Gretel leave behind in the woods.

'The fact that you made it through the night on your own is incredible to me. You were only a young woman.'

'Your father could be out of town. In order to avoid more discussion, I have decided not to discuss it. I should have kept my mouth shut. It's over. It's time to move on. If you don't pledge to keep quiet about it, I'll have to take legal action against you.'

Yesterday when I was with my mother and before that, what had she been up to before I went for the day alone in that mansion? She informed me that I was the first person she'd told. As if it wasn't bad enough, I had to leave her behind. She seemed to be very powerful, competent, and whole, but I saw now that her fullness was more like the way a snail is finished by the hole in its shell.

When I wanted a break from my mother, I'd go to Fingal Bay. Before going out for a drink, take a stroll down the beach to catch some waves. It was tucked away in the woods, far enough from town to seem like a secret.

At the end of the drive, we were assaulted by a sea wind as we emerged from the vehicle. This stretch of sand was deserted. It was Cassandra's turn to wrap her neck in the scarf she'd just wrapped around her shawl. In keeping with her usual style, she arrived so well-prepared. As for me, I had pants and a T-shirt on. It did help to cleanse my mind. We removed our shoes and socks and went down the grassy hill without them. Cassandra showed me how to avoid sinking on the soft sand. It brought up memories of my mother telling me about guys she had seen in The Italian canal city walking on water. She quickly backed away from me, practically sprinting, before turning around and beaming with delight. However, I'm a sinker at heart, so I made a beeline for the firm sand right immediately, putting up with her amusing jabs the whole while. It was difficult to connect her with the lady I'd left shackled to her chair two days before since she seemed to be so light and happy. At one point, she nearly danced around me as I trudged down the lengthy path to the river. As painful as it was to contemplate the last time she did anything similar, I couldn't help but smile. I hadn't even gotten it halfway down the beach when she lifted her skirt up to just above her knees and was already at the tideline. All that naked leg was quite a sight, and it made me dizzy as well, taking my focus away from the breathtaking surroundings. When I raised my head, it seemed as if someone had raised the ceiling, so far in the sky.

Winds of rage dissipated as we proceeded. It was a joy to be able to spend time outdoors. No matter how hard I tried, I couldn't think of a way to start the discussion without ruining it or seeming to bite the hand that fed me. Cassandra drew me closer to her by tying her arm around mine, her body radiates warmth like a sun that's only a few feet away.

She said, 'Are you having a nice time?' Even though she leant her head on my arm, she was able to keep pace with my feet. It was supposed to be uncomfortable, but it wasn't at all.

As I kiss her head, I add, 'It couldn't be better.'

It's a look I've never seen from her before, and I can only describe it as mischief. She kisses me passionately on the lips as she pulls my chin into hers.

Inquiringly, I ask, 'What was that?' With my mind racing and a racing heart that feels like I've just raced the length of the beach. We hadn't even reached the midway point.

'For me, it's a way of treating the guys I like.'

The question was posed, 'And how many of them were there?'

Her response is, 'I'm not a counter, but I'd say that you are the only one.'

Once again, it tore at me, as if human affairs were subject to tempests that may last for all time. Seeing her uncle through the keyhole, her father was skeptical. Between them and me, there's nothing but void. Me? It was too good to be true. Sighing, I uttered the inarticulate scream we frequently make when we become conscious of the heat and weight of the boiling lava within us, which is a vapor release. She was grinning again. But how could I ever tell her what was going through my head? They couldn't be transferred. What good were they if they couldn't be transmitted, if sighing was their only utterance?

For now, let's just sit and talk. 'I'm terrible at this.'

'What?'

I pointed at the long expanse of sand remaining in front of us, the bluish light, and the little island at the far end, which the approaching tide had separated from the rest of the beach. 'Exercise.'

Her expression was one of disbelief. 'You said we should come here, and now you're giving up? No,' she said, 'you are not going to go to the end of it.'

She tenses up and thrusts her hips forwards, as if challenging the wind to a contest. I can't stop staring at her. She resumes walking with my hand in hers. No other option is an option for me. It's the only reason I'm here. Aside from booze, walking is the most effective way to relax one's tongue. Putting it at the top of a torturer's list is essential.

'My mother brought me to see The Wizard of Oz as a child, and I fell in step with her as we walked side by side. I was able to make her laugh so hard that she had to leave the theatre to collect her breath. Years later, she told me this story. Apparently, when the lion appeared on the screen for the first time, I informed her, "I've got long strands of head keratin, a visual apparatus that operates as expected, auditory sense organs that are sensitive to sound, and the ends of my arms can be used to manipulate objects and hold them if I like. As a big predatory cat, I must be." "Whoa dude," you could say. Once again, she burst into laughter and halted her path. Mum added, "I couldn't stand to watch him terrified." Everything hurt made me sad.'

Taking her arm, I hugged her tightly and kissed her for so long that my ears began to tingle. The skin on my arms resembled that of a chicken that had just been deboned. I could see seagulls landing and tucking themselves up beneath their wings behind her head. The scent of her hair reminded me of the little girl who believed she was a lion.

The tale she has just told me is quite a tale, so I ask her. 'Are you sure you don't want to go back?'

'Let us sit down."

After a time, she finds a little dune of soft dry sand to hide behind. The wind has kicked up again since we started walking. It seems as though the sun is playing hide-and-seek with a few stray clouds in the sky. In order to show off most of her thighs, she places her hands on her knees and pulls her skirt up beneath her. She's able to tell that I'm freezing. As soon as I kneel down next to her, she unwraps her shawl and wraps it over us as a blanket. My hand is working on her thigh as if she doesn't even know I'm there. This is due to the fact that there is nothing missing from it. Like the sound of the sea in an empty shell, I can hear the blood rushing to my ears. My temples are twitching with excitement, even though she doesn't flinch. She also doesn't say anything to me.

Her response is, 'I haven't questioned you about your mother,' she continues. 'How's she doing?' For the first time since I started recording my chats with her, she's taken a week off work and hasn't visited my mother. If nothing else, talking about my mother is a distraction from the task at hand that I'd rather be doing with my hand. I wish we weren't talking about my mother right now. On the beach, there are no other people around, and this has already occurred to me many times. The chances are slim, and even I wouldn't risk damaging what we have here - two peas in a pod, as the saying goes. The beach, the sea, and the pale sky are plenty for any man, and I'm more than happy to sit there like a trembling sea creature and listen to everything she has to say, which is more than I could have expected.

'She says she wants to die,' I overheard my voice say. When it comes to my sister, I keep quiet.

She glances up at me and then out to the horizon, where I've been staring for a long time. It's one of the most amazing vistas I've ever seen.

Then she replied, 'she is joking'
'She may, if I'm not mistaken.'

She clenches her fists around her knees and turns her gaze away. This is something we've never discussed before! She believes that he will be able to continue caring for my mother indefinitely. She does it all the time. I don't have a map if I'm going somewhere new. It's best to end now. However, it's already in the air between us, hovering there like a ghost. It's possible that if my mother wants to die, I won't object to her wishes.

Her last words to me are, 'I believe you should explain what you're saying,' as she slowly moves away from me but still within my reach. For the time being, the shawl resists being yanked off my shoulder. A look like that of a guy who has just admitted to seeing another woman enters her eyes as she turns to face me. When she looks up, she doesn't look down. I take a step back and wrap my arm around her waist, leaning back into her. There's no one around to give a rat's behind about it. Until the sea is dry, we may play about in the water, which was exactly what we need to do. I'm not sure why I'm opening my mouth now. 'As far as I know, she's made her mind up. She's had it.'

'Isn't it her decision?' she inquired. She raises her shoulders and moves slightly away from me again, but this time it's less noticeable.

'This is the reason I haven't visited her in all this time, you know. You never asked. It's possible that you mistook me for a sibling.'

'Why not tell me right away? The best time to do something is now.'

She's finally freed herself from my arm and turned to face me, removing the shawl in order to have a closer look at me. What she seems to be witnessing bothers me. I can still taste the sweetness of her hair on the back of my tongue.

I say, 'I don't want to ruin the morning.'

'You may not,' she said. She doesn't seem to be persuaded.

'I'd want to change the subject. The awful news can wait till later.'

I grin at her, but it doesn't do much to persuade her. If only there was a way out in the future. She doesn't talk, but I can tell what she's trying to convey because I can hear it.

'We both know that we were never the best of children, and she was never the finest of parents. No, I'm not inconsolable over it, because that's what happened. It's impossible to play at happy families if the tank is empty. I came up with the concept for a nursing home. She resisted my every move. When I first met her, she wasn't quite as terrible. She misunderstood my motives. Despite the fact that this was accurate in its own way. I knew I couldn't take care of her on my own. Despite the fact that she was still in charge, I was unable to care for her. After that, she requested me to allow her to end her life. As a means of helping her die. I told you I couldn't. Instead, I placed her with family. She yelled and swore as she stomped her feet. She informed me I was no longer hers. The last time I saw her, she said she never wanted to. I'm ashamed to admit it, but for almost two years, I believed everything she said about her. We'd had our disagreements in the past, of course. Her absence from my life would last months at a time. It was a relief, to be honest.'

Despite the fact that I had no clue what I was going to say before I began speaking, it was clear that I had avoided disaster. There would be others to come, but for the moment she could see that it wasn't as it seemed, that I didn't support my mother in her wish, that I was reprieved, and we could go back to being newlyweds (well, almost) on a honeymoon stroll with the promise of everything that lay ahead in the bedroom later. As far as my mother was concerned, was I willing to give up my new frame of mind and explain to her my new condition of affairs? Keeping the pledges I had made to others. When I found out that my son was coming to help me with something I shouldn't have asked him to do (he'd already made his own conclusions about the cloak-and-dagger visits, to which he had made no allusion aside from the shoebox), I was mortified. That we were going to assist in her demise as a group? No way in hell. I'd walked away unscathed from a potentially deadly situation. I was determined not to shoot myself in the face again!

'They're struggling. Before I began taking care of them, I never gave it a second thought. You don't learn about it in school. It is, nonetheless, of paramount importance. You have no idea how many of them rely on my assistance. What caught my attention was the expression on their faces. I don't make snap decisions. It doesn't matter whether they're in agony or if they've given up hope; it's not my responsibility to interfere. It's neither my right nor theirs. I was concerned that you would have a different opinion. It gives me comfort to know that you feel the same way.'

She returns to my side, hugging me closer than before. Under my shirt, I can feel her hands squeezing my waist. They exude a sense of comfort and purpose. Maintaining balance is a struggle for me.

As I nod in agreement, I cast my gaze back towards the horizon, terrified of what she may get a glimpse of in my eyes.

In order to have a better look at me, she removes her hands from around my waist and spins herself around in the sand. A worried expression might be exchanged with a cheerier one. She asks, 'What's on your mind?'

I have no choice but to keep my lips quiet for the time being.

My anxiety of saying what I was afraid of shrinks quickly and leaves me just somewhat weak when I say, 'Nothing,' Thanks for saving me from standing up. When I go back to the office, I'll have no clue how to proceed; my knees seem frozen in place. When I hear the awful words 'You can't,' I convince myself that I don't have to tell them all. How can you not... what?' Is it possible to save everybody? Is this possible? Is that what you want to do? Is it possible to eliminate pain? But that's not what I have to say today! 'What gives you the right to tell me that right now?' I say that with a smile on my face. It has a welcoming vibe about it.

'My belief is that God gave us life and only God can take that life away from us. In the end, I decided to tell you because I was afraid that you might think differently, and if I didn't, we might start to feel so good on the beach that we wouldn't have the courage to tell you, and that would have been wrong and unforgivable.' he said. 'I thought you might think otherwise, and I wasn't sure if I could be with you.' A sudden pause is made by her hands as they rest on my chest. '... that I was pondering this here, right now,' he said. Her chin is out and her oyster eyes are completely shucked as she nods at me. 'This way, you can tell me what you're thinking,' he said.

Although I'm sad she's so concerned about the future and respect her concern, I add, 'I appreciate you looking out for me.' If I could put off until tomorrow what I might say tonight, with her hands still restless on my knees and the beach empty except for possibilities (I can still picture us intertwined together in the shade of this dune for a second or two), I would. Even though she has a keen sense for the silences of others, she has spent most of her adult life analyzing the signals of those who have lost control of what their own signals mean because they no longer know themselves. She senses in the half-heartedness of what I've just said not only an evasion, but also a signal of deeper darkness, my withholding of the truth. When a mother becomes a kid to her son, she must be diapered and fed from another's hand, but she is now a baby who is not aware of this need and is so full of shame that it burns and burns but isn't enough to incinerate. She must beg for aid from another to put it all to a close. Surely, who am I to refuse my mother this aid, to deny her a merciful end to her shame? But who was I to tell Cassandra, whose only mother was a ghost she had created in her mind?

Her agitated lips twitched. 'A mature man like him required caring after,' she added, as she moved her hands away from his body. This is simply a conversation. When individuals converse, they say what they mean and not what they mean.

In an instant after she spoke those words, we both realized it was all over and that what was about to happen (our partial undress, her lovely naked buttocks on my knees as she climbed on top of me) was not going to happen; and our excitement, having reached its zenith, started to diminish. Afterward, she gave me a pat on the knees and a grin that she had been wishing she could offer me for a long time. It was followed by a kiss on the cheek that seemed like it might have been given to a loved one who had passed away. She rose up and put her hand on my shoulder as if it were the most natural thing in the world. Unnoticed tears film my eye like a lens, and I have to stifle their flow. My despair was not entirely unmixed, however, when I thought that anyone can fail the difficult things; the wonder is when we fail what should be easy. I'd sunk so low – I'd been sitting for too long; my knees ached; I was in the middle of many and great troubles, and my nature seemed so frail, it seemed, that I wondered if I'd ever be able to stand again.

The white cloud above has collected and is pulling against the sky like a robe being pulled over a corpse's shoulders. A group of youngsters runs by, barefoot and with their tracksuit trousers pulled up to the knee, unnoticed by us, even though there is now space between us, yelling with joy at the prospect of finally being liberated.

The tiny, red, dog-like animal that some liken to a sexy woman or whose nature they use as a metaphor for cunning, knows a lot, but the hedgehog knows a lot more than the tiny, red, dog-like animal that some liken to a sexy woman or whose nature they use as a metaphor for cunning, does.

In the chilly dawn light of a cold Saturday morning, Bobs Farm, just outside of Dualipa Bay, seems to be everything but picturesque. James is scheduled to arrive at 7:31 p.m. I'm hoping he has his winter coats ready. In spite of the fact that I'd awoken in the dead of night, I hadn't really been sleeping. No, if you think of sleep as a break from worrying thoughts and fears that are intensified by the onset of nighttime. To be alone in the automobile, cocooned like a grub, is an enjoyable experience. Wouldn't it be nice if the trip could go on for months? In reality, sluggish learners (sometimes known as 'late bloomers' or 'idiots') need longer lifetimes. The more time it takes, the better. At the very least, you'll learn how to pick yourself up by the bootstraps of your own messes. An opportunity to screw things up even more, that is. Whatever the situation may be, I'm grateful for the opportunity to get out of the house and get some exercise. Cassandra's situation was worse than it had been on our walk earlier in the day. Of course, it's my fault. How could I have ever imagined that they would move in a different direction? Bad memories, like four-legged companion animal pee on telegraph posts, have been my only meaningful legacy.

The sky seems to be painted between the trees outside my window. In the fog, the rising sun appears as a faint halo. We expect James to be flying above Bellingen by now, eating his in-flight meal. In fact, I've travelled this stretch of road so many times that I could do it blindfolded. Mum relocated here, I'm sure, to make it as difficult as possible to see her. There are few things more lonely than cows staring out from weedy paddocks. It seemed as if the flat, dry soil had become loose and had fallen off the endless sand dunes. There are patches of thickets of half-blackened, half-rootless sclerophyll on the fence lines of paddocks that are thickening into the bush; they are ugly, alien, and ramshackle fence replicas, with their wiry branches barbed with thorns, their mole burrows knotted, bowled and whorled, and their arthritic trunks scabbed with lichen. Greyhounds restrained and muzzled, smoke billowing from chimneys, and desultory weatherboards, the waterless riverbank with sand orange and swamp teak trees. It seems strange that such a country, a bipolar region, could exist, since cities must have an edge.

If the world in front of me isn't just a dream, I take a glance back. In the backseat of that car, I wonder if my mother isn't there, too, returning from one of our endless visits to Wollongong Hospital and the specialized barracks that hang in stationary orbit around it – gerontology, cardiology, audiology, clinical pharmacology, ear, nose and throat, immunology and infectious disease, medical imaging, neurology, palliative care, podiatry, rheumatology, stroke (as if the past could be anything other than a form of reminiscence). It seems to me how little we keep in our brains, even of our own lives, the enormous abyss of oblivion into which everything finally must fade away.... Isn't it possible that the web will survive the spider, too?

I'm surprised by how rapidly the drive is going. I can see Davidtown in the distance. Only a few minutes had passed. There is a lone horse scratching its behind on the high wire fence over which two crows jump and caw in the final pasture before the RAAF base. The twin-engine General Electric F404 turbofan engines (James was an aeronautical nerd there for a time) of the F/A-18 Hornets would shake the automobile where it stood when they took off for early morning exercises when James was only a youngster. What the horse thinks about it all is anyone's guess. When James was approximately five or six years old, he begged me nonstop about getting him a horse for Christmas. My annoyance was so great that on Christmas Eve, after he had gone to bed, I got a sack of horse crap from a barn in Randwick and put it in the garden of Bronte. On Christmas morning, he hurried down the stairs as soon as I informed him that Santa had come and left him a gift in the backyard. After running out of the room, he returned minutes later, speechless and weeping. Looked out the window and made a great deal out of it. I told him it had to have gotten over the fence somehow. The lesson I was attempting to teach him is beyond me. I hadn't told Anne about the stuff that had happened. When James was twelve, she divorced me and we split up. I can't believe she lasted this long without giving up.

James is a sad case. I don't know what condition he'll be in when I get to his door. My initial thought was that it was the wrong number when I called his cell phone three nights ago to explain my predicament. In his usual exuberant manner, he offered me advice and promised to fly down to help me out once he'd taken care of his own headaches — the Russians again! — and set up things for his mother, Anne, who had stayed with him since my last visit and showed no signs of wanting to leave, as she'd been since the early days of his short-lived marriage (I didn't like the syllables to it). It gave me a lift, but I didn't allow it to become anything more than a fleeting sensation. It didn't help that I was still apprehensive about what I was trying to ask him. Since moving his Nanna into the home against her wishes two years ago, he'd made it abundantly clear to me that he supported her right to die in the home, and that was a point of contention between us (not to mention his secret visits, which I had yet to bring up with him and, given what we were about to embark on, for the moment at least, would no doubt keep to myself unless my foot found its way into my mouth yet again) that I was unwilling to discuss.

Although he's always been a master of the unexpected, his comment, 'Dad, have you ever considered the reason you've held out so long against it was not because you loved her, but because you felt so awful about hating her?' definitely took me by surprise. What more could a twelve-year-old possibly know? After that, I considered telling him about my sister since it seemed so surreal. Though I might get into a frenzy, whatever anger I may convey to him would be a fabrication. Even though it had been only two days after my mother dropped that bombshell, I had not felt a gossamer thread of connection, and when I remembered that final discussion with my mother, if I was honest, I was really just dramatizing my pain in order to hurt her. As a challenge to James, I'd want to challenge him to spend 50 years living near a glacier and not turn to ice. However, even in this declaration of innocence, I am not totally truthful. That's because, even though I felt bad for the baby, all I could think about was my mother, what she had to go through and how much it must have cost her. My thoughts would not go farther than that, it felt like a dull rumble in my mind where the sensation should have been. Though she had only been my mother's sister for two days, I wished she never existed and wanted her to vanish and take with her the desolate desert she created of her life, and the desolate desert she thus made of my own existence. The loss of everything I may have had was replaced by the loss of all I might have had in her memory (my father included).

My inner mewling kid (who may not be the worst of me) is not something I'm proud of. I have no idea how I managed to give birth to such a beautiful boy. You should focus on him, who strangely loves you and forgives you without allowing his forgiveness to interfere. When I talked to him on the phone, I had even considered playing him one of the recordings. As a result, our children continue to wow us, which should come as no surprise yet does. In spite of the optimism he instils in me, I have no clue who will walk through the Arrivals door when he does.

Despite its size, Wollongong Airport is a pleasant place to land. It's like those demountable structures you find in practically every schoolyard, a mini hangar, if you will, in that it lacks permanency and seems moveable. To be honest, I wish I had more of an excuse to come here. Parking is simple, and the walk to the terminal is quick, so what better way to pass the time? We don't spend nearly enough time gazing up at the stars. Sub specie aeternitatis and all that jazz, is surprisingly refreshing. I'm sure the speck from James's jet will emerge in my eye in the next few moments (I'm trying to avoid thinking about the biblical log, but I know it will eventually turn into a forest).

I order a coffee from a huge Sikh wearing a light blue turban who is standing behind a little coffee cart inside the main entrance. The chill in the early morning is as cunning as a spider. There isn't a soul in sight. His first client is me. As long as I keep my eyes on the reward, I can talk to him about anything under the milk wand's constant whirr. I usually like my coffee Americano, but I haven't eaten yet and, according to Cassandra, milk helps lower stomach acid (a constant issue). I'm crossing my fingers that James will be game for a seaside breakfast with dad and son bantering above the waves' rhythm. She is a wealth of knowledge when she is in a good mood, particularly when it comes to matters of the heart and stomach.

Face of the Sikh is black and pocked in the manner of a golf ball, Sikh. While his cab company is slowing and his wife is pregnant with their fourth child, the man informs me that he also works as a bartender in the evenings. When he's not driving or preparing coffee, his wife works as a cleaner. They reside in Mayfield, Ohio. A bombing in Amritsar claimed the lives of his parents and mother. He didn't see much of a future there. While he may not conceive of his life as a short narrative, the way it seems to me is the same. He's really forthcoming about what he knows. In exchange, I tell him what I'm up to. I can't wait to spend a few days with my adult son. In Surfers, I add, and smile like a fool, I am a property developer. That's something he's not entirely sure how to handle. We should leave it at that, considering what he's told me about his parents. There's no need to go into specifics. My mother's identity is best kept a secret. They're essential for storytelling, after all. I congratulate him on a successful day at work and send him on his way to the arrivals lounge, where I wait patiently for my flight.

After our frigid walk down the beach yesterday, we returned in near silence, and I was still hopeful that I might salvage anything with Cassandra. Even though her offer to visit her home was just half-hearted, I happily accepted despite its underlying warning. Even still, as I got out of the vehicle, I felt fatigued, like I had just completed a long jog in the sand, with heavy legs and a severe pain in my back.

There is a security panel outside, and Cassandra punches in the code (which she's also given me: 9234#) and it lights up green. She switches on the light in the hallway before walking me down to the kitchen, even though it's still early in the day. The centerpiece of the table is a glass vase filled with local flowers, a white dish of soft cheeses, a long baguette, and a bottle of red wine. Glasses, forks & knives, plates, and linen napkins are all provided. This is a heartbreaking sight. My heart shattered at that moment, and I didn't even know it was there. After our short trip, she was clearly hoping for a better ending, and she wanted the floor would open up and take it all.

The muscles near the top of my jaw are starting to twitch. What had I done to deserve this? I couldn't have imagined such a lady even in my dreams. As far as she was concerned, I was the finest thing that had happened to her. How much effort did you put into convincing her that she could succeed? Before she gets a chance to speak, I open the bottle, pour myself a huge glass, and proceed to the balcony.

Although the weather is still frigid outside, the clouds have begun to dissipate, much to my surprise and delight. The magpie is strutting its stuff on the grass. In the distance, Cassandra appears behind me, but I don't respond. After wondering forlornly whether or not she'll pick up where we left off half an hour ago on the beach, she takes my arm and gently turns me around, looking at me squarely, though still gentle, through those deep, dark eyes that seem to take in even the birthmark on her cheek and glow with wonder at all they can see. But this isn't the moment for such bareness; I'm not in control of what she could see, so I turn away, but hopefully not in a manner she'll interpret as a rejection. Rejection is the farthest thing from my thoughts. I really want to kiss that one stripe on her face. A want to never speak again and live in a perpetual state of silent pleasure (I already have a triple-bypass, so I'm already Lazarus). That's a nonstarter.

She thanks Penny for her insights.

A tortoiseshell barrette holds her black hair in place, but she wears no additional jewellery. Even as I write this, the salt on her skin is still lingering in my mouth. Her pearly whites are dazzling. The spherical bowl of wine is still in her hands, but she hasn't yet taken a drink. It's as if we're hanging in mid-air, waiting for someone to turn the power back on for us. A four-legged companion animal barks and a door smashes in the yard behind hers, then becomes quiet.

Prior to all this, I tell you, 'I was thinking about you.' In any case, I do hope she understands the essence of what I'm saying.

'Before?'

'Your father and uncle live in Sydney, yes. Sad business, to be honest. I'm grateful that you told me, but I wish you hadn't done so... What I'm saying is that it hadn't...'

Those are the mornings when I wake up in the dead of night and lay there, eyes wide open, waiting for my father's face to take shape and for his voice to come into focus in my head, a face and a voice I don't recognize. Or how about the dream I had last night in which two guys were peering through a keyhole at a young girl who was nude in the bath. What might I have done to prevent it? I was clinging to my cell phone, completely stumped. In the darkness, I was murmuring to myself, 'Only a dream, only a dream,' when I awoke abruptly. What happened to the girl in that home with her father and uncle may have been similar to radiation poisoning, which mutates and persists long after the corpse has decayed. If my own childhood's residue is the same. But now isn't the right moment to bring it up. That's why I'm suspicious of what she says next, the way she attempts to deceive me. Perception of regular occurrences, on the other hand, is as enigmatic as ESP, and it has the extra benefit of being grounded in reality.

Her sudden question, 'Are you excellent at your job?' came out of nowhere and she vanished into thin air. She's still near to me, but she's no longer clutching my arm in her hands. 'It's a good job you're doing. It's very appealing to me. Your mother always brings up the subject of you.'

It brightens my day. Because I have no understanding why she dragged my mother into the picture or what that X means, I respond, 'I'm not sure what you're getting at.' It's the most honest thing I've spoken since we arrived. No matter how much time has passed, after my mother's death, if she believes that my mother (and so I, and by extension we) may still be rescued, she refuses to say so. Regardless, it's uncomfortable to stand like this, so I take a seat in one of the two outside canvas chairs that overlooks the yard. They seem to be fresh, however one of the armrests has a fleck of white bird poop that can be easily wiped off. I believe the offender is there in front of me, parading about on the spongy grass as he surveys his territory. Cassandra has nothing to say to me. In her spare time, she enjoys photographing birds. She follows me down, but not quickly, as if she wants to make sure I'm going to stick around.

In a casual conversation, she tells me, 'You create stuff that people want to see,' as she sits down next to me with her wineglass propped up on the table next to her.

I assure her, 'It's not difficult. In every film I create, the characters are the same: average people who do awful things. Because of it, I feel confident.'

As though the ice that had existed between us had finally been shattered, she now exclaims, 'I don't believe you.' She bounces back and forth in her chair as if it were meant for it.

'As a non-performer, I want my work to be in the shadows because it is easier to see.'

'Your job is considerably more difficult,' I reply, 'now that I'm on solid ground. In my opinion, I wouldn't do it for a penny. Better than mine – and essential. That which you must deal with is genuine.' My heart is aching and I want to tell her this with all my heart, but I don't know how to teach her how to suck eggs. My want to bury my face in her hair, stroke her forehead, or her waist has unexpectedly resurfaced in my thoughts. I reach uncomfortably over and kiss her on the cheek before moving on to the neck, where the kiss makes me shiver.

Though I'm unsure whether she is kidding or telling the truth, 'Easy now,' she tells me. That's not to say she didn't try to meet me halfway.

She can still feel my breath on her neck since I'm so close to her neck. As my breath passes through her fine down, it seems lighter than her hair against her dark skin. But she just gives me a cheeky peck, then walks away and stands with her glass still untouched in her hand, staring out at the grass across the street. I have no choice but to follow, leaning against the balcony rail as casually as I can while sipping from my wine glass. I'm lost and confused because I feel as if I've violated a rule. Whenever she stares at me, I don't know what she's thinking or feeling; it was as if there were an invisible barrier between us, I have no idea where the palings and cracks are. In an ideal world, I'd be doing just that. But she has other things on her mind, and adds, 'Let's eat some of that stuff in there before it goes to waste.'

'Why not?' I follow her gaze towards the kitchen as she says something to me. 'It's the chilly weather,' I thought.

While cutting the bread on her huge wooden board, she throws crumbs all over the table and calls for me to join her. She then places a couple rounds of bread on my plate. She peels back the foil surrounding the cheeses, allowing the cheesy goodness to spill out onto the table. With my hand pointing to the bottle, she nods, and I pour myself another. As though I've stumbled over a crack in the pavement, I'm getting to the point where there is nothing I can do to stop myself. It's hers that I leave unattended. None of it has been consumed by her.

'You asked whether I was thinking about my mum.' Finally, I state.

'Why?' she asked inquiringly, 'Are you?'

Using a question to answer a question is a new phenomenon, and I'm not a fan of it at all. This woman's passive aggressiveness is much more in line with her personality than her authoritarian charity, which is understandable - after all, no one wants to spend their whole life taking care of the insane for financial benefit! I'm referring to your mum, of course.

To which he replies, 'Well… Well… Well… Well… Well… In light of our previous discussion,'

'No,'

'You're better than you think,'

'I was thinking about you.'

On paper, it's a nice idea, but I'm not buying it for a second. 'Believe me, I'd want to be there, too.' In fact, if you were to stand on Jupiter, the debris I've left in my path wouldn't look much better. Whatever the reason, I'm crossing my fingers that this distracts her from what she's about to say. I'm no longer interested in finding out what she's thinking. 'Perhaps that is all I am,' he thought to himself.

'This is what people say if they don't want to change,' he said. 'As soon as they make a decision.' There is something about her expression when she takes her first drink of the wine that suggests she was expecting something different or was hoping for a miracle that would convert it into water. I've never seen her drink anything other than water before now. She gulps down a sluggish slice of bread. 'When I woke up this morning, I had a hunch that something was off. That's a thinking I haven't had in a long time. I was eagerly awaiting your arrival.'

The past tense once again. Human hope is in a terrible state right now. Isn't it the case all across the place? Then it dawned on me how lonesome I was (though in my mind was also her father and what he had done to her). The words 'I hope you haven't stopped looking ahead' make me angry. But I was in desperate need of a life raft, and all I had were sticks. Every piece of bread that I eat, I have to fight with my jaw and cheek to get it out. Let her know I'm ready to take this on. That I am capable of becoming such a guy. I'm getting the feeling that I'm going to grin as I write this. It's a good thing I'm blind because it would be hilarious.

'Why is that smile on your face?' she asks.

'What can I say? I'm at a loss. Are there any reasons why I shouldn't be here?'

Like an old-fashioned fortune-teller from her area of the globe (and it is), she stares into my eyes and wonders what sort of riddle she might conjure up for me in order to discover what's lurking in me. While stretching, she extends her arms over her head and joins her fingers, as if I've tangled her up in some way and she has to untangle herself. The joints are creaking softly, as I can hear. As soon as she returns to her seat, her face softens and her eyes seem to be filled with a mixture of tenderness and sympathy. Throughout the course of the story, I've found myself admiring her calm demeanor, her patient approach to problem solving, and her ability to think on her feet. However, I now believe she has a more serpentine nature, as if she's been lurking in the shadows, waiting for the right moment to strike. And it's too late to go away. She reaches for the bread once again but decides not to eat it. A strange quiet pervades the landscape beyond my window. This has become so bad that even the magpie has lost his cool. There will be no one around to witness the carnage if it does take place.

'The only thing I would want us to do is return to our previous location.'

'And exactly where was that?' I'm surprised she doesn't mind if I thrash about on her hook as much as she does.

'Prior to today's arrival at work,' he said. 'I'm referring to the beach,' I said.

I can see that she's thinking about what she should say since she keeps it hidden from my view. Her birthmark is the sole indication that she could split in the winter sunlight streaming in through the kitchen window. A delicate balance is in play, and she is the most beautiful I've ever seen her. Just loving her and keeping my mouth shut can't be that difficult, can it?

'Do you really want to assist your mum die? As a result, you're hesitant to speak it out loud.'

Finally, the genie has popped out of the bottle, so to speak.

'No, not at all,' I respond. My mum has always encouraged me to pursue a career in law. The vocation of a real son of immigrants. Was it a writing job? Sophistry was all I was adept at, but surely you needed something more solid.

'When I first heard it, I had no idea what it meant. For every red light, there's an equal number of green lights. That's impossible. Many individuals have died in front of me, and I'd rather not have to tell you about it. There's no going back from this point on. That's as precise as it gets.'

I recall the willy-willies that would sometimes sprout up in the school playground, plucking up leaves and wrappers off the tarmac and hurling them into the air. I suppose she was taken aback by the intensity of her emotions, as if they had been fermenting for far too long; a storm created just for me. She took a long breath and held the base of her glass in her palms before releasing it from the table. It didn't help, but the fact that she cared so much about me still took my breath away. But I couldn't figure out what was going on in her thoughts.

Nevertheless, because we must see this through to the finish, even if it is the end, I say, 'I wish it was as easy as you say,' because we must.

A paper napkin is used to wipe her nose while she sniffs. Hair is pulled back from her face and her fingers are rubbed through the strands. In the past, I've shared a bathroom with a lady, and the smell of shampoo and conditioner brings back memories of that time. There's no other fragrance like it, unless you count a newborn baby's head. She shakes her head as if to remove all of my thoughts from it. In her gaze, she conveys a mix of skepticism and hostility. She asks, 'Then tell me. What you say matters.'

'I'd rather not,' I respond. 'I think I've exhausted my supply of words. In my opinion, they haven't done anything for me.'

She adds, 'Well, you're a good writer,' as if she knows how to scoff. 'Isn't that a little juvenile? Putting your head in the sand?'

Here I am, she's got me! My eyes are shut and my hands are over my face. 'John, where are you?'

'I think so, too. And if that doesn't work, I'll bury myself even farther. The classic joke goes, Have you heard of it?' In the belief that women and children are the only two sorts of individuals, there's nothing in her expression to suggest that she considers that humorous - or correct! The jokes I tell cut too close to the bone, and they're not funny at all; they're an invitation to the axe, and that's not how I want to be seen. In the end it comes to be clear to me—foolish as I am—that I have it all wrong, and she wants me to show her otherwise. The taste of my own foot appeals to me, something one would think I'd have learned to flee from by now. To satisfy her, I've been acting defensively from the beginning, and she's been calling the shots (a forgivable blunder considering who owns this particular piece of high moral ground), while all she's actually wanted is for me to take charge. If nothing positive is going to come out of it, I ask, 'Why bother if the only thing that can happen is that the terrible situation will grow worse? That seems harsh to me.'

Something horrible has just become worse, and I don't even have to look at her. I might just as well have referred to her as my mother's tormentor. Nevertheless, why can't she comprehend that even death isn't always the worst? Do you honestly think it's that difficult? After seeing my mother chop up her fish and put it in her cup of tea last night, she could have been more understanding of my mother's actions if she'd been there. What rational person would say no to someone who was desperate to escape from that? Of course, I don't have to say anything. If I'd kept my lips shut, we'd be upstairs right now. Alternatively, if you must say anything, why not tell a lie? Even if the fire of imagination is in them, lies are more intriguing. What a bizarre bit of advice my mother offered me — odd for a mother to give, but I didn't find it unusual at the time — when my head was on the block and the axe was already cutting through the air. The remarks stayed with her since she wasn't a big fan of folklore wisdom. A personal question, she answered, 'You're completely allowed to tell a falsehood if someone asks.' I was probably sixteen or seventeen at the time. I'm not sure how or why she brought it up to me at the time, but I've followed this counsel my whole life, despite the fact that it has caused as much damage as good. In order to be a master in the art of lying, you must also have an uncanny ability to recall details. Even if the deception has persisted and been kept a secret for decades, it is advisable not to divulge the truth until the very end (no deathbed disclosures, please)!

'What is life to you?' asks the question. Cassandra makes her presence known. It's not a subject of peacemaking, the implication here is that I've suddenly become an unwanted intruder, an outsider from a different moral universe.

Even when things go bad, there will always be something worse ahead of us. That's the joy of life. Fear of something worse may even be used as a way of defining what it is to live.

'It's not something I give much thought to,' I respond, as if she had asked me whether I like cabbage or daikon radish. 'I'm not sure I can answer that. Why is it suddenly so important?'

'It seemed like we had something here.' When I hear her voice, I know it's time to get serious. Listening is all I can muster. Poison would be poured into your ear for certain utterances. I'm hoping they aren't the words; 'to know what type of guy I've brought into my home.'

'When I say, a decent guy, I say it too soon, then take a few steps backwards. At the very least, an honest guy who has a hard time distinguishing between his a** and the ground. A bumbler, he's spent his whole life living in fear of failure. After meeting you, a guy thought there was no hope left for him in the world. What type of guy are you looking for?'

At this moment, she's a searchlight and I'm a rabbit. Maybe tomorrow my response will mean something to her, move her in some way? This might be the case. However, I have little faith in talks. 'I want to know whether you're a fan of life.'

Finally, from a lengthy list of awful options, I guess I've twirled my tail around the elephant long enough. She needs a straightforward response even if it means that I'm announcing my own demise. She's looking at me with her hands clasped, as if she's asking for a miracle, and she seems to be praying. My response is, 'It's not as easy as you believe.' A hundred different responses, all of which seem persuasive to me at the moment I say them, are at my disposal should you ask what I think about X. 'For as long as I live, I will continue to provide you with solutions. Never in my life have I made the proper choice. I may avoid making a choice by going to a nursing facility. Despite my best efforts, my mother still holds a grudge against me. However, I had the pleasure of meeting you. In other words, did I get it right or wrong? Red and green lights are mutually exclusive, as you said. On the other hand, when it comes to the major things in life, we are precisely that. It was both proper and wrong to bring my mother into the family home. Almost all of my work is. People that approach life with a fire in hand and illuminate the path, inspire me.' That final one didn't get enough consideration from me. I had no intention of sending a fiery arrow her way. However, she was unquestionably a torchbearer in this regard. She only asked me that question because she already knew the answer to it. When I see these kinds of folks, I usually flee a hundred miles away. Even if I tried, I couldn't stop myself from plunging headlong to the earth — if that qualifies as flight. My saner, more atrophied self, of course. Not to overstate things, but my mum is not an easy person to deal with. She's got a drive in her. If I don't step in right away, she'll figure it out on her own. As far as I know, that's what she told me. She's refusing to consume any food at this time. She'll die of starvation. You'd want to see this before I was unable to complete the task. When I first brought her in two years ago, I wish I hadn't been able to do this. However, there is a new dynamic. I'm not sure what's going on. What I'm doing is in the best interest of humanity. Isn't it obvious to you?'

'Why are you so opposed to it?'

While I had anticipated her repeating what she'd said to me on the beach, that it was all a matter of right – or lack thereof – she kept her own counsel. As if I'd never grasp the answer if she'd had to ask, she stayed quiet, as if I was the only one who'd ever asked the question. There you go. The Holy Trinity was a mystery to me, and no one, save for Thomas Aquinas had even begun to scratch the surface of that mystery in his thirty-odd works. She was well aware that nothing she said would make sense. She may as well respond to me in Swahili, if that's what it takes.

Her response was: 'I think you can be persuaded out of such a strict stance, don't you? It seems to me that you meant "not being able to trust your own judgments" when you said that.' A full wine glass was in her hand as soon as she said this and she got up, raising her arms and twisting herself to the side as if she was handing me a knot to untie as she spoke. I didn't expect her to use my own words in this manner, with her own little twist, and hang me on my own petard like a rising star of the Persecution of Jews and other non-Christians that happened on the Iberian Peninsula around the same time Columbus was looking for the West Indies. For a brief minute, I was dumbfounded.

'If you ask me, I'd never think so. But then again, I guess it depends on who's saying it.'

For what they were, my remarks' levity and underlying assumption that nothing is unrepairable were taken as a given by her. Her gaze drifted away from me as if I were no longer there. As a result of my own suffering and thanks for her efforts, I'm tempted to rise from my chair and embrace her (I'm still here, they say) and cradle my face in her hair and rub my lips and nose against the neck of her luscious locks. There is a feeling of progress, but there is no reciprocation: her eyes remain fixated on something out in the yard as if she is ignoring me.

Her response is simply, 'That's what I thought.'

No matter how long it takes, I'm willing to wait if it means delaying the inevitable fall just a little bit longer. I have no clue where I stand with that, and I'm not sure what it means. After all, whether we're nine or ninety, the thinnest membrane is all that stands between us and the emptiness. As a result, a single second might seem like a lifetime.

I tell her that she is the most gorgeous lady I've ever encountered, bright, practical, and giving, she embodies the finest of what nature has to give – barring a miracle, of course – when it comes to qualities. When I think about my strong feelings (how surely everything pales into insignificance in the fierce light of that fire), I feel old butterflies in my stomach (and maybe even in hers), a rapid flutter connected to a feeling that announced itself hours ago and won't go away, and I sense she's only waiting for me to admit – because she is too kind to rub my nose in it – which is why I think she's waiting for me to admit it. 'You and your mother have a lot more in common than you think.' My readiness to assist her die is just the tip of the iceberg. To be honest, I'm quite sure I'm all tip!

When she walks out onto the porch again, she does so without looking at me or gauging how I may react to what she knows is a very gnomic statement, and the screen door closes with a scarcely detectable click (a precisely calibrated closer – what else) behind her.

Now that everything is peaceful, I don't mind standing alone for a little while longer. Something else is going on in my head, and it has nothing to do with my present love situation or any kind of internal debriefing. With what I've learned, I'm certain that nothing is as horrible as one would imagine it is, and that it is often preferable to let the aftermath to deal with itself, which will happen regardless of our involvement. The sea salt fragrance is wafting up from the nearby casuarinas, where I can see it blowing. The water is less than 100 yards away, if you fly. A crow like that? For now, I'm not thinking about flying. Even if it's a ragtag bunch, I may be able to salvage anything. Even if it's not, I can only wonder whether our conversation is somehow reminiscent of what occurred with her uncle and her father all those years ago, when she packed up and left without saying a word to anybody, which in her own mind may well have been the case, but that nothing was everything to her.

It's hard not to be impressed when James walks through the gate like he's on a mission. The opportunity to act as a father figure to one's father appears to excite a son like nothing else. I can't recall the last time I saw him so cheerful. A jingle comes from the bottom of my coffee cup every time I rise to meet him. Fortunately, it's empty, even though I have no recollection of having consumed it. Despite my best efforts, the Sikh is preoccupied with a long queue of customers and doesn't seem to care that I'm slacking on mindfulness. Even in the best of circumstances, some baristas demand an appreciation of their trade, if not downright devotion. Despite this, I can't help but feel a pang of sadness when James comes running towards me, his bare arms extended to wrap around my shoulders and pull me into his barrel chest in a hug that transports me to unexpected weepiness, despite my best efforts to keep such embarrassing fatherly emotions hidden deep inside my heart and not be a pity party. Even though I'd like for my son to believe his grandfather is depending on him (and I have no idea where to get the cocktail we'll need), I'm not comfortable leaving him in Surfers, and I'd like to provide him with some home-cooked advice along the way to help him navigate the rough terrain ahead. I'd like him to believe his grandfather is depending on him, but the truth is that I'm not sure he's ready to leave. Actually, I'd want to see him get married, have children, and be happy — he's still an appealing prospect to people of the opposite sex – but I'd rather he not follow in my footsteps. The experience wasn't all bad, but like with a lot of our childhood, James's benefitted him in precisely the places where it also injured him. His parents' inability to see beyond the fog of what was actually covert warfare for years gave him mental independence, no question, but it also led to a coldness in human relationships that no woman has ever been able to penetrate (even his ex-wife). It's hard to believe that I was standing there with those enormous arms around me, and that I was that fatherless father who never in a hundred years should have been permitted to provide where it hadn't been requested some good old-fashioned life advise.

Because there were no other adults around, I was the only one who could provide my kid with anything greater than what I could give him. As a result, I would have to make do, despite the fact that I am not and never have been a doctor enough to heal myself. Love - big weepy gouts of it, if not wisdom, if not authority - was all that I had, plus a nice winter dip in the Pacific and breakfast at a seaside café, and a few beers over lunch later in the day, et cetera, et cetera. As a result of this, we are once again father and son even if neither of us wants to speak about what has brought us here.

'So, Dad, after I've recovered enough to step out of the harbor where I worry I've overstayed my welcome, it's nice to see you, and I do so. However, you should be aware that you were under no obligation to do so; hire automobiles are an option.'

My son's stagecraft brings a grin to my face.

'What?' he exclaims in surprise.

'Nothing. Surely a parent can't help but be happy to meet his son? I think you look great.'

Exactly so. It looks like he's shed some pounds (did I notice this in Goldie?) and that suits him. His face has returned to its former vibrancy, his Magyar jaws can be seen peeking out from beneath his cheekbones, and he's spent time, as he used to, selecting his outfit: black docs, black jeans, a long-sleeve band tee. Being able to perceive him in this light makes me happy: as a dedicated seeker of fortune while on vacation. His father invited him to spend the weekend with him.

He adds, 'You too.' As though there's something trapped between his teeth, I can see his tongue making its way up his face. I'm hoping he hasn't had any food in him. This is the second time in less than one minute that he's asked me what I was gazing at him for.

It takes me a little while to go back to where I was before. 'Have you had anything to eat?' I ask.

Looks at the pricey watch on his wrist dramatically as he removes the sleeve from his jacket sleeve. 'Seriously? When did I leave, do you have any idea?'

Again, the lightness strikes me in the heart. Many fine creases may be seen on his face when he grins these days. A guy I've known for so long has shown these early indications of ageing, and it breaks my heart (and with whom I used to have such banter). I've learned that if you look at problems from the appropriate perspective, you can deal with them. These creases are the product of a lifetime spent attempting to make light of the most difficult situations, like a father who, despite his best efforts, felt helpless and could only repeat what his mother had taught him not to do and pass on his ruination like the color of his eyes and hair. They're a heroic thing's death warrant, like Sisyphus' calloused hands. Since reading this, I've come to see how one may come to accept such changes, like a long-lost sibling one never knew.

I replied, 'Then let's get going. My preparations are in place. When we get in the vehicle, I will tell you everything about it.'

'Please, add bacon and eggs and a huge cup of coffee in one of them.'

Again, he chuckles and pulls the handle of his little luggage and drags it like a weightless object as he makes his way to the door. That's all there is to it for now.

As he pulls into the traffic circle and joins the effective transition of Weekend traffic out of Davidtown toward this big soot of Wollongong, James appears ready for a snooze, but he's clearly as wide awake as a rooster. This morning, James has offered to drive. His big hands rest complacently at ten and two on the wheel. In the parking park, while we were strolling, he informed me that he seldom had time to relax, and that my huge Subaru Forester would be a wonderful break from his Audi sport. I get what he's saying. At 6'1', he has a Russian peasant build with broad shoulders and narrow hips (my mother calls them 'cubes'). A fight with his stomach has plagued him since the age of twenty-one. Since childhood, his limbs have been restless, and even while he's sitting on the pedals, his feet tremble nervously. Despite his angular features, he seems to be both weighty and light at the same time. His hair still falls over his forehead to cover the scar from his skateboard accident into the paling fence at the foot of our hill, even though he should have outgrown such vanity by now.

He hasn't said much since we passed the 24-hour McDonald's and sped down the long length of open road to Fern Bay. Because of his divorce, I've noticed he's started to exhibit moody, deep-cover states in which the tip of his tongue sticks out from between his closed lips like a lizard's head, while taking deep, meditative yoga breaths and frowning at whatever he finds in his head. He even scratches his eyebrows as if to make sure they're still there. Although, I'm well aware that my knowledge of this area is limited and that I'm not one to let the truth get in the way of a good narrative, these gestures seem to be common in the business world and in the business of generating truckloads of money, a type of secret masonic handshake. The two of them aren't much of a concern to me this morning, and I'm grateful for the opportunity to be chauffeured by my son, who seems to be aware that I might not be quite the young ram I once was, and willing at last to give me a glimpse of the kind of care I might expect as I grow older and to take in the scenery while shunting anxious thoughts to the back of my brain—a trade in which I've never had much success, but I'm still prepared to try my hand. At the very least, his sheer size has temporarily distracted me from thinking about Cassandra, even though the real reason we're taking this journey is as personal to him as it is to me. If I may use Latin to describe those elbows, Et in Arcadia ego. After all, no one does death quite like the ancients. To be clear, we aren't just stopping by Wollongong to take in the sights. However, it would be good if we could inhale some scent on the way.

As a businessman, James is no different from the majority of people who believe that generating money is a good thing, and for the genuine Francis Nightingales among them, a 24-hour profession, a true calling that enables them to sleep peacefully at night (if only on their feet). Of a certain, there are criminals. A handful of them were in bed with James at this point. The man's efforts to leave that bed gracefully — or at the very least, with all his bones intact — were commendable. And who knows, maybe it was also a part of the process of discovery. That in business, like in life, the majority of the experience is one of suffering. He once told me that if you're willing to violate the law, there are many ways to get money. He may have been pleading for aid with that statement. I'm not sure whether I could have done more to aid him. For the most part, it was easy for me to assume that he had gone outside my area of expertise — which he did — but what I didn't take into consideration was that such demands might be made for non-technical reasons as well. Besides, I didn't want to dwell on it just now; scarred skin is usually tougher, and if coming down here to assist me was his way of distracting himself from his problems, he could always return to them later. Unfortunately, disappointment and its underlying financial woes weren't just James's to bear. The Russians, however, were not the only ones who were brutal. Similar to the list of dodginess, you'd want a large amount of paper to compile such a list. You don't really know who you've been sleeping with until they take their clothes off, which is a common occurrence. In other words, when it's too late.

In my heart, I understood that James's disappointment was greater than his effort. All around him, it slammed into him like a sledgehammer. It seemed like a waste of time when he wanted to devote his life to a greater purpose. Individuals like James — people who want to produce things – show the real essence of our time better than anybody else because they take use of all the chances our time has to offer, good, terrible, and ugly. To put it another way, if poets aren't what we're looking for these days (and apart from Shakespeare and Sophocles, maybe they never have been), then perhaps philosophers are. I'm not so naïve as to not wonder whether I'm any better or worse than the rest of them. Despite the fact that James's desire to build and grow was a good and necessary thing, and that the face he looked at in the morning mirror, disappointed and depressed, could turn sour at times, the currency in which James traded was an abstraction (money, although an end in itself, must always stand for something else) and outside of himself, whereas what I sold was something that I could identify with.

A thick layer of traffic has formed at Wollongong Golf Club on Nelson Bay Road, and by Stockton Bridge we're in major congestion. People are waking up early these days, driving their children to school in the mist, or resignedly accepting a seven-day workweek. Idleness is an unaffordable luxury in today's rental market. My mission (which I try to downplay because the alternative is unthinkable), will arrive later in the day, so for the time being, I'm content to take in the scenery and wait for the breathtaking view from the bridge's vantage point, which never fails to take my breath away, despite how many times I've seen it. When the Pacific swifts (on a winter break from Siberia) fly above, they write their names in blue-black ink and blink their wings. They leave just a memory, thrown into space by quick changes of direction, hairpin twists, fast wing-glides, accelerations, and gear switches. It would be nice if I could point them out to James, but I don't want to draw his attention away from the birds as he speeds up the bridge's steep rise. Despite the fact that we're driving faster than the speed limit, I'm still able to glance to my left and see a river mouth, the ocean, and a city rising up from the harbor to the Cathedral that encircles the hill.

Before I placed Mum in the home, I used to bring her here on Sunday mornings for years. Jobbys Beach, located on the eastern outskirts of the city, would be the perfect place to pitch up tent under the shelter of the harbor groin. This is what I'm seeing now as James makes his way down to Crescent Island, the terrain thinning down to meet the water, and the small strip of road that connects it to the harbor below. After lunch, we would go carefully down the groin, where fisherman would stop and smoke, staring up from their lines to a coal ship floating into the harbor, which was only a few feet away from them. There was usually a group of lads removing their wetsuits on the sand at the beach. To get a better view of the BHP Steelworks, which is now a skeleton and rimmed in coal dust, I'd turn around and stare back at the enormous bridge I'm gazing at this recollection from, and underneath it the BHP Steelworks (a corpse, rimmed in coal dust, rough like whiskers to the touch). The lighthouse and the city may be seen in the distance behind us. Returning to the vehicle, I saw the little concrete cage erected at the foot of Jobby's Head to house the city's defense cannons in case the Japanese invaded, but they never did. These eerie reminders of a war that never happened littered the streets of Wollongong.

That elderly mother so near the end (how wrong I was) with that small baby just starting on her lap, I used to fear that Mum wouldn't live to see James grow up. Seeing her swollen spirit pressing up on her weak heart made me feel sad for her. Honestly, I didn't realize half of what was happening. Perhaps discovering that I had a sister had a greater impact on me than I had previously assumed. It was not what my mother had to go through or how much it had cost her that bothered me, but the fact that someone else had been involved.

It comes out of the blue: 'I told you Mom is still living with me,' James adds. 'I'm concerned about her safety. My opinion is that you should meet with her. You could call her while we're in the car, if you wanted to.'

His idealistic outlook is admirable. It's been a long time since he's seen us grow up, but he hasn't given up faith that we'll one day become the happy family he never had, even after all these years. He's dying to know what happened. There have been twenty years of bursting. If that's the case, he may be worried about his mother. That was a long time ago, when I was much younger than James is today. Can anybody really blame you for being on the defensive when you've messed up other people's life as well (and whose kid isn't father to the man)?

It is hence my belief that she will be able to overcome the challenge since she always does.

'You need to be aware of the fact that she isn't as tough as you believe she is.'

In light of the uncertainty surrounding her strength, I decided to let that one go. She might be vulnerable. When James snuck up on me unexpectedly on my recent trip north, I was horrified by the figure she cut. She'd had an even worse time with Colin, the orthopedic surgeon (James's stepfather), her second husband, than she had with me, but it took longer to see the rot. In that respect, marriages resemble trees. For a hundred years, a tree may not exhibit signs of death. Anne, on the other hand, did not need a long-distance, meaningful conversation with her first husband over a shaky mobile phone connection. What James saw as a crisis was most likely just a bloated case of wackiness, which is usually amplified with age. What do I know about this? It is impossible to comprehend someone if all you've ever done was oppose them.

I respond, 'I'll call her,' since there are wrinkles on his brow that I'd want to see disappear, 'if it makes you happy. But we'll have to wait till breakfast. The time has slipped your mind.'

As a result of my having spoken what he wants to hear (and how difficult could it have been?) his generosity has returned, along with a sense of nostalgia, as if he can simply go back far enough in time to a happier period. Yet, I'm taken aback by how far he's willing to go back. When you think about it, that's a long way to go. In that instant, I see us smashing through the guardrail and plummeting headfirst into the frigid Hunter River below as we turn his head to look at me, but whatever he's seen on the way back cannot be transported over but can only flow through him like a hole in an urn.

How did I get to be such a weirdo? He keeps his eyes on me, as if he's expecting something from me.

Compass points north and south. It always works out for James. It makes me cry. Cars appear to be going in every way, and I'm wishing he'd turn back to the road. He hasn't slowed down even a little bit. In an attempt to flee something, we're hurtling down the bridge at breakneck speed. On the other side of the river, a gaping hole in the haze marks the site of the BHP's disappearance.

'I can't recall,' he said. I say this, despite the fact that it's not the right moment to be honest. 'You were only intriguing to me when you could speak,' I thought to myself.

You can't solve anything without talking about it, so I chuckle to let him know it's all in jest (even if I'm telling the truth). But I'm sure he already understands this since he's earned a fortune in business. It seems to me that his issue is that he's never been able to reconcile the idea that we're both more immoral and more moral than we're aware of. Even today, my ability to do hurt even when I want to do good is astonishment to me. In spite of the fact that one may fool oneself for years (a lifetime) and get away with it, there is no mystery to self-deception. Why? Because there's one fundamental life skill we all lack: how to deal with situations we don't fully comprehend. Isn't that all there is to say?

He adds, 'I don't believe you,' as if to show his disbelief. 'Dad, I'm serious. My opinion matters to me.'

'What? How could I not know?'

'Dad.'

'What do you want me to say? I'm not sure, James, all newborns are the same in every way. The only thing that sets them apart is their ability to communicate.'

'Why do you always have to do this? In my mind, you already know what I mean by that.

'If you still don't know, just ask.'

I don't know why I've suddenly been so adamant. I didn't plan it that way. Somehow, he makes me angry at him when all I want to do is hug him and tell him everything will turn out just fine.

Finally, we've arrived at the roundabout on Crescent Island. The gas station to the left of here is completely sold out. Walking through the nearby vacant lots, you'll see they're covered with dew. It's as if the wrecker's yard's massive wooden gates are opening up to reveal a terrible mediaeval memento mori of mangled metal corpses. But the company name, BAD KARMA PARTS, is written over the fence in brilliant neon, which appears to speak to the contrary and contradicts any finality, even death. Squirting profusely out of his back-to-front baseball hat, an older man with a padlock the size of his palm ties an enormous gate chain around a fence and locks it in place. One of the lanes we exit the roundabout onto is now a deep hole in the bitumen, with a huge group of hard-hatted men staring down at other hard-hatted men who are enacting yet another Commonwealth Government Initiative, as is stated on the sign ahead of us. There are enormous slagheaps to our right that feed even more enormous and voracious ships, locked as if they were in some aquatic constellation (how could such vast beasts float) through the draglines and conveyor belts that pass above, restless, like death.

His voice level and chin up, James keeps the seat pulled back to the limit of its range to allow him to stretch both of his long legs slightly and maintain his hands on the wheel away from his torso. 'I know, I know,' he adds. 'You weren't always like that. You used to be a lot of fun. In no way am I asking you to divulge any of those tremendous mysteries. We're on our way to Wollongong, and I simply want to chat to you and ask that you take up the ball once in a while and consider running with it.'

There is no way I can know what's upsetting him since I am not psychic (it's basic arithmetic: assuming the worst makes you accurate most of the time). Also, he has been to the wrecker's yard to view the vehicles. It's possible that his mother's condition causes him to worry about me as well (particularly when you consider the reason we're travelling to Wollongong), which causes him to wonder about his own marriage (was non-failure ever an option?) and his future as well. What are the possibilities? When you're sixteen and you find yourself driving your father to Wollongong to purchase drugs to help him murder your grandma, your only relief is looking back, as some of us find out early on, it's like seeing through deep water, and that's no accident. For the duration of the trip, why should I hold him responsible for wanting to revert? Even though he's come in from Surfers to assist me, I know he can't help himself. Is it really worth it to me to chase him away from refuge because he expects to get a glimpse of bliss in his early infancy (which is all he wants from me now) before his memory kicks in and he sees the wreckage of his recalled past as the only future he can see? He's right: I'm a scumbag because I'm trying to make him stronger. We live in a difficult environment, and I don't want him to face the same fate as myself. Nothing can separate us from one other like the everlasting return that binds us together like two poles of a magnet.

As a result, after mocking the game, I'm now going to pick up the ball. Exhilarating, not because it all comes back, but because it does. 'In my life, I've never seen a newborn appear happier. You scurried about like a four-legged companion animal, gnawing on anything you came across. Once you'd been weaned, you wore down the nail on your thumb by sucking so much.'

When I saw him at the grocery checkout, I couldn't help but grin as if I'd just bumped into a long-lost friend. That's all I need to say to let his mind go wild. Unlike Anne, who could only sit in the sandpit for a few minutes before heading to the nearest café on Johnson Street, I could spend hours watching him use the toy front-end loader to load a bucket full of sand, then spin the bucket around and dump it on top of the mound he was determined to build into a mountain the size of himself. Alternatively, you may watch him slither down the slick slide on his stomach, or climb the rope pyramid to the top.

A fig tree's root system almost snatched me off my scooter as I rode down the trail.

When we weren't swimming on the weekends, I'd take him with me instead of his mother. I, on the other hand, choose to ignore the comment. Joy might be found in the recollection for a little period. Suddenly, I'm smiling along with him. Those latter years had slipped my mind. Delight and death are always within a heartbeat of one other. The past may be compressed into a single, joyful plane if you're skilled enough.

Because it comes to me, I add, 'I remember the first time I brought you to the barber,' and she laughs. Normally, Anne would clip his hair, but I believed he needed an introduction to the art of manhood. 'The brothers, Tino and Dino, who lived on Clovelly Road, may have been familiar to you.' His expression is open to the idea, and he wants me to continue because he knows that one word may bring it all back to him again. 'You yanked at my hand and attempted to flee when you noticed a bald guy exiting the business as we were about to enter. When you woke up in the middle of the night, you were as terrified as you were now. From our beds on the opposite side of the house, Mum and I could hear you. You'd run down the corridor, slam into me, lay over on top of me, and fall asleep as if you'd never been awake until your head touched the pillow. That made me a little nervous.'

The most beautiful thing in my head right now is like an infinite stream of winter light. So I halt, not just to allow him time to recall and come in. In fact, even while looking at him from the side, I can notice the same thing. He is simply interested in soaking up the sun's rays.

'I was forced to bring you in.' he said. In contrast to this, 'after Tino hoisted you onto the giant cushion he'd placed on the seat, you sat there calmly and still, and you sobbed the most silent tears I've ever seen that flowed down your cheeks until it was over. Tino's expression was so sad...'

Some emotions, like ideas, appear out of nowhere and draw you in, but as soon as you step inside, the door shuts behind you. He has no recollection of it, but that won't stop him from remembering it now. He's making fun of himself, and I'm making fun of him as well. It's a hoot! My apologies for not handing this up to him sooner. Rather than having to walk on eggshells because I gave him eggs to hurl, I should have given it to myself instead. Even though he attempted to be a nice kid, which was understandable given his age, I was a father figure to him even though I wasn't there physically. We recall the period when he started feeding on this guilt and using it as an excuse for everything that went wrong in the course of his life, blaming me (and his mother) for it all. He found it in me, ate it up, and got fat on it like a tick feeding on fat. When I saw it, I despised it and as I despised it, my sense of shame only deepened because what else was there for me to do? That's exactly what he said I was, plus a whole lot more. That's why, whenever I attempted to distance myself and let him to develop, it simply fueled the guilt and made me feel even worse. As to how we came to this conclusion (we never discussed it), Anne and I decided that by keeping our issues to ourselves and acting as if they didn't exist (as if you can't see the battle raging around you), we might somehow shield James from their effects. It wasn't enough for me to just wish to be someone else; I had to do something about it. Even though we believe we're free, we're still tethered to our past.

Rachel was the wrong woman for James. There's no way he could have replicated my errors more precisely. He understood that I was against it. Then, he was earning money and she was a lovely girl at the time. He was pulled to the debris like a moth to a flame, even if she was insane as well. He would have been like way even if we had built him like this. Just when he thought he had everything figured out, he was shattered. If a dominant lobster loses heavily in a battle, its brain dissolves because it lacks the sophistication to handle the change from king of the heap to court jester without full disintegration and regrowth. It develops a new brain in a subordinate. Humans, I believe, are one and the same. You don't have to run away from risky things. Maybe they're just that way because you're fleeing.

Even though it's too late for me to tell him now, I should have told James something very simple when I saw how miserable he was becoming from all the guilt and knew I had a responsibility to spare him from it. It was so obvious it felt pointless to say it. I should have said, 'Stand up straight, son, push your shoulders back. Treat yourself like someone you're responsible for helping. Make friends (and marry too) with people who want the best for you.' – In hindsight, I wish I had given him this discussion sooner rather than later, since I had been so paralyzed by the concept that I had to first get my own home in order before I could begin working on his.

While he's finally talking, swinging his left arm around, as he remembers me bringing him home brown paper bags filled with coconut-dusted, chocolate marshmallow logs from the Chocolate House on Bondi Road on Friday nights on my way home from work on Friday nights, I have to acknowledge that somehow he's successful, too, he's made a pharaoh's-load of money and buildings as large as the pyramids (though it's a bit of a stretch). None of this was given to him by me. From the beginning, I was content with the low-hanging, and now ripe, fruit. So who am I to argue with him?

Mayfield and Tighes Hill are behind us now; the sun is finally breaking through. For now, I take James through Wollongong's seedy west end and then the rest of the city eastwards to the coast, since I know this area better than he does. The doctor he's arranged for us to meet is an old buddy from Sydney Uni. The chocolate marshmallow logs have brought us closer, but there's no time for reminiscing now. We're both still basking in the glory of their sweetness. Our proximity has brought us closer, but not near enough to enable me to talk any more.

In a similar vein to James, I've never been one to let sleeping four-legged companion animals lie, and the thought of his doctor friend and the reason we're driving through this fraudulent city – these filthy, industrial suburbs – where the country town is constantly playing hide-and-seek, brings to mind, with a vividness so much brighter than the morning light outside, the dream that seems to have followed me into waking, though I'm sure it wasn't real. James is following the road along the harbor to Jobbys Beach, where we swing around to where we can already see the pink art-deco entrance to the Wollongong Ocean Baths, and I'm breaking every rule in the book I only just wrote for myself a moment before and telling James about this terrible dream I'd had just moments earlier.

For some reason, it's not terrible when it's described. I tell him it's because I had a dream that I was the one with dementia, not my mother. 'I had a feeling it was mine. Knew it would only get worse from there. I had the idea that I should commit suicide. Then, I drove to the beach, Jobbys Beach, the one we just drove by; I remember you were with me; we went to the sea together, I didn't undress, but when I entered (I only got as far as my knees), it was too cold and it was impossible for me to go in. I tried to stand in the flowing water, but it was too much for me. I was still in the dream, and I pondered why it is that in dreams we are unable to do the most basic tasks. Even if we can't put up our top button on our shirts to stop things from boiling over on the stove, we can fly out the window and soar over the town or swim to the bottom of the ocean to communicate with the fish for hours at a time. Although I had a plan and just needed to take a few more steps, the water was too cold for me to even consider moving.'

I tell James that I awoke from my slumber in a chilly sweat. All of my worries had been reduced to a single worry: the fear of becoming insane. While James is busy parking the Subaru now, he's still paying attention to the sudden stillness, and he's pondering whatever ideas my dream has placed into his mind as a result. Nothing about it made me afraid of dying or being dead, I reasoned; my greatest concern was the gradual deterioration of my mental faculties. All of this mortality pales in comparison to the terror of losing my memory, of no longer being myself. Then, as I do now, when I watch my lanky and neurotic kid fixate on the road markings with his tongue protruding from his pursed lips, I realized that we weren't supposed to get this old: to the point where we no longer dread death. It's not right. Everyone's pet has a death phobia. When a person reaches old age, he or she is no longer merely another species, yet he or she is no longer genuinely animal.

Regardless of how much we wish it weren't the case, it is what it is, and will continue to be until death brings it to an end. An elderly lady contacted me on the day I placed my mother into a nursing facility in the lizard place over two years ago and she invited me to come along for the ride. She was decked up in a blue linen suit, a flowing flowery scarf, and huge gold-splattered sunglasses, as if she were going on a voyage on the Titanic. She ordered a gin and tonic and expressed excitement that we would soon be sailing away. Her derangement's luscious normality threw me off my game. She was slumped in a wheelchair the size of a huge truck next to her bed when I returned to her room to say, 'I don't know what.' She snarled at me, saying that she no longer cared about me or wanted to see me. As I already said, I accepted her word for it. Even deadly curses may have great force, because there is bitterness in the hearts of those who have been cursed, as well as in those who have been cursed themselves (without craziness, we would have never come up with the concept of gods). There was a deep pool of suffering inside me, both then and today. The identical scenario played out in every room on every level in my head. Dissolving brains in the form of a mosaic. A person's nightmares can no longer be restricted to their sleep. No, my mum did not. Despite this, I had left her with them.

I'd been abandoning her to them for over a year. However, I had returned. At the very least, I could have saved her from the remainder of what she'd been forced to go through, even if it was too late.

At the moment, there is no one using the Wollongong Ocean Baths. When we exit the vehicle, it's nipping at our toes. We both put our hands in our pockets and stomp our feet a few times. It takes me a while to straighten out after a long journey. As I breathe, I can see both my own and James's. At this point, I can't keep up with his pace of pulling his things out of the boot and exhaling. People dressed in tracksuits, beanies, and gloves are strolling swiftly towards Jobby's on the walkway. They seem to be bracing themselves against the wind, their expressions grim. However, the early air is crystal clear, overcast, chilly, and quiet. It's the ideal time of day to commit suicide. Your mother, if you'd choose.

So I say, 'Let's do this,' and make my way over to the bathrooms.

Nothing comes out of James's mouth. While I don't know what he's thinking about, he quietly stands one step ahead of me and seems to have reserved the right to leave at any moment.

An enormous wedding cake in Art Deco design, the pavilion has long been a favorite of mine. As we enter the dressing room, we immediately undress, snorting loudly to emphasize how chilly it is and how foolish our decision is. Like horses, we're both afraid of everything. Slapping him on the back and shoulders brings the blood to the surface of the skin, which fades fast. I do the same for him. I'm inconsolable right now, and I'm sobbing. My guess is that it is the slapping that re-ignites the memories. Momentarily, I can't hold on to a clear picture. There were so many things I loved about him, from his dimples to the black pimple on top of his eyebrow to the itchy left ear when he was scared to the way he sang after we'd put him to bed without realizing we were listening to him and the way his voice cracked upon calling for us after a nightmare. Right now, he's staring at me. The cold, I explain to him. He doesn't express what he's thinking. We hastily embrace each other in our speedos, embarrassed by the sight of so much skin, and then sprint outdoors, shouting like crazy people. 'A barnacle is the last one in!' As the waves pound against the rock, I yell, my words unaffected by the twenty years that have gone since their previous utterance.

Compared to other ocean pools I've swum in, this one seems to have grown organically from the rock platform, albeit it's a little more luxurious than the convict bathing hole dug in near the beach's southern end. This ecstasy that comes when the cold grabs my breath and everything that is exposed is drawn back into my body while I'm in the water. Shocked clarity and glacial isolation from the outside world are the result of my increasing wooliness. I swim the first lap like a shark, gasping for air and going faster than I can. In the corner of my eye, I catch James's gaze. He's a good distance away from me, closer to the water. Incredibly, he's an excellent swimmer. His powerful stroke maintains his head above the water, like he's hauling himself out of an underwater hole. There's no indication from him that I'm following him. Observing the water, I'm struck by the simplicity of its patterns, which repeat themselves wave after wave. Even the simplest things aren't easy to grasp without a full grasp of the subject matter. Because rationality is in limited supply when confronted with the vastness of the universe. That's why we're rushing to the perimeters. The view over the rock to Wollongong Beach and the beginnings of the city can be seen when I lay my chin on the edge of the pool. I could float about here all day if it weren't so freezing.

This is the end of the line for James. This morning, he came in because he knows I used to bring his Nanna here, and I'm guessing he's just come in to be pampered by me because he's picked up something vulnerable in me. My heart thrills at the sight of an insect's love sense. Now, Surfers Paradise has the feel of being a world away. As though the difficulty was the distance. It takes me two more laps to catch up to him; instead, I concentrate on my body alignment and displace as little water as possible while crawling over a bed of sharp blades. However, there is no such getaway in my head. For the time being, this is enough to keep me from succumbing to the depths. Enough to savor the tingling sensation on my skin and the euphoria I get when I emerge from the water.

James has already bathed and is frantically stroking himself with his towel as I enter the changing room. I'd want to say a hundred things, but now isn't the right moment. I just take a brief shower. It's colder than the water in my swimming pool, and it freezes my brain's plumbing every night. He's all conspiratorial when I return, pointing at the wall behind me. A guy swaddled in *filthy blankets rests his head on a large canvas duffel bag on the long wooden bench. When I came in to change, he was still sleeping, so I know he was here earlier. Is it possible that we didn't see him? Slender cheekbones protrude out of his face awkwardly, his skull has an odd shape, and his eyebrows are pointed like crescent moons. When I walked in on my father in the toilet and smelled something neither good nor nasty, it brought up memories of that moment. I can't bear the closeness any longer, and I'm forced to look away. For a split second, I wonder whether James's scent is the same in me as it is in him. Because he's tying his laces, he's not looking directly at me. He, like me, is just interested in escaping at this point before the guy awakens. In order to avoid waking him up, we kept our mouths shut before the lie (which neither of us wants to admit).*

Out there, the sky remains cloudy. There's a sign that says, 'Pavilion Entrance Kiosk Blocked Up for the Winter.' Rather of driving, we opt to stroll down the beach to the café. I think we make quite the impression on the horde of walkers we pass, both cold and shivering. For so long, we've kept our mouths shut, yet the rattling of our teeth has kept us amused, even if we're unsure how to proceed. The lone illuminated window on the first level of Noah's Hotel catches my eye as we pass the children's pool.

I'm not sure what I see at first, but I have a feeling James has as well. A nude lady is drying her hair with a huge white towel in front of the shuttered glass of the balcony door. She notices us as well and pauses, perhaps contemplating turning away and returning to the bathroom, but instead she straightens, exposing her breasts above the balcony rail, and examines me as if she's just emerged from many depths, winking (I think that's what it is) and lifting the towel once more to her head. Even if it's a show, I think it's a gift, since she seems to know why I'm here, and I'm an elderly guy now, so I can flirt freely. The only person in his life outside his estranged mother should be his mother, not me.

His undershot look returns as I refocus my gaze on the road. We've got a long way to go until we see each other again. Compared to James, I'm always renegotiating the conditions. My trust in the long-term appears to be waning. That's why every time I express my fatherly feelings, they surprise and humiliate him, please him yet raise distrust in him. Is my parenting adequate? No, I don't think so. Is it true that I am madly in love with him? I'm positive I can only respond yes to one of them. For the most part, the troubles he has with me stem from my own lack of self-discipline.

I return my gaze to the glowing window and remark, 'Nice.' It's not the right moment for father and son to show off their softer side. However, James has turned his gaze elsewhere for some time now. It's possible he didn't see her at all. It breaks my heart more than words can express.

We're the first customers to sit down at the café's new location. I feel dizzy when the temperature suddenly rises, but it immediately subsides. However, I am content to remain seated. An off-screen skirmish like a film set battle has left me feeling exhausted. Our journey has taken us to a tiny town where we've gone swimming and are now enjoying a hearty meal. Is there anything more commonplace and unexceptional? It's like a set of stairs heading to nothing, just to vanish as quickly as they appeared.

I haven't been back in over two years, but it used to be a frequent stop on my way back to the lizard place after seeing a movie with my mother and having coffee and cake the Italian way. She was enamored with the scenery. It's impossible not to like this. At first glance, the ocean seems as if it's hanging from my window in a spectacular quicksilver curtain embroidered with little coal ships and cartoon clouds. I can see the pool where we just swam, while James stares out into a grey expanse with nothing to separate the sea from the sky. It's as though we're perched precariously on the precipice of something huge.

It's cozy and toasty inside. Coffee permeates the air. James is hunched over on his chair, as if he can't quite keep up with the size of his person. His knees are pressed against mine as we sit at the table. The fact that he doesn't flinch when I touch him is a positive indication in my book. We take a close look at the offerings on the table. Just far enough away, I can make out the waitress's swooping movements like a bird. This menu is extensive. We haven't talked since the last time we met. Even though we're working in quiet, it seems like we're two artisans in a studio. We've been pushed inside by the weather, but there's no rush to reopen. The day is ours to do as we choose, and all we have to do is hang out with each other. Since I cleaned his small body in the bath and prepared him for bed, and laid with him in the restless dark, until he fell asleep and I fell asleep with him, I've never felt tethered to him as I am now.

I'm never good at making decisions. I'm tempted by practically everything on the menu, and I'm about to tell the waitress which meal I'd like to get, but I won't be able to explain why I've chosen that particular dish over another because I'm at a loss for words. What's the deal with Anne? What are the benefits of working with a screenwriter? Whence came these jackets and pants? When I refuse to let my mother to die, I'm turning her against me. Why am I agreeing to do what has made my life so miserable for the last two years? Who better to involve than my own son? Instead of saying what Cassandra wanted to hear, why not say what she wanted to hear? My nose isn't the only part of my face that I'd want to remove. What's the point of robbing Paul to pay Peter? I wish I could tell myself what to do and force myself to follow through on my plans.

What's on the menu? With honeycomb butter and caramelized bananas, these ricotta hotcakes are delicious. Tomato and fontina atop a toasted baguette. Porridge made with five grains and stewed winter fruit. Sweetcorn fritters topped with bacon, wilted spinach, and an avocado salsa. Bread with coconut and lime jam. Cherry compote on Belgian waffles with vanilla yoghurt and house-made syrups. Toasted Uprising sourdough bread with thyme and taleggio baked mushrooms. Scrambled, poached, baked, and fried eggs are all on the menu at this restaurant. Raspberry-rhubarb coulis over an oatmeal/nut/chia base. Banana pancakes with passionfruit syrup or cream cheese and smoked salmon buckwheat pancakes. Beans prepared at home in Boston. French toast with ham and gruyere. A bread with oatmeal, pear, and raspberry. Goat's curd with sage omelet...

'Would you want to share your opinion?' In what I believe to be a loud voice, I state the obvious.

After swimming, James adds, 'Swimming has made me so hungry,' and then chuckles, realizing what he's going to say, 'I could devour a horse and pursue its rider.'

It couldn't have been written any better by the writer. This entire time, I have no doubt that he's been thinking about what grace was like at my mother's home (her, fuck-you God). I chuckle as though I've just rediscovered what laughing is when I place my knees on my son's. For a split second, he clenches his teeth and trembles with excitement when he hears those words. It's so easy to overlook the fact that he feels the same way about her. When you're half a globe away or on the verge, it's impossible to adore her. At the table with us she appears as a ghostly apparition and it fills us with delight since we have created her together from thin air, as we always do when she is not around. This vivid waking dream is so beautiful to us that we don't even see the darkness lurking in the background.

The waitress, too, appears out of nowhere. On her left wrist, she has a little tattoo. Colorful flowers adorn a wreath. In her early 20s, she has the physique of an athlete who is no longer in training, with flabby muscles and voluptuous spandex. She asks, 'Are you ready to order?' Almost as though the words conjured it, that alloy of kitchen odors now in the air that is like a residue of the menu we've just read, the perfume of words, left behind in our remembrance of their departure, is there. Is an amalgamation of what is present, as well as what is not present.

While I'm not sure what my mind is doing, James orders the omelet with goat's curd and sage and I ask the waitress to surprise me. There are times when I wonder whether I should have taken the cowardly route years ago. As a result, my life couldn't have become any more miserable in the event when at every intersection there is a crossroad. If I'd pursued the route I ultimately decided against, how much worse might things have gotten? Any option is only a figment of our imagination, a way to fool ourselves into believing that we are in charge. It seems as though we are able to negotiate with the world. To the world, I should have told you that you were going to mess with me regardless of what I said. If it had been the case, I would have lost James, Anne, and maybe Cassandra. No one, not even a complete moron like me, would return such tickets. In the end it was only a matter of time until the next chapter was written. Nothing could be undone; nothing could be erased. It doesn't matter if the waitress is astonished by my order, since it won't show. I don't know whether it's just me. All she says is, 'Coffee?' and then she's gone.

Once we've eaten our morning meal, we'll travel to Hamilton, where James has set up a meeting with a medical friend of his. The deal should be done without me, but James feels I have a 'way with people,' a point of contention with practically every individual who's ever come my way, including him. I have told him that. Of all, our mission is the kind of mission that always fails, no matter how well-intentioned everyone is. ...and as King of False Words, I should know that something doesn't have to be difficult to be messed up in an infinite number of different ways. However, Future Me will have to deal with it. Until then, I want to enjoy this seaside breakfast for as long as possible. At the very least, wait for an hour.

James remarks out of the blue, 'I never understood how Nanna lived in those early years in Sydney, before you were born.' When did he start having these thoughts? Before now, he'd never shown open curiosity in such matters. Even so, it is the perfect time to do it. It's something I'm experiencing as well. It's a type of nostalgia for guilt, much like hope.

My response is, 'That's because she never brought up the subject.' Angry feelings are out of the question now. 'She was a self-confident lady. She was humiliated by it.'

'What? No, I don't think so.'

'Then, when I was a child, it was a very different experience for me. Upon the passing of your grandpa, you know, in the richer suburbs in Sydney she worked as a cleaner for years. Not until we stumbled across an elderly couple in Clovelly years later did I learn about her past employment. That was the most desperate I've ever seen her. Your grandpa, on the other hand, was a night shift train cleaner and a day shift laborer. I'm not sure how long ago he slept. Prior to the outbreak of the big war of the 1930s and 1940s, he worked as an electrical engineer in Russia. All I do know about him is what I just said. You know that your Nanna won't talk about him. In the course of the big war of the 1930s and 1940s, I have no clue what he was doing in Italy. All I can think about is running away. He didn't speak any Italian, and she didn't speak any Russian. The whole situation is a puzzle. According to what I've gathered, they began studying English while on board the ship.'

It had been a long time since I had contemplated these issues. However, James's thoughts were elsewhere. My family and I had never discussed my father's suicide before. Of course, James had never met him; he was only his father's father; his Nanna's spouse. He existed only as a byproduct of that relationship. My opinion wasn't swayed by it. Why would he do this? Without sifting through the past for extras, he had everything he needed in his own existence. In other words, without offering him my own. Besides my DNA and my flaws, what more could he possibly require from me? We'd never talked about my father, either. The moment had not come for them to renounce their faith.

'How did she end up as a floral designer?' I was dragged back to the table by James's persistence.

'I believe it's luck.' She found a work at a business in Bellevue Hill after a recommendation from a client she cleaned for. She has a soft spot for flowers. She taught you all you know about running a company.' Now, James had a smile on his face. Inheritance brings so much joy. You can see he had no interest in what I had to offer him. After a few years, she was able to purchase a home in Double Bay. In fact, she wasn't the first newly arrived Australian to take this route.'

With James's omelet and my long black on the table and what she tells me is the special of the day, a trio of really cool crumpets stuffed with rose and orange blossom ricotta, as well as fruit and nuts with a honey dribble. She's hoping I like them, and she's all grins as she waits to find out. I'd like to invite her to sit down (the café is still virtually empty) and introduce her to my affluent son (who, it appears, just has eyes for his omelet) and allow them to have some alone time. On the contrary, I return her grin and tell her I believe it's a Cézanne on a platter, then praise her for her decision. All around, everyone gets hugged and kissed.

However, it isn't until my second experiment that I really grasp the gravity of my error. My own statements are the ones that surprise me because they are the ones that no guy should even stumble upon on the most remote shelf in his shed. That's what growing up is for, right? To pick out and discard everything that doesn't promote indirection via filtering, weeding, and winnowing.

'You can tell me the truth, James, because I know how much you mean to me. As a parent, what do you think sets me apart? My question is this: Would you have preferred me in another form?'

Because he's chomping down on his sourdough so intently, it takes him some time to answer. To be honest, if I had the option of either retrieving those words or falling into an infinite abyss, I would choose it. In the end, he tells me that 'to be honest with you, Dad, I haven't been around long enough to know.' It's another day of wonders at the weird (though freeing) disproportion of words. His grin is engaging, as if he had won a gold medal at Little Athletics and gave it to me to admire because what I'm hearing does not match up with what he's really spoken.

'How can it be?' Throwing it back at him, with a smile on my face, I am sure, like a lunatic. I don't know what to expect this time around. What bothers me most is that two times two does not equal four, he said. I didn't give it much thought at the time. Most of my friends' dads were abusive. You remained an enigma. Whenever I saw you, you were usually in a jovial mood. Get over yourself.'

That's where I should have left it. However, he'd given me a window of opportunity. The absence of guilt in a man's life breeds his ruthlessness. That is, if you don't include guilt. This is how quickly sins are transformed into virtues. 'Perhaps my absence was for the best for you. It taught you to not let your first true encounters with failure get you down. If it helps, I didn't intend to be such a bad parent. Both your mother and I were forced to escape before all-out conflict broke out. Let me tell you something: violence is not a mystery. It is simply to commit acts of violence. The wonder here is that there is calm. Like two blind individuals looking for a wall, your mother and I went at it like that.'

As for the rest, I'm sure he understands it all. Even as a child, James was privy to a slew of experiences that he chose not to divulge to me. Anne, on the other hand, had her own tale to share.

Father: 'It's OK; I think we're alright.' He's less chirpy these days. He's had enough with this exchange. Scab-picking is something he avoids, but to me, it's just a red flag that someone is trying to get my attention.

'How did Rachel fare?'

In other words, 'I don't want to discuss it.' Gentle but firm. Anne was proud of her son since he was taught to be a gentleman. After that, he brought down the shutters and closed the store. Even so, I didn't feel bad about giving it a go. We'd never discussed his marriage with each other.

The café was starting to fill up and there was a buzz of conversation. Also, the agitated state of mind that is brought on by battling a cold. Suits, scarves, jackets, and caps were in plenty. I had no idea Saturday was a working day. In the midst of a stampede. In the meanwhile, I'll focus on the food in front of me. Allow James time to speak. It's up to you whether or not you want to. However, despite the fact that they are no longer warm, the crumpets have a delicate honeycomb structure to them that I like, and the perfumed ricotta and rhubarb are not as sugary as I imagined. I savor each bite while sipping on a mug of lukewarm coffee. The waitress returns and asks James if everything is good, if we want anything more, and so on. As she goes away, James gets another coffee and fixes his gaze on her. As a positive indicator, this is fantastic news.

He has a hard time remembering where he placed his phone when it calls. The tune from Austin Powers is used as the ringtone. However, I allow myself to be affected by it. I'm looking forwards to finding out. to decipher his nonverbal cues, for example, the organized crime syndicate from that huge Eurasian country where they had the big revolution in the early 20th century or a lady he prefers not to discuss with his father, even though such conversation would make his father ecstatic? What if it's an old acquaintance? Inquiring minds want to know: On every level, I'm dissatisfied. Obviously it's his mother, whose body language is as unafraid as a newborn's.

'Hello, Mom,' he says cheerfully. 'How are you?'

It's as if I'm watching a tennis match with a mime, since I understand everything Anne says without having to pay attention to a single word she says. A volley of questions from James about what we're actually up to in Wollongong later, it becomes evident that she is calling because she wants to speak with me. Has he pre-arranged this? Mime is clearly not my strong suit, and James passes me the phone. Obviously, my abilities are not quite as advanced as his are.

Since we used to speak so much as children (to paraphrase Clausewitz, discourse was the continuation of sex by other ways), I'm still surprised by how tough it is today. My mind has been transformed into a black hole from which not even the tiniest whisper can escape, as if language had suddenly become a tool only for the purpose of concentrating my self-consciousness. Anne, on the other hand, arouses in me a deep sense of humiliation that no amount of apologizing would ever be able to remove. With it as a starting point, there's only one direction to go: down. However, I'm curious to hear her thoughts now that I have James's phone in my hand and he's looking at me eagerly. In James's last week, she seemed to be a bit out of it. A razor blade I'd married was difficult to reconcile. The sight of her in such a state of decline tore at me, even though a little bluntness could have helped my cause.

'If you could hear me out there, I'd want to say hello.'

She asks, 'John?' as if she's on the other side of the dark, peeking in. 'Is that you, John?'

'Yes.'

'Is James still there?'

'I am concerned about him, and he is, too.'

'Me, too,' she said.

'I want to know why he is with you again.'

There is absolutely no need for me to open that bag of worms with her. Under any condition, the fact that he's here to assist me in the murder of my mother is not going to reassure me. Her tears stop when I tell her 'He's listening,' and I wink at James to let him know everything is OK.

'No worries, I'm sorry. Later, when you're on your own, give me a call.'

'What's that?' I say this because she's been seeing him for a few weeks now, and a mother's instinct can sometimes be a second sight, even if she's a little crazy. Like gazing at the world through the wrong end of a telescope, on other occasions

In his presence, I'm unable to speak. Is this the beginning of something annoying?

'Why did you call me at this time?' I inquired.

'I didn't, I phoned James.' Her voice is loud and tremulous, cracking slightly, yet it is also ferocious and threatening.

She comes back into my life at the most inconvenient times, reminding me that progress in anger and annoyance control is only a mirage, and that only when she's completely out of sight (and hearing) can she genuinely be out of mind. Her huge green eyes, slim nose, and hair piled on top of her head like an overflow of personality, too big for her body, made this lady, the mother of my kid, a beautiful woman even today, despite the difficulties she caused me (and I for her).

Whenever she was escorting me to the dry cleaners after court, she was affectionate and touchy-feely, as if her confidence in her ability to win had freed her feelings for me. Because she was fond of me, once. She was a strong lady, but she was also weighed down by her responsibilities. Straight out of the gate. Getting out of bed to cook breakfast had become too much for her after all, if what James had told me was accurate (and why would he lie). I was tempted to feel sorry for her, but I couldn't help it. That was until I recalled the holes in her stockings and blazer, as well as her breathless appearances in the courtroom. When it came to defrauding me, Machiavelli had nothing to offer her. A Pandora's box is a person's heart unless you're a saint, and if so, where do you locate one? Not in my case, for sure. Was it my fault that she sent me to the dry cleaners? Against the terrible irrationalities of life (Auschwitz, Siberia, Cambodia and Srebrenica, to name just the iceberg's tip), our only hope lies in pitting ourselves against them an equally illogical dedication to the possibility of good. Despite the fact that I'm rooting for the less favored four-legged companion animal, that is I mean, the four-legged companion animal that could be said to be under, I'm not the only one! Even if evil never really leaves us, at least we may now conceive of a better alternative and who wouldn't climb into a lifeboat if one were available on a sinking ship?

'OK, I'll put him back on,' I said.

'I think so, too. What are your thoughts about him?'

'In the best possible way. His heart is broken by the loss of your presence in his life.'

'That's natural,' she said.

'Nothing is natural for him,' says the man.

'He misses you with all his heart.'

'What are you expecting me to say?' I asked.

'His Christmas preparations are already in motion.' If you'd forgotten, this is his first Christmas without Rachel. His expectations for your presence are high.'

'It was your idea, therefore I said no to it.'

'Is it because you're already too famous to act like an average parent one day?' Only a matter of time until I'll be forced to sell my soul to the mighty devil once again. 'I told him you were coming,' she said.

'Me? There's no way. This is what he would have heard if it had not been for you.'

'If, before I was born, you had given me the story of my life and asked me to live it, would you not have accepted my invitation?' he asks.

I hand James his phone and play dumb for a moment, hoping that whatever is going through his head fizzes out like water on a hotplate and disappears. And then the line goes dead. I say, 'I love you too, dear, speak to you soon,' in the dying tone for poor James, who's been sitting and watching the whole thing.

This comes as a surprise to me.

And he stares at me as if I'm the guy who fell on the ground, got up and went to the restroom. It's possible that things might have been worse.

The cafe is a hive of activity right now, a kaleidoscope of voices, as the day begins. She returns to the table with James's second cup of coffee, which makes her feel a little saddened by the lack of company on his side, reminding him he's still an attractive young man. Once our dishes and cups have been cleared away, she pauses and surveys the scene. The young guy in question has yet to be found. She tries to say something to me, then decides against it and heads back to the kitchen behind the counter.

'I'm hoarding my good fortune.'

A young, fashionable couple sits at a low table under the counter to enjoy their meal. They have that late-night rather than early-morning face, which suggests they've been up for a long time. What a week! Observing the waitress as she approaches, the guy seems to be thinking about something. She almost touches his ear with her hip as they grip.

'You can't rescue bad luck.' Even though I don't intend to, their sounds have caught my attention.

'I'll do that,' I said.

The hip that is so near to his ear could be a good place to start.

Despite the girl's desperate attempt to respond, her voice is drowned out by another lot closer to me, but behind, so I can't see its source. Whatever he is, he's having a great run of it thus far. There is no need to turn around and look at him; his speech suffices.

'Everyone is wondering, "Why bother with a universe at all?" Howeevr, "Why bother with anything?" is a better question. Even if it's obvious, what would nothing be if there was no nothing? When there was nothing, how did anything come into being?' In his inflection, he asks, 'What does the word, exist, mean? Where did you get that? What have you gotten out of it? Who is responsible for this? It makes logic to cease to exist. That's not a problem for us. It's not only a matter of 'coming into being' [the university town accent], such a question isn't designed into the human brain. No one knows what the term 'nothing' really means. Everything but nothing happens to us as soon as we're born.'

His words make me think about my mother and what will be there tomorrow in her place, for some strange reason. My mind refuses to accept the concept. Because I'm convinced she'll always be a part of me. But what does she care about that? In the lizard place, I had been staying with her for the weekend, and when I awoke to go to the bathroom, the light in her room was on but she was nowhere to be seen; the panic rushed me like a wild four-legged companion animal, and I raced out into the street and I screamed, 'It's her! She's gone!' She was taken back to her house by police. When I returned, they were already there. She'd made it all the way to Nelson Bay in her nightgown and no shoes. Her feet had been slashed and bled. Once the bleeding had stopped, I treated and wrapped her wounds as she reclined in the shower chair. In my mind, that was the worst thing I had ever seen—worse even than losing James or wandering the streets in hope-fueled panic—but it wasn't the worst because at least she was able to see the reflection of herself in her wardrobe mirror, whereas all that will remain of her in me tomorrow, she won't even be able to see.

When a woman tells a younger version of herself, 'I never told you this, but I made a bargain with your father and promised him I'd help him battle it to the end,' she's referring to her cosmetic surgery. At a little table near the entrance, their hair is blown by the wind, and they pat it back into place in unison whenever someone enters. If the confession that the elderly lady is about to make makes it to the stage where people may laugh, it will be a great vaudeville performance. Despite her mother's best efforts, her daughter seemed to prefer listening to anything other than the words that are going to be said to her. That's why her mother's telling her right now, isn't it? 'It's better not to make any promises. You didn't notice how sad I was when I realized he was dying. Because I couldn't control myself, I ended up making this mistake. My response to him was, 'It's okay for you; you'll soon be out of it.' Because of this, I'm the one who is being left out. For a split second, she stares at me as if I'm the one at fault. I can't see her daughter's face, but I know what she's thinking. After her mother began talking, she would have stopped her immediately if it was anything else. I'm not sure how nasty that would have been. 'I didn't know whether I should feel sorry for you or envious of your father's death.' The truth is, I don't know.

On a chilly Saturday morning at a packed Wollongong Cafe, you can learn a lot. Even though it has started to rain in the outside world, the rain is still just a grayer grey and not heavy enough to be heard. The coal ship I had previously saw on the horizon has vanished. His parents' nasty phone conversation is nothing more than an act in another play when James comes to the table and sits down. His cup of coffee is raised as if it is part of this new present without a history, too. I can't help but be impressed by his capacity for obscurity in order to start again from scratch. Instead of telling him about the strange appropriation that makes every coincidence seem dramatic and noncoincidental, I try to think of anything else to say to him now that he's back. We could need a little fatherly advice to help us get moving.

If you have to ask, how is the bathroom?

In fact, we have been regulars since James was a youngster (along with the thousand and one other divorced dad) — the first to make a visit reporting back and commenting on whether or not it was worth a visit. We've been connoisseurs since then. We've had to alter our lexicon to reflect these unsuspected delights, such as sloping black granite and subdued light, or gardenia blossoms floating in porcelain bowls as though nothing would satisfy you more about the dish than its departure.

James's always had a smile on his face when he's happy. This is one of the many qualities about him that I like. I can tell he's been thinking about it the whole time he's been sitting in there, waiting for me to bring it up. That is, if I'm still the same parent and he's still the same kid. I'm not sure why this subject is constantly raised in relation to sons (not having much experience as a son myself), but it appears to be the cornerstone of the discussion. Surely, if anything, the query should be directed in the other direction?

'This is modern,' he says with a smile, Central European country that was unified in the 19th century and was famously geopolitically aggressive in the 20th century-engineered, stainless-steel, waterless urinal, mounted on the wall, soft curves, cream porcelain, in-wash and drying functions with temperature and positioning adjustment (seat warm to the touch), user detection and night light, water supply pressure 500kPa, 4.5-litre full flush, 3-litre half flush, soft-close, quick release seat, state-of-the-art; rectangular in shape

'So, I've had it. A few more minutes of this, and I'll be there all day.'

Towels aren't necessary here. At this point, he's giggling softly, like a bruise that's just come to the surface. Anyone who heard that would say, 'Wow, now we have a father and son!' For a little period, we are the Platonic Ideal: The Real Deal.

'Do you remember that Broken Hill pisser,' he asks, referring to 'the one where someone speared a beach umbrella through a hole in the cistern so that you could pee in the shade and you hung your hat with fishing line from one of its ribs and took your shoes off and left them facing in, so that from outside – it was just a knee-to-shoulder wall, remember? – it looked like the invisible man was standing there.' He's on his ten-year-old roll now.

The fact that I had no recollection of it didn't really matter. I still remember how much fun it was when he did it. It was, at least, for a little time. For a brief period, there was a hint of thicker veins. In such times, there was a belief that time could be abolished since the whole bloated past was entwined in them. Hence, indefinitely. And who knows, maybe it was for all time. I don't know how to put that into words. In the end we ended up arguing over the bill since the coffee was gone and James was reaching into his jacket pocket. As wealthy as Croesus, he seemed to be my own son, yet I knew nothing about him.

'I need to use that 3-liter half-flush,' I say and rise, but he doesn't believe me. It's a ploy I've used time and time again to confuse him. Grabs me by the hand and keeps me there as he knows where I'm going. To be honest, I'm beginning to wonder whether I could stand here for the rest of time if he wouldn't let go. I feel as if I'm being held by a child's hand. I'm confused as to where in my family line there are males of such heft. However, I've learned more in the last week, at the very least, on my mother's side of the family. A smile spreads over his face as his hands remain tightly clasped around her waist. And I'm squirming about like a fish while softly tugging. My peripheral vision catches a glimpse of the waitress. Plates, bowls, and glasses are all balanced on her wrist and hand.

I tell James, 'Behave yourself.'

'No, it wasn't the final shower that brought me down.'

'That doesn't seem to be the case, at least for Freddie, who is visually impaired.'

So, we're back to playing his favorite childhood game of exchanging cliches and oxymorons.

'What if I don't have enough sandwiches for a picnic?'

'Does a fat four-legged companion animal fart?'

The question, 'Does a digger like to drink?'

'Yes, he is a Catholic. As a matter of fact, this is a well-known fact.' It was a 'timeless' moment, 'Is that your first impression, too?'

'I never make generalizations.'

'In the absence of a willful error,' he said.

'No, I don't think so.'

'Do you think that's a reasonable estimate?'

When he lets go of my hand, I break myself free and flee. He tries to sneak up behind me, but he realizes he's too late and retreats. I turn to face him from behind the bar and mutter the words 'puckered butthole' in his ear. Instead of moaning about the pain, he just wipes it away and goes on to battle another day. After all, we still have lunch to deal with. Then there's the little issue of what happens afterwards. Everything we've done up to this point (the airport, the drive, the swim, the café) has been a delay (in the sense civilization itself is a postponement) of what must happen next. That's when it hits me as the girl takes my card and asks if I like it. Death is the only thing that follows after.

Even if the rain isn't torrential, the boardwalk is a no-go zone. When we get back to the vehicle, we're drenched to the bone, so we use our beach towels to dry off. We don't talk since we don't want to disturb the tense atmosphere. The last time we were this close, I had to go through a full library of file cards to figure out where they were. That was the weekend before I packed up my things and headed out of Bronte, leaving him with his mum. On the weekend that I was supposed to inform him about this, I ended up doing it instead. I believe he still holds himself responsible in some unsaid sense.

What happened to your mother was all my responsibility, and I continue to think about it like a whale that has to emerge. In the event a whale had a foot and was able to place it in its mouth.

We're back on the road, and James is still behind the wheel. In the hopes of drying ourselves off before we reach Hamilton, we've set the air conditioner to its hottest setting. James can't see well from the front or rear of the car since the windows have started to fog up. Both of us are shaking violently. In spite of my best efforts, my final words are still hanging in the air. I've compelled him to respond in kind.

'Why go over it again?' he asks, wiping the side glass with his arm. Everything that can grow will, since this place is like a glasshouse.

'My Nanna informed me that marrying your mother was a mistake, and divorcing her was much worse. Even if she may have made the pill more palatable – even though it was never her way, she never had any true love when it came to me, it was only you that demonstrated she still has some type of heart pounding there - she was correct. She was able to see my mistakes in a more objective manner than I could have ever imagined.'

I laugh in an attempt to put a smile on the face of the person I'm with. However, James is no longer in the mood for lightness.

He adds, 'You're like a broken record at times. You should have done something sooner rather than later if it bothered you as much as it did.'

Of course, he's right: it's far simpler to whine after the fact than it is to act when the outcome is still uncertain. Certainly, but isn't it also appropriate to express one's sorrow? In the words of James, 'This is not about me.'

'Oh, no!' moaned the man. 'Dad, I don't need to feel sorry for you. If you and Mom were the happiest couple in the history of human marriage, then what happened to Rachel and me would have occurred. What better way to learn than through observing what is going on around you?'

He was annoyed by the discourse. For some reason, it seemed like I was always on the lookout for a little crack in the castle walls because it's as if, ever since his divorce, my entire goal has been to get access.

'It may come as a shock to you, Dad, but the world isn't only about you and your wife.'

As quietly as he could muster, he continued to try. A fight was not on his agenda. For my part, I had no such luck.

'To have children was out of the question.'

'All right, I've had enough. I'm on my way to Wayne's operation now, as per your instructions, and I'll see what I can do. Both for your sake and because I believe it to be correct. It has nothing to do with what you just stated if I'm unhappy. I just wish we'd been able to assist Nanna sooner.'

He was saying that he wished you had realized it was the proper thing to do two years ago. So what if I tell him I agree with him? Having to leave his mother made me wish I hadn't had to do so. Wishing that two was not four would have been better for me. Just like he said before, some individuals take action, while others only desire. He's mistaken, though, if he believes that just the well-wishers are bereaved. Guilt doesn't make a difference in my opinion. There's no need to lecture at this point in time, though. Having a bigger gun would just serve to shoot myself in the foot, so what's the point? My mum is to blame for getting everything started. The last time I spoke to her, I was on the edge of my seat. The phrase 'you learn from what you see' wasn't a joke when I told James it. Where was there any hope for me? That said, he's correct: what you perceive is determined by your point of view.

Seeing requires concentration, and concentration necessitates prioritizing one thing above all others. But that's just the beginning. Things that are not in front of your eyes are indistinguishable from what might or should have been since you can see them all the time. What's the point of all this constant foresight and retrospection? Is it worth it to endure a life of pain and discomfort? In other words, you strive for what isn't when you compare what is with what may be (and how do you get there), because no one ever lives in reality while they are enslaved by hope or guilt. It is just you who is to blame if that is your goal, but James and I aren't saying anything of the kind. Not at this time. Not right now.

Once again, we've arrived at our destination on the shores of the harbor, but I'm unable to see anything. The rain has become worse, and the fog is making things worse. With my handkerchief in hand, I've started cleaning a little porthole in the windshield in front of James. It's a physical act that takes me out of my head and into the world. I can't help but giggle at the ridiculousness of the situation. Hope James has the same sentiments! I can see the sweat rising from our breeches now that the vehicle has become such a sauna. Since James has never been one for jeans (apart from those odd gardening outfits I recently saw him in - James gardens), and since I'm getting on in years, I can no longer dress how I believe he should (i.e. young).

One benefit of not being able to see where we're going is that I can still follow along. Since my mother moved to the lizard place about 30 years ago, I've travelled this road so many times that I can navigate it with my eyes closed (It seems that there are advantages to not seeing as well). The only time James and I speak is when I give him instructions that he must follow far in advance of their implementation. To him, it's obvious that I can't resist the temptation. Unfortunately, I'm not much of a travel companion. Also, I'm all twisted up. Even more than normal today, but not as if it's a shock to him. I've come to believe that he knows me better than I do. The answer is, of course, yes. Only if he could get inside my skull and take control of the situation would I be able to go on (when it comes to his mother, I'm not so sure.)

The road is congested (we were at the café for a long time; the dashboard clock says it's almost eleven o'clock now). Even though the rain is slowing things down, we're not in a rush. We're barely five minutes away from James's doctor friend's appointment, which is scheduled for

11:15. At the Civic Gates, we cross the railway tracks onto Hunter Street, then turn left into Tudor Street, through a car yard and a service station, and finally turn left into Lawson to get to where we're going.

A big red-brick Federation home with two paperbarks and a gigantic Ficus of some kind dominates the block where the office is placed. Physician and Geriatrician (according to the gate sign), Dr. Danny Pembleton provides comprehensive care for people later in life, specializing in cancer (ovarian, breast, prostate), dementia (including Alzheimer's disease), diabetes (including type 2 diabetes), epilepsy (including Parkinson's disease), heart disease (including hypertension), osteoporosis, and sleep disorders. Pulling the vehicle against the kerb, James shuts off the engine and walks away from it. It's deafening to hear nothing. My window is at half-mast and I can see two ragged magpies in the paperbarks above me. As we approach the wide covered verandah, we find Dr. Wilson waving at the vehicle as if he's been awaiting us (the sign also indicates he doesn't practice medicine on Saturdays — at least not life-preserving medication). It's understandable that he doesn't want to get his toes wet. Even though the rain has subsided, it continues to fall.

In spite of James's initial desire to do this with me (because of my 'way with people,' as he called it), he's changed his mind since breakfast and now prefers to go in alone. That's OK with me. If I was nervous before, I'm paralyzed by the notion of what lies ahead. When the curtains haven't yet been opened in one of the gloomy rooms, there are medications that Dr. Wayne Wilson (geriatrician and notable euthanasia supporter) plans to retrieve from a cupboard? Refrigerator? selling my mother's life-ending medications to my son in an ethical and humanitarian manner. You're welcome, I tell James in my brain. That's when it dawned on me why I was asking him. Why? Because I know it can't be me. I've known that since I was a child. For all my other crimes, I am cowardly while my kid is a greater guy than me, but can I truly ask him to provide the deadly amount in only a few hours?

I don't see any indication on his face that he was expecting me to dispute. He has never before been so gloomy, focused, and in command. Possibly, it's his conciliatory demeanor. A look at his demeanor when confronted by sharks could be to blame for this. To be clear, I didn't say he was a superior guy to me in jest, but up until this point, I don't think I've ever felt that he could survive the world without my support. He should know that if the tables were turned, I would be unable to function on a single moment's worth of food. After tonight, he'll be the only one I have to fall back on. I finally respond to him, 'You're correct,' even though there's no need for a response at this point. In my opinion, I'm the wrong person to be in there, asking the wrong questions.' After a short grin to let me know he understands I'm not kidding, he hurriedly exits the vehicle and makes his way up the walk to the verandah. Dr. Wilson gives him a hearty handshake and a chuckle before turning to face the other way to allow him pass. His nose finishes in a white bulb, which gives me a different sense of him in this quick profile. It's unusually white, and I wonder whether he's ever been out onto the porch to bask in the sunlight. Gypsum comes to mind. Nonetheless, the opening and shutting of an aperture is all that is necessary. It's as though James just walked in the door and the good doctor's wide back whisked him away. At my wit's end, with no idea how long the transaction might last (they were friends in their student days and hadn't seen each other in some time so a cup of tea might be in order) and knowing only that I couldn't be alone now even for an instant, I open the glove box and pull out the brochure I'd intended to read while waiting for James at the airport but had forgotten to bring with me and left in my car. The last time I saw Cassandra, she handed it to me. I'm not sure what she was thinking. Would you believe that before I brought my mother into the house, I hadn't already read all I could get my hands on? It would be great if I could point out the irony to her. That's what this leaflet was truly for: reassuring me that there was hope.

She couldn't function without it. So now I was a guy actively seeking the end of hope, right? When it comes to some questions, it's best not to ask at all. That's not really a problem for me.

'What Is Dementia? Alzheimer's, Parkinson's, and other neurological disorders are included under the umbrella category of dementia. Is something that has been seen in humans for centuries. Before the Industrial Revolution, dementia was a relatively uncommon phenomenon since fewer people survived to old age. Alzheimer's disease, as we know it now, was not coined until the middle of the 1970s. As we've learned, dementia isn't an inevitable feature of ageing. It is estimated that over a hundred different illnesses are capable of resulting in dementia. Alzheimer's disease, vascular dementia, and dementia with Lewy bodies are the most prevalent causes. Alzheimer's illness is one example of this. As many as 70 percent of dementia sufferers are affected with Alzheimer's disease.

Dr. Alois Alzheimer was the first to notice it in 1907. Auguste Deter, a middle-aged dementia sufferer, was the subject of a case study by Dr. Alzheimer. People under 65 were deemed to be at risk for Alzheimer's disease over the following 60 years. It wasn't until the 1970s that Dr. Katzman boldly proclaimed (at the time) that is oldening of the mind and brain' and Alzheimer's disease were the same disorder and that neither was a natural part of ageing. It is possible for Alzheimer's disease to be sporadic or inherited. The most prevalent type of Alzheimer's disease, sporadic Alzheimer's disease, affects humans at any age, but is most frequent after the age of 65.

A mutation in one of multiple genes causes familial Alzheimer's disease, which is very uncommon. Alzheimer's disease often strikes people in their 40s or 50s who have altered genes. The human brain in good health. A network of arteries, veins, and capillaries provide the brain with blood and oxygen. The brain is isolated from the rest of the circulation by this highly regulated vascular system. Blood–brain barrier protects the brain from infection yet many medications are too big to penetrate barrier, making treatment difficult if a brain infection does occur in the search for Alzheimer's disease treatment drugs, this barrier must be crossed in order to reach the brain. The temporal lobes of the brain are located just above and below the ear canals and temples. Speech and working memory are both handled by these areas, as well as 'higher' emotions like empathy and remorse. The limbic system and other basic brain areas may be found underneath the forebrain. In all animals, the limbic system handles our wants and a wide range of emotions. This part of the limbic system includes the hippocampus, where new memories are formed. When we ride a bike, we don't have to think about what we're doing since our cerebellum has stored our muscle memory. The most rudimentary parts of the brain are located in the midbrain and the brainstem.

Body activities such as heart rate and digestion are controlled by the sympathetic nervous system (SNS). The connections between brain cells known as synapses mediate all of these intricate processes. 5000–10,000 synapses link each of the 100 billion brain cells in an adult human brain. Every second we are alive, we create a million new connections in our brains. This means that no two minds are exactly same, since our brains are continuously rewiring themselves. Memory, habits, and personalities are formed by reinforcing some patterns of brain activity and erasing others in these shifting connections. Synapses in the brain allow several types of communication between brain cells. Neurotransmitters are the molecules that carry signals across synapses. One brain cell sends a neurotransmitter to another cell through a synapse (connection), which links the neurotransmitter to a receptor. The message may then be passed on to other brain cells by the receiving cell sending out another rush of neurotransmitters.

Alzheimer's disease-afflicted brain tissue. Alzheimer's patient Mrs. Deter died in the 1900s, and Dr. Alzheimer studied her brain. He discovered a decrease in the size of the cortex, the outer layer of the brain where functions like as memory, language, and judgement are located. When a person's brain seems to shrink, it is because brain cells have died. Mrs. Deter's brain was likewise determined to have two forms of deposits by Dr Alzheimer.

Neurofibrillary tangles (also known as 'plaques' or 'tangles') were detected in the brains of patients with Alzheimer's disease. Synapses between brain cells are hindered by these 'tangles.' Tangles disrupt the flow of nutrients and energy to brain cells, killing them. Magnetic resonance imaging (MRI) may reveal the shrinkage of the brain, which is caused by the death of brain cells (MRI). There is a tendency for the illness to begin at the outermost regions of the brain. Memory loss in the short term is hence one of Alzheimer's disease's initial signs. Long-term memory loss occurs when the illness spreads deeper into the brain. Many other parts of behavior are affected as a result of the disease's impact on the brain's other processes.

There is no known cause for Alzheimer's disease, other from a few people with familial Alzheimer's disease. Alzheimer's disease is a condition in which plaques and tangles grow, as well as other chemical changes that destroy brain cells. Environmental influences, metabolic abnormalities, and immunological processes are just a few of the things being looked at. One thing or a combination of variables may be the cause of a person's inability to concentrate.

Signs and symptoms of Alzheimer's.

Alzheimer's disease's early signs and symptoms might be difficult to detect. As a result, memory loss and difficulties in naming commonplace items are common occurrences.

Persistent and recurrent memory problems, particularly with regard to recent events, are other possible signs.

Routine chores take longer to complete due to a lack of interest in previously enjoyable activities.

Inability to understand queries and directions.

Deterioration of social skills.

Emotional unpredictability are all symptoms of Alzheimer's disease.

What is the progression of Alzheimer's disease like?

Individuals with the condition develop at different rates. During times of stress, weariness, or illness, a person's talents might deteriorate, even if just temporarily. However, the condition does ultimately lead to total reliance and death, generally from another ailment such as pneumonia. Eventually, the disease. Alzheimer's patients may expect to survive anywhere from three to twenty years, with an average of seven to 10 years. As of right now, there is no remedy.

I had reached my goal: a place where there was no hope left in the world. You may stop here. In any case, there's no time - has it really been half an hour? James has returned. As if he's gone through some kind of battle or rite of passage and returned more than man, he's changed in some way (I'd say he's grown up, but what does that mean).

'What happened?' I enquire. The only thing left to do was get a cup of coffee.

'I'm not sure whether including him in this is the best course of action. A door inside of him could be opened, but it couldn't be shut again. But, if that's what these second thoughts are, they've come too late. When I instructed the horse to fly down, he fled. There was an emergency with one of his patients, and he had everything ready for me, so he only needed to coach me through it...' Although he's acting like he's just taken a nitrous oxide cylinder full, his demeanor is otherwise uncharacteristically calm. The fragrance of burning wood fills the air. Rain has ceased and he seems to be taking his time returning to his vehicle. He holds a featureless cardboard box in his right hand and a little plastic bag in his left. It's as light as air when he holds it. I don't know why I felt death had to be heavy. If you're going too fast, I say, 'Hop in,' to calm you down and bring you back where you were. Despite my best efforts, I'm unable to look away from the bag. A chill must be in the air. He responds, 'I'm OK. Instead of sitting, I'd like to stand. What do you want to know?'

'No, I don't, Of course,' I respond, 'yes.' Driving with the windows down and James standing outside is odd. To see him, I have to stoop and stretch my neck. I unlatch the door and follow him out of the vehicle. Even though the vehicle is soaked, we lean against it and stare across the street at the weather-shuttered homes and the billowing smoke coming from their chimneys. A cloud forms around us when we exhale. I'm waiting for James to say anything. He's going to provide a description of what's within. When I ask him how his grandma will die, he says he'll tell me. Those phrases might need a little help from the sky. Wayne said that it's easy and painless to do. Barbiturates, which slow down the nervous system, are often used as anesthetics in surgery, according to certain sources. Large doses cause the brain to shut down the respiratory system and cease instructing the body to keep functioning, thus breathing stops.' His emphasis on me slows him down a little, and he stops for a time to check in on my mental condition. I'm grateful for the automobile since I doubt I could stand on my own, but I'm hoping the attention in my face is just that: curiosity. I feel like I've just finished a lengthy race in my heart.

'There are a total of a hundred mils of pentobarbital (Nembutal) combined with sugar syrup and twenty percent alcohol. Everything about it works. There have been no reported side effects from his usage of it hundreds of times, and the amount he's given Nanna is precisely what is recommended in the Netherlands for a merciful death.' As soon as she's swallowed the combination, the genie will be back in the bottle, and we'll be ready for business.'

'That's good news,' I respond. 'How about a drink?' If he had answered no, I'm not sure what I would have done. 'Yes, he is a Catholic.' Repetitive refrain. He's got a bird's chirpy voice. It's not as if I know anything. Who am I to tell someone how to deal with adversity? He, and not I, entered the room. It's even better if it's all medication to him. There can be no worse calamity than thinking that what someone else is thinking may be discovered in your own mind. Where I could not, he had gone. Enough for him to return.

'James,' I say, turning to him and grabbing him by the arm closest to my body. 'I appreciate it.' The skin surrounding the barman's face droops like a damp towel, revealing his black eyes, which sparkle. It's too early for lunch, and I'm not in the mood to eat at this time. For myself and James, I pick up a Scotch and a lager, along with a bag of salt and vinegar chips. On Hamilton's main drag, there's a tavern with the name of the Kent. The earthquake wreaked havoc on it. The awning collapsed, killing someone. Rather than walk, we chose to drive. It seemed to be raining once again. We were able to get a spot just in front of the building. It was a good day to go to the park. A tradesman had just pulled away. Before returning to James, I finish my Scotch and place another order at the bar. After the earthquake, the bar underwent renovations. I'd bring my mum over for lunch from time to time. Everyone was looking for new customers. There was something wrong with the previous version. Hamilton is Wollongong's most Italian suburb, although we didn't know it when we first arrived there. 'Hamilton' As a child, my mother enjoyed listening to the elderly men share their stories over a cup of joe. After all, it was a matter of her dialect. I'd ask her to interpret from time to time. She seemed pleased with herself, I imagined.

We are seated at a table overlooking Beaumont Street at a mostly deserted pub. Two young women dressed in black singlets and shorts are seated in front of a giant television. A lot of cleavage is on display. Both of their hair has been bleached, but the darker roots are still apparent. It reminds me of a terrible Guinness pour. They're presumably students, based on their appearance. As you can see on TV, they're getting ready for the race. On the track, there are greyhounds being walked. When it comes to the females, no one seems to notice.

I'm starting to unwind after the second Scotch. There is a sense of relief throughout my body. It seems like a coat hanger has been removed from my shirt in my reflection in the glass. As James drinks, he makes a circle around his mug of beer. To my knowledge, this is the most he's ever been drunk. This is our first time sitting together in a public bar, I realize now. My jaw muscles twitch uncontrollably as a result.

He asks, 'What?'

'Nothing.'

The question was, 'Are you reconsidering?'

That is not the case.

When I look into his eyes, it's as if he has no idea who I am. This is as though you don't believe in my abilities. I'm running low on stored information. I'll have to keep spinning them till they're done. Recollections of James's formative years. Happy memories of James.

'What! Why can't fathers be content?' I think so, too.

You have a unique way of expressing yourself.'

'I don't exhibit it very frequently,' he says.

In silence, he rises from his chair and places it closer to mine. As he does so, he bangs the table, spilling his drink. As the glass self-rights, I watch the bubbles rise to the surface. He leans forwards and pats me on the shoulder. I believe he's going to kiss me on the cheek for a split second. His breath has a distinct odor of booze and nostalgia.

'You know, we don't have to.'

Saying 'I know' is an adequate response. 'I think so, too.'

'Excuse me,' he said.

Vampire: Guilt is Guilt. 'That was something you said once,' I recall.

I assure him, 'It's not that.'

'So what?' I asked.

In the absence of knowledge, I am unable to answer. 'You and Nanna, as well as your mother and I, are responsible for all of this. It could have been so much better...'

'A total fuckwit could only take the world seriously, as the saying goes.' In typical Russian tradition, he shouts the phrases loudly and obnoxiously before downing his drink. I've never been able to tell whether he's being serious or not because of his impeccable poker face. Only by following him with my Scotch can I keep myself from exploding within. I'f you don't recall who I was paraphrasing, I'll remind you now. He was a brilliant naturalist. When I informed him I was leaving Rachel, they were his exact words. Then, can you recall anything else I said? In your attempt to comfort me, don't forget. Only thing is, if you're on the inside of the joke, it's not that hilarious from the inside.'

It's like trying to stop a sneeze for me. As the tears stream down my cheeks, I decide to give up the struggle. James shifts his gaze. Assuming this is the case, I'm afraid of spreading the disease. If anything, it makes things worse. I had no idea he was listening to me. I remember him as always being so self-reliant. I had no idea how firmly he believed in the utter insignificance of everything.

His big body is bent at the waist, the trunk of his arms circling me and sucking out the air as if he thinks I've swallowed poison (which I have). I cough and he does kiss me on the forehead and pat me on the back, and all that's missing is the gently whispered 'Chill out', before he turns back again and disappears with our two glasses lost in the wells of his h, our two glasses in his hand.

In response to my question, he yells back over his shoulder, 'Let's get angry.' They're the most luscious words in the English language.

It's a beautiful day outside, and I gaze out the window. There are a lot of people and a lot of automobiles banked all around me. The vapors float through the air like ghosts, giving everything a carnival-mirror quality. The tears may be to blame. There's a blurring effect. At school, I was reading an essay about Martin Place and the guy who was wailing. Then, I began to wonder whether there was a phrase that could include both happiness and grief.

James and I agreed to record cassettes for each other and send them in the mail, even though I had just relocated from Bronte to Bondi at the time. Almost like a rebirth, they're breathtakingly gorgeous. I listen to them while driving all the time. So many times throughout the years that it's like a second language to me. I can recite them word for word. On my phone, I used to tell him tales before he went to sleep, but on his, he was more talkative. He was ready to take a bath in one of his first recordings, but he had to wait. This has to be delayed for reasons I'm not going to share with you right now. No big deal, but what's the point of wasting the tape? I laughed out loud. His response to my charge that he didn't answer my questions came later, when he was finally in the shower (he must have left the recorder on his vanity). It seemed as if he was repeating what I had said to him: 'I ask you plenty of questions and you don't answer them.' Yet he continued, 'Do you know why

I don't answer them?' he said. 'Because I don't bombard you with inquiries. You ask so many questions that the answers to all of them would take up a whole cassette and then some... I don't respond because I don't have the energy to address each and every one of them. Although I remember to answer a few of them, you ask so many questions that it becomes difficult to keep track of them all.' I died a thousand times over this, even though James wasn't to fault, given that it was just the new order of things, and he knew I knew quite well that my seat at the table (and in his mother's bed!) had been replaced. It was a gift from Colin, he told him (he was getting into his pajamas now). 'The toy koala was only as large as both hands could grasp, and it came from a different nation like China or something, but if you observe, there are a lot of toy koalas made in China, or Japan, or anything like that, so why manufacture one if you're from a different country?' he said.

In the meantime, I'm thinking about the fact that I'm wondering whether or not that particular koala was already packing his bags for Surfers, and it's soothing to think of him in his bath, thinking about me and all my infernal questions, while his mother cooks dinner downstairs and Colin the orthopedic surgeon gives him soft toys made in China. By the time he returns with what appears to be a double SC, I'm calmed so powerfully that I'm ready to go. He had a dejected expression.

'So, let's play some games,' I remark in an attempt to indicate that I'm still in the mood for romance.

Opens the bag of chips and stares at me hopefully as he reclines on the stool next to me. 'What are your plans?'

'As you may recall, Nanna, who has no religious beliefs of her own, forced me to memorize a text from the Old Testament during my last year of school at Rose Bay Public School. Mom had me repeat it to her over and over again when I arrived home and she was preparing supper, until I had it memorized. It sounds like a song. It's something I'll never forget.'

He looks at me like I've gone crazy, yet he still indulges me. He asks, 'What was it?' If I say it's a game, it's a game for the time being.

To quote Friedrich Nietzsche: 'Our life is a short one, full of sorrows, and there is no treatment for it when a man gets to his end.' My gaze is fixed on him, but I'm really staring within because I have no clue whether the words I'm about to speak are still there until I utter them. 'Due to the fact that the air in our nostrils is smoke and reason is a spark ignited by the beating of our hearts; because we were created by chance and hereafter we will be as if we had never been. The body will be reduced to cinders and the soul will vanish into thin air if the flame is extinguished. It seems as though the traces of our existence, like the mist pursued by the light, would fade away, and no one will remember our efforts; we will be forgotten like a cloud.'

'That is your game, isn't it?' he says. He seems nervous. While there may have been some uncertainty, his concern is far more serious than it was before.

I give him a wink. 'Yes and no. We may call it a prologue. I'm more interested in what happens next.'

You may count on me to listen attentively. Neither he nor I raise our glasses. 'Salute, sir!' He yells in response. 'From top to bottom,' So, as a group, we down our booze as one. This is the first time I've ever seen him in this state. It's remarkable and requires a lot of work to get there; more than a decade of work lunches. How little we truly know about our children. The concept itself is comforting.

'The time we have together is like the passage of a shadow,' I say, as if my finger was lingering on the last word I'd said. Let us then return to our youth-like enjoyment of the pleasant things that already exist and use of the creation to its full potential. Come on, let's drink all the expensive wine we can get our hands on, or whisky and beer, if we must and don't let a single spring blossom pass us by. Until the rosebuds have faded, let's crown ourselves with them. This is our lot and our part, so let us all join in the celebration and leave tokens of our delight everywhere we go.' This time it's contagious. He already knows what I'm about to advise before I ever say it. I arrive, panting, but I'm overjoyed. 'That Nanna moment!' I exclaim.

'My mother would wash my feet in the washing tub before allowing me to enter the home even though I was wearing shoes and socks, so it was simple for me. In those days, she was as strong as a vice and would massage them so firmly between her hands that they ached. Eventually, when I was old enough, I would have to stand in the doorway and raise them for myself. I was astonished, though, at how she got you to comply. Remember?'

I chuckle and say, 'She still does.'

'I bet she asks the lizard place nurses too,' I thought.

In spite of how ridiculous that sounds, he's laughing as well, and he understands what he's doing. He then adds, 'Your turn.'

In light of the fact that my mother is nearing death, everything seems insignificant. A little bit of fun. That cardboard box in the automobile is no more somber than a circus clown, it would seem. In the cafeteria only an hour earlier, I had contemplated informing James about my sister, and only by a stroke of luck managed to keep myself from spilling the beans that would have tarnished his memory for the rest of time.

'In the event that you're looking for battle, we have it. That's no problem for me,' I reply. When I was younger, I had to categorize the universe into "living" and "sleeping" and I never informed you about this. Everyone and everything that moved was alive, and when it slowed down, it went to sleep. I was able to quickly identify the sleepyheads. For a week, the waste bin was dormant. For a long time, I couldn't tell where one thing ended and another began since everything in the room was always in motion. At the time, I had no clue what was really going on: your Nanna was moving things about the home as I slept. I waited patiently for hours to get a glimpse of the movement. People lived throughout the day, and when they slept, the furniture walked about the home as if it was them. Even I have had the experience of waking up in strange places. In the dining room, the living room, the foyer, and, on one occasion, the laundry room. After a while, I was able to adapt to it. In the end, I gave up attempting to witness the movement for myself, content to believe in furniture as much as I believed in dinosaurs There's no telling where I'll wake up if I go to bed anywhere. But wait, there's a catch...' I take a breather and raise my head to see James leaning in for a closer look. And there, in his eyes, was the youngster he'd once been, rising to the surface to take a sip of the water around him. It occurred to me that I should have told him this tale sooner. 'I remember being six years old and waking up in the middle of the night. I drank too much water before going to sleep since it was so hot. I could hear a lot of sounds coming from down the hall. As I walked down the corridor, I was on my toes. With Dad still in the bed, Mom was pulling it.'

He says, 'You're fabricating.'

'No way,' I said.

'When I heard you were considering cheating, I was shocked.'

'What makes you think I'm making this up?'

'Do you really think I'm telling the truth?'

'Well, what can I say? 'It took place.'

'This will all be OK, but I'll put it all in parenthesis just in case we need to bring in the stewards. You used to bend over and ask me how much methane I believed was being emitted into the atmosphere when someone was bullshitting, don't you remember? Another drink will be on its way.'

'It's not your scream,' I yelled. 'We'll take one for the road.

It's not until I get up that I realize how inebriated I am. My head starts to spin and I have to hang on to the table's edge to keep it from falling over. When James stares at me, it seems as though he has mischief in his eye for all the world to see. The entire thing seems contrived to me. When his father is in this state, he seems to like it. Just as though we should do it all over again tomorrow. In contrast, he appears like he hasn't had a drink since his birth.

I stumble my way to the bar while I try to keep my balance. I don't recall the last time I drank to this extent. I can, but I'd rather avoid it. That's not going to happen right now. Not right now. Remembering my mum in this way seems like she is still alive to me. The lady we're slouching towards isn't, therefore we need to be alive to talk to her because it keeps you alive, it is the worst insult of the disease: it kills you at the same time. She doesn't have to go out for the dead; she needs to go out for the living. And she's having a hard time keeping them apart. Despite the fact that her mother is both dead and living (often in the same sentence). When I tell her how much I miss her, she cries and begs me to go home and get her passport from her nightstand so she may fly back to Italy to apologize to Cassandra. She has requested Cassandra to purchase her ticket and plans to return to Italy the following day. 'You know, she's a terrific opera singer, but she's getting old and needs a little TLC because you were never attracted to her,' she wonders. I'm stumped. I guess I should have been. As far as I was concerned, she was not my grandma. She's my sister, and I tell her that I'm far more interested in her than you are. She assures me she is, too. She wants to visit her as well when she returns to her hometown. She wants to know how I'm doing. In her mind, she's concerned about her living on her own there. As though she's still alive, but somehow hasn't matured into the grownup she could never have been. Like she hadn't been submerged in a marsh for so many years. I feel as though she sees me in her thoughts about her. As though the same time has been reversed and I've failed to mature into the kid I could never have been in my own body. If history were a gambler, it would seem. Need to defecate. Across the bar, there's a restroom that you may use. The first stop is a tiny area filled with slot machines, followed by a lounge with a massive fireplace. It's a pity no one is here to appreciate it.

Empty toilets are also found. The urinal is filled with porous bricks that smell strongly of antiseptic. I wink in the mirror next to the urinal when I see my reflection. My cheeks twitch. As a youngster, I used to do it in an attempt to fool my own reflection. In the moments before realizing what I was about to do, I asked Cassandra the last thing I wanted to know before I hung up and called James, who knew precisely what I was about to say.

'What am I, Mum?' I inquired of her. And she said, 'I know you, you're my father,' without blinking. As if that wasn't enough to make me happy, she also reminded me that I am the father my mother has never met, just as she is her mother and I am my own father's son. As a result, not only is the passage of time muddled, but so are the memories of everyone you've ever met. When I looked at her, I saw a fusion or, more accurately, a conglomeration of every age I've ever had, as if they were all happening at once, collapsing on top of each other with no space in between. I was an adult dressed like an adolescent in my first pair of shoes! 'John, why aren't you in school?' When she glanced up at me, it was always with a question in her eyes. She seems unsure about herself. This is how it seems to me that she woke up and had no idea how she had gotten here. 'Today, would you want to go for a drive with me?'

'My lunch is here for you. Anne isn't feeding you enough, and I don't know why. I don't feel like eating. It's still warm in this area.'

'Mum, you informed me that the food is bad.' Yes, you read it correctly. In the end, who's going to be fed? Her perversity angered me (same mischief in her eye I'd just seen in James's), so I became agitated. Because we had fought, I could stand before her in her final room with all the scars that should have burned and she'd speak to me as a kid talking to a child, as selfish and demanding as she had ever been: 'Where have you been?' 'The reason I'm here is a mystery.' 'You should get a haircut.' 'Your weight is increasing.' 'I'll chop your steak for you if you just hand me the knife.' 'What's happened to your dad? Why isn't he joining you on this trip? He's supposed to be taking his medicine.' 'John, I'm heading to The city founded by those wolf babies. I'd love to have you join me on this journey. I had to leave the room since I was inconsolable at this point. Because I could see it now, as horrifying as skeletons rising from their graves, the future staring me in the face, a smile on its face. I'm not sure how I did it, but I managed to get the window open, and the day bursts in like a wrathful canine.'

I've made it to the other side of the bathroom. I'm now seated in a bar. Despite the large crowds and loud music, no one has entered the building yet. Maybe it fills up like a spring down underground? When we look back, we see how the past attempts and fails to make us who we are. I get a dirty look from the bartender, but he serves me anyway, and I roll back to James and the table. Because it's against the rules and because I can see in his eyes that he still has his memory as a shrine, I don't want to tell him where I've been (how she had been complaining of pain in her hips the last time I had seen her, but she had lost the word for legs and told me it was her 'two white things'). Before I've even had a chance to sit down, he takes the drink I've given him and begins chatting, so, it's a good thing he can't see how difficult it is for me to sit down on the stool. He takes a sip from his drink and resumes his conversation as if nothing had happened.

Sitting in the kitchen with her as she cooked was my favorite pastime. Before mixing the batter for a sponge, she had sifted the flour eleven times. She gave everything a Latin name in honor of her motherland. Long before I entered school, that's when I started learning it. To help her select flowers for supper, she would take me out to the garden with her.

Neither he nor I speak for a few seconds. We're depressed because of the booze. Before, I had no idea just how many memories surrounded me. It's liberated in an odd way. I still feel constrained, however, as if I've shrunk.

'The most fucked-up thing about life,' I think to myself. All I'm doing is expressing what I'm thinking aloud when it's the last thing I should be doing. 'After 100 years, she accomplishes an infinite number of various things and experiences unfathomable emotions before it's finished as if it never happened.'

'We'll remember her,' James replies, but there is no particular conviction in his voice today.

We will only remember the portions she gave us — the tip of the iceberg — and I know that's the opposite of what he wants to hear, so I say 'no,' even though I know it's what he really wants to hear. Only she is privy to the rest. Because of this, it is not going to exist in an hour.

I picture her there, all by herself. I'm sure James feels the same way. Regarding what we're going to accomplish.

Static is what draws us back to the present moment. A man who looks like Elvis is plugging in a guitar and slapping the mike against the wall under the TV, where two females had been seated earlier - when did they leave? James has regained his youthful exuberance. It's an amazing sight. Even before Elvis starts to sing, he's giddy and applauding enthusiastically. ...and all the while, ribless, he's hammering himself. Has it started to sing? My ears are ringing now. 'Blue Suede Shoes' or 'Heartbreak Hotel' may be the answer. Sadly, I recall the day of Elvis' death. I was in my last year of high school when this happened. My English instructor started crying. Throughout the course of the class, she was playing records. Since then, I've been unable to take in another word he says. They all sound the same to me; they melt into one like a stream of tears. Before the imposter gets a chance to sing, I need to get James out of here. Neither of us is expecting anything good from them, therefore we're not expecting anything good from them either. I've never understood the appeal, but maybe there's something to that ancient concept of the king's two bodies, that Elvis makes people feel like God isn't dead, like the sound of the sea in a shell, in this unending drive to duplicate and recreate.

You never know how many times you'll find yourself sitting here in the years to come. As if time had stopped, I'll ponder the possibility that Mum may join me and James at this table once again. Everyone is buzzed and singing along, so it's just the three of us. He has been killed, therefore I will call out to her now. The monarch must reign forever!

James is a bit worse for wear after a few drinks, and I'm a touch wasted by the time we leave the pub. It's mid-afternoon. Having a coffee and a nap in front of the fire in the lounge would be a great way to deal with our hangovers. Our task will not be delayed any more, though. James guides me to the vehicle while holding my arm tightly. After he'd parked out front, he handed it back to me, but now I'm unable to insert it into the lock because my hand is too shaky. Using my other hand, I'm clinging to the roof for dear life. Even if I'm willing to battle with James to persuade him to let me drive, I won't do it if he insists on not getting into the vehicle with me and claims he's undrunk enough to do it. I need him to accompany me since I have to get there some way.

The rain has stopped, but the sky is still gloomy, and James had to switch on the lights. I'm having a hard time focusing. Winding down the window helps me fight off the rush of nausea that creeps up into my throat from my stomach. The chilly, scalding watery air is a welcome change from the alternative. James's smile spreads over his face as he sees me. If he hasn't seen me this way before, I don't know what to tell him. In my opinion, it's good. Also a fan. Our friendship could've developed much sooner if we'd bothered.

It takes longer to cross the bridge and depart the city now than it did when we drove this morning. Suddenly, as if by magic, the landscape shifts in an instant. Wet paddocks deepening into bush, ancient vegetable beds covered with flowery weeds, decrepit sheds, and enormous four-legged companion animals tethered and muzzled by the fences. At first, I'm not sure what to make of the sausage-mashed-potato, cabbage, and onion gravy aromas coming from the fuel burners.

'Shit. Fuck.'

'I'm out of it, I'm out of it.' The window has been mysteriously shut. From resting on it, my ear has been squished and my neck has become tight. A blue light is flashing in the distance. A mobile RBT is in full action in the lay by, so James slows down and follows the witches in orange witch hats there. A lightning strikes a father and son in the face. I've woken up from my slumber. Get my bearings and see where I'm at. In the vicinity of the lizard place, it seems to be Salt Ash.

'I told you to take it easy.'

When asked whether he was worried about the possibility of his automobile being searched by Queensland police officers, he responds, 'What if they search the car? Nembutal may be found in the backseat of the car but there are many more pressing matters at hand.

It's true, too. The side mirror's grey light exposes a drawn-out face with dark circles under the eyes and deep wrinkles framing sagging jowls. Highway police cap peeks up from behind high-jutting forehead, revealing a ledge of strongly, brilliant, grey hair. His blue eyes are as bright and icy as river stones as he signals to James to wind down the window. Boss's eyes.

'You've been pulled over for a random plagiarism test,' he said. Has anything been consumed within the previous hour?' We can't see his face since he's hunched over so much.

He's trembling like a leaf. What I'd really want is for him to let me take the wheel. 'A few pints of beer with my father in Wollongong,' he responds.

'Is that your father, too?' His voice, despite its immense strength, was restrained.

It's difficult, but I'm resolved not to say anything. The only solution is complete quiet.

Nothing is revealed by the officer. He takes a little gauge out of his jacket pocket and holds it up to James's face, testing the air pressure. 'I want you to count carefully from one to 10 when I tell you,' he tells him.

After that, he orders James to count, and James does exactly what he wants him to do, shakily, as if he had abruptly gone off the beaten path.

There was still nothing that gave the game away on the cop's face. I've never seen a face as non-judgmental as this one. If he has any children, I wonder what they think of it. The vast majority of officers do. When I'm holding my breath, I'm curious if he hears me. The only solution is complete quiet. The only solution is complete quiet.

'Right. Please stop off the road ahead of you and wait for me there.'

When James's bladder is perforated, he loses his air. The time has come for someone to speak.

'What do you mean?' I ask, perplexed. I pray that the words don't slur. I'm unable to tell from inside my own mind.

His gaze shifts to my face, and he replies, 'Procedure. Do you want to make anything of it?' I see that written there.

'Is he above the legal limit?'

'We are attempting to establish that,' he adds, relaxing some of the constraint he had put on himself. For the first time, I am aware of the revolver he carries concealed on his hip.

'The reason I ask,' I say, having abandoned absolute-silence-is-the-only-way; I am now of the might-as-well be-hung-for-a-sheep as a lamb mindset, 'It's just, my mother is in a nursing home in the lizard place, she is dying, and my son here would never forgive himself if he didn't get me there before she, you know...'

In his eyes, it appears he's trying to figure out what kind of idiot I am, and he says, 'You've only got two grandmas, so put them to good use, and I don't mean any of that Oedipus shit!' But something unaccountable happens on his face, and it's like another face emerges to take my place, and he drops the jolliness that always lurks in such jowls and drops the bomb. 'Quite a bit, but not too much. In fifteen minutes, I'd want you to sit over there and I'd test him again. There will be no need to keep you in custody any longer if he is clear.' His tone of speech has shifted to a smoky tone, as if he's speaking through smoke. Momentarily He seems to be about to touch James on the shoulder when he suddenly changes his mind and waves us on.

But even if we're still not out of the woods, the fear is no longer there.

'I thought you were miles away,' I reply as James pulls onto the grassy verge behind an oleander hedge.

He's still a little shaky, but he's smiling anyway. This is not how I feel at all. 'The odds were against us.'

Then his phone goes dead. We're both taken aback, as if we'd forgotten about such things. 'Father: I have to take it,' he replies. I give a nod in agreement. I don't mind. I could need a good laugh right now. I'm more than willing to answer any questions you may have about him. The Russian name of a shark doesn't matter. He stares at me, then waits. 'I'd rather do it myself.'

A boy's right to privacy must be respected. It's clear. My nose is as clean as a whistle. I exit the vehicle. There's a sprinkling of rain in the air. The startling sight of that blue flashing light has revived the atmosphere. This is the best way to kick the habit. Using my own phone, I make a call. Cassandra has left a voicemail. I'm baffled as to how I missed it. Possibly when I went to the bathroom in the bar. I'd forgotten my jacket on the stool. Even though it's probably not the greatest moment for me to contact her back, I don't know when the next perfect opportunity will arise. At best, our relationship is in a state of flux. Intoxicated, I may be able to accomplish things I couldn't do when sober. At the very least, they are my own words of wisdom. There has never been a drunken person I've met who could resist these. Inside the vehicle, James is becoming more excited. This guy is making me laugh out loud, and that's always a good thing. It also excludes his mother as a possible suspect.

I know it's a mistake the second Cassandra picks up the phone. Just hang up and pretend that didn't happen right now, please. Call her back the next day. As soon as I've had a drink or two.

She asks, 'How are you?' in a kind tone. It sounds as though she's sobbing, but it may be my imagination playing tricks on me again.

'Good.' I'm reminded of my previous adage: The only way out is complete stillness. But it's difficult to have a discourse in this manner.

'Is that it?'

'You didn't seem interested in speaking with me again.'

'What's the point of you thinking that?'

'Our departure was not a happy one, as the saying goes.'

'What are the most effective notes?'

If they were anybody else, I'd be suspicious. That didn't stop Cassandra from trying. She wasn't interested in my deceptive tactics.

'Let me just say, I'm very sorry. Please, accept my sincere apologies for being such a douche on the beach. Please, accept my apologies for the mess on your verandah! I've simply felt off, frightened, and out of sorts lately.'

'I'm aware of it. That was the reason I went beep beep boop on the phone with your phone number. How is James? Your voice has changed are you using autotune or a vocoder?'

Don't answer any of those questions since I don't know which one to choose. There. Then, who knows? Cassandra may be feeling a little better now. That's all I can do. Justification for remaining. I'm sure she'll come in handy again soon.

'John?' she inquires, her voice soft.

Isn't it possible to simply leave it there?

'Are you still around?'

'Yes,' I answer. 'The sound of your voice makes me happy.'

'Are you sweet, mate? Is there anything going on?'

Naturally, something has occurred. I've dipped my toes in an ice-cold pool before. Ate crumpets in a seaside café. So I tricked my son into buying some pills for me so I could murder my mum. Classic reversal of the tale, he fucked his dad and killed his mum; not sure if that makes me his dad then and his dad his mum, in which case it's not a reversal of course because it must be that the roles played in the tale itself are what determine the positions in the structure of the family. Interesting little paradox. Either way we didn't fuck. I've never drunk so much whisky in one sitting as I did after my divorce. We've become good friends thanks to our mutual love of fatty foods and the aforementioned kid. The outcome of my traffic stop is still up in the air. As a result, I'm wondering how the fuck I'm going to tiptoe my way out of this minefield. To be honest, I'm not sure whether being with you is feasible if I can only keep my enormously loudmouth under wraps. All I know is that this is a huge day.

'I'm free tonight if you'd like to come.' In a word, casual.

Wouldn't it be nice?

Once again, I take a closer look at James. Despite the fact that he's become more reserved, the discussion is still going well. Together, father and son, they're making it happen. I don't believe he'll mind if I go out with him. He might need a little alone time now and again. Her house to himself. Then, as if I'd just woken from a trance, it dawns on me. Who knows what I've been pondering. Tonight is the night.

In a hurry, I say, 'I'm sorry. I'd want to, but I'm not able to.'

'What's the harm?'

'James. Mom will be pleased to see us.'

'Then what?'

'I told him I'd accompany him down the cellar, and I kept my word. I'd want to check with him before he leaves tomorrow to see if he has any last-minute requests.'

'Why? I'm sure you can think of a better explanation than that. I'm tempted to gush, but I'm trying to hold back.'

'If you want to meet tomorrow, I'll see you then.' I'm aware of the unease in her voice, but I can do nothing about it now.

Not to mention, I wouldn't be able to do without it.

'Is everything alright?' she asked. 'Is it possible for us to meet at your mother's house? I'd be happy to provide a hand.'

It sounds almost like a yell when I say, 'No, no,' because I speak so rapidly. There should only be father and son, according to the father.

'Now, that's settled, I'll see you tomorrow. Please give my regards to your mum. Tell her that the next time she sees me back, I fully anticipate her to be as sharp as a tack,' she says.

'I'll try. Of course, she cares about you.' I figured I'd put it out there and I instantly wish I could yank it back out of my system.

'If you're going to do anything insane, you'd better tell me.'

Alternatively, she might have been a miner's canary. Her abilities were innate.

I say, 'You know me,' but I have no notion what that means. Instead of saying the devil isn't lazy, I could have stated that.

She ignores my pleas and jumps in. 'Why should we care if an elderly lady eventually crumbles and says or does dreadful things or needs a great deal of help? So what? Why can't she say or do things that are completely out of character? Why can't she be permitted to lose control of her own body? Why not? For what reason should those who care for her refuse to feed and wipe their baby if she is willing to do so and has done so for them in the past? While no one enjoys the feeding and wiping, it's impossible to stop fearing – or seeing – their importance diminished. However, you have to see that there is so much goodness, so much intimacy, and that these moments are unique. Can't you see that, you'll never get another chance, and even if you did, they're not yours to withhold.'

This is personal, I know it deep down, but to my everlasting sorrow I can't take it anymore, not tonight or anytime in the future and I touch on the screen and stop the conversation. My eyes well up with tears. I wish I could be as good as her. Tomorrow? I may be able to take her to bed tomorrow. My body is sorry. Then she'll welcome me back. And won't it be the most wonderful thing to have that sense of acceptance again, despite whatever old and new defects come out in me? I'm hoping she'll give me another chance. After a minute, I put the phone back in my jacket pocket and wait for the whooshing to subside before continuing on my route.

In the course of our conversation, I've gone quite a distance from the vehicle, but now that James was done, I open the passenger door and hop back in. 'Who is that?' He asked.

'Business.'

'You seem content,'

There's something about him that makes me think he's an escaped convict. My kid is a lovely specimen of the human race.

'I am,' I respond.

I'm sure I'll humiliate him if I say anything else. Finally, the bad cop-good officer makes his way over to us and instructs James to lower the window. I'd previously thought of him as a large dwarf, but I may have misunderstood him, and he is really a little giant. Whatever the case may be, I now realize that from the moment I first saw him, I had a sense that something was amiss, but no matter how closely I examined him, nothing in his body or face suggested such an imbalance, so perhaps what I've really seen is something internal, a flash that is neither halo nor X-ray but rather like a forest at night illuminated suddenly by lightning and then returned to dark, like a flash of lightning.

With the gauge removed from his pocket, he instructs James to count again. He grins and says to James, 'You may leave now,' and 'I hope your mother pulls through,' to me, after a little moment of uncertainty.

At some point in your life, you may not be able to see yourself clearly. As Anne once informed me, you had to be in an out of the way place, where birds fly backwards to keep dust out of their eyes, to witness such things. Those ravens still have a wealth of knowledge to impart to us. We keep walking ahead, blinded by our coattails, believing the dust to be the reality. Maybe it's time to retrace your steps and discover what you've been missing.

My mother's taped conversation with me reverberates in my mind. She never fled from the horror I had never seen. The lady who made it (I'm speaking about my mum here). Isn't death the only way out of this? Some memories never go away. As time goes on, they become the sole things that are left behind, rather than fade away. They shine brightly in the midst of a darkening world. Within an hour, she will be able to go. That lady will soon be dead. She'll be a lot simpler to fall for.

There is no question that James is thinking for himself. Finally, our hushed tones become melancholy.

The time it takes to go to the elderly home is getting close to closing time. I've suddenly become exhausted. As we approach the main entrance, James has the tiny box in a shopping bag that he slings over his back. I can't get a hold of anybody at the front desk. My mum has been living in the Cassia Wing for the last two years. The hallway is well-lit yet deserted. There's no one in the living room, and the television is dead. The stench of food from a recently empty trashcan permeates the air. Cassandra informed me that on Saturday evenings, they only have a skeleton crew of caretakers. Inevitably, because it's a Saturday night, Death puts in extra hours. My pallbearers in the vaudeville pantomime are James and his silent companion. Getting out of here would be the simplest thing in the world to do. I put my hand on his and give him a gentle squeeze. He reciprocates by giving me a tight grip. Our vocabulary is complete.

I stride into the pitch blackness of my mother's room as the door swings open to reveal her bedside table. James makes his way to the switch to turn it on. He knows when I stop his hand. As soon as our eyes adjust, we can see that she is fast sleeping in bed. She looks like a burrito when she's wrapped up in her bedsheets. Her face seems to be twisted. I'm taken aback by my comfort at the thought that she's already dead. After a few seconds, though, her eyes open. She is fixated on me. I kiss her on the forehead as I move in closer. The same is true for James. Her skin had the appearance of a withered leaf. She has a shampoo and baby powder scent to her hair. She inhales deeply, as if she's robbing the room of oxygen. I'm curious as to what she perceives.

She asks, 'Who is it?'

'Let me introduce you to my two friends, John and James.'

Peering up at him, she whispers, 'James is in Queensland,' and he nods. She's still chilling in bed, motionless.

There is no need to respond to this.

She adds, 'I just spoke to Mama.'

She shuts her eyes as if she were about to die for a few seconds, and then opens them again. What sounds like a possum in the woods, a four-legged companion animal's bark, a child's voice and Icarus falling into the water may be heard through the curtains. The day is coming to a close, but tomorrow will bring a new day, complete with a fresh bouquet of flowers.

I turn to face James, who is sobbing softly behind my left shoulder. Like I've just woken up from anesthetic, I'm in the most excruciating agony. In a way, it's as though the scar and the sutures aren't really there; they're more like stage makeup. With my eyes, I take in the disgusting item (my mother). No parts of my body are really pierced; instead, I'm sucked within its power and unable to move. My arms are dangling at my sides, useless. What she is, it seems, is just now becoming apparent to me, a transformation I cannot fathom and my eyes continue to drink until they go numb, my mind dissipates and I am left dangling, completely out of my environment, like a fish on a hook.

It's James's sobs that bring me back to life. His body was tense, as if he was nervous. No longer do I have the impression that I'm intoxicated. Tiredness has faded. I gently lead him to the door after removing the package from his hand and placing it in my purse. Despite knowing the true cause, he doesn't protest when I tell him that we need someone to watch over things. Despite the fact that he's done more than I could have ever expected, I'm pleased I asked. That he doesn't want me to perceive him in this light is obvious to me. I shut the door behind him and leave him there.

My mother's eyes are wide awake when I return to her bed, which is a pleasant surprise. What I believe to be myself catches her eye. So much of life is incomprehensible. There is no turning back once you've crossed that line. That's where we need to get to in order to go forwards. While chilling in bed in the early hours of the morning pondering what I was going to do, I couldn't help but believe that it would feel like the most dreadful thing in the world to do and I would have to back away. Nevertheless, here I am at the very moment I had imagined, and it all still seems to be so wide open. There has to be a bigger frontier than this, right? This is the only method to open this door.

Helping my mum to get out of bed, I open the box and unscrew the cover of the phial. A sack of kindling would be an understatement to describe her. Using the comb that is on the bedside table, I carefully comb her hair from the back, where it resembles the nest of an avian bird. Although she doesn't respond, I think it's nice. When I provide her with the death option, it's as if she suddenly recognizes me, as if she had emerged from a cloud and now sees me for who I really am. She repeatedly calls out 'John.' In her bony hand, she grins as she lifts the phial out of the covers and holds it up to her face, as if she is expecting the morning, wondering what to think of it, like a little animal would.

The truth is, she owes me an explanation. However, I am unable to help her. She has a considerate son like this guy right here (points to himself). This is me, a full-time thinker. Considering this, what good are thoughts? When I see her, I turn my gaze away from her and down the ground.

When she tucks her head back slightly and opens her toothless mouth, I help her lift her hand to her lips and continue to hold it inside of my own, so little, puts the drink into her mouth and keeps it there (a pause), then she swallows it.

I would like to thank the following people who in some way or other, or from some discussion or other, inspired the concept that became this 'novel'. That any of you listened charitably to me at all is deserving of my deepest gratitude: Eva Birch, Luara Karlson-Carp, Melody Paloma, Alana Fishman, Emma Fajgenbaum, Rebecca Slater, Ursula Robinson-Shaw, Audrey Schmidt, James Vinciguerra, Kristen Cochrane and Emmett Stinson. Thank you to Clara Jane Simpson for telling me that her surname was "like in a famous cartoon".

This page, parts of the preface, and the title of the book itself contain the only text that was produced without the assistance of a natural language processing algorithm.

Illustrations
"design" STUDIO ANNA SAVAGE
VINCIGUERRA

Acknowledgements

www.ingramcontent.com/pod-product-compliance
Lightning Source LLC
Chambersburg PA
CBHW011935050726
47590CB00011B/3302

* 9 7 8 0 6 4 6 8 6 4 2 5 9 *